"Reading Don't Fix No Chevys"

"Reading Don't Fix

LITERACY

IN THE LIVES

OF YOUNG MEN

No Chevys"

MICHAEL W. SMITH

JEFFREY D. WILHELM

FOREWORD BY THOMAS NEWKIRK

HEINEMANN
Portsmouth, NH

Heinemann
A division of Reed Elsevier Inc.
361 Hanover Street
Portsmouth, NH 03801–3912
www.heinemann.com

Offices and agents throughout the world

*All of the boys' names are pseudonyms, chosen by the boys themselves. When we talk about students' school performance in the *Meet the Crew* chart and Interchapters, we considered their track or learning community, grades, teacher reports, and what they told us about their previous school histories (e.g., their class rank, suspensions, and so on). We want to stress that we see an important distinction between school performance and academic ability. Some very able students may have been low achievers in school for a variety of reasons.

The boys represented in the photographs throughout this book are not the boys discussed in the book. The publisher and authors wish to thank Epping High School, Epping, New Hampshire, with special thanks to Principal Gary Tirone, Athletic Director Jamie Hayes, and the following students: Ben, Danny, Derek, Justin, Keith, Logan, Mack, Ryan and Ryan, and Starr.

Library of Congress Cataloging-in-Publication Data

Smith, Michael W. (Michael William), 1954–
 "Reading don't fix no Chevys": literacy in the lives of young men / Michael W. Smith and Jeffrey D. Wilhelm.
  p. cn.
 Includes bibliographical references and index.
 ISBN 0-86709-509-1 (alk. paper)
 1. Teenage boys—Education—United States. 2. Teenage boys—United States—Attitudes. 3. Language arts (Secondary)—United States. I. Title: Literacy in the lives of young men II. Wilhelm, Jeffrey D., 1959– III. Title.

LC1390.S65 2002
371.8235'1—dc21   2002019168

Editor: Lisa Luedeke
Production: Renée Le Verrier
Cover design: Catherine Hawkes/Cat and Mouse Design
Cover and text photographs: Putnam Ercoline
Back cover photograph of Michael W. Smith: © 2001 Rutgers/Nick Romanenko
Manufacturing: Louise Richardson

Printed in the United States of America on acid-free paper
04 03   RRD   4 5

To Brian White

Thanks, Brian, for helping us keep our eyes on the prize.

CONTENTS

Foreword   ix

Acknowledgments   xiii

Preface   xv

Introduction: Two Very Concerned Teachers   xix

CHAPTER 1   WHAT'S GOING DOWN: A REVIEW OF THE CURRENT CONCERNS AROUND BOYS AND LITERACY   1

Interchapter: Meet the Crew   22
Ricardo   23
Bambino   23
Pablo   24
Bodey   25

CHAPTER 2   GOING WITH THE FLOW: WHAT BOYS LIKE TO DO AND WHY THEY LIKE TO DO IT   26

Interchapter: Meet the Crew   54
Zach   55
Gohan   55
Haywood   56
Yuri   57

CHAPTER 3   DO THE RIGHT THING: THE INSTRUMENTAL VALUE OF SCHOOL AND READING   58

Interchapter: Meet the Crew   88
Buster   89
Ian   89
Alucard   90
Geo   90

CHAPTER 4   MOSTLY OUTSIDE, RARELY INSIDE:
              SITUATIONS THAT PROMOTE LITERACY   92

              Interchapter: Meet the Crew   135
              Bam   *136*
              Wolf   *136*
              Stan   *137*
              Larry   *138*

CHAPTER 5   MAY I HAVE THE ENVELOPE PLEASE? THE TEXTS
              BOYS ENJOY AND WHY THEY ENJOY THEM   140

              Interchapter: Meet the Crew   178
              Barnabas   *179*
              Aaron   *179*
              Mike   *179*
              Marcel   *180*

CHAPTER 6   A PROFOUND CHALLENGE: IMPLICATIONS FOR
              CLASSROOM PRACTICE   182

APPENDIX A   MAJOR CODING CATEGORIES   205

APPENDIX B   READING LOG DIRECTIONS   206

APPENDIX C   CATEGORY SYSTEM FOR THE PROTOCOL ANALYSIS
              AND DISTRIBUTION OF MOVES BY STORY   209

              Bibliography   211

              Index   219

FOREWORD

A couple of years ago I began to notice a pattern in my son's required high school reading: he moved from *Catcher in the Rye*, to *A Separate Peace*, to *Lord of the Flies* within the space of a few months. While I like all of these books, it *did* seem like he was in the Prep School Boy Reading Series. Preppie flunks out of school and goes to New York: Preppie accidentally kills his best friend; and Preppies go to a deserted island and run amuck. It was a needed reminder that for all the work on gender equity, male authors and their male protagonists have hardly moved off center stage. It also explains the skepticism of many female educators about the attention now being given to boys' difficulties in school, particularly in reading and writing. The canon has hardly been reformed to anything approaching equity. And just as the young women are beginning to make real progress in traditionally male subjects, these reformers can see this shift to male underachievement as an attempt to reinscribe male privilege.

There are other minefields, as well. If we want to discuss "boys" resistance to school reading tasks, just which *boys* are we talking about? Is there some uniform description or construction that fits all, or even most boys? And if not, how can we generalize about gender at all? Or, perhaps, the problem is that, when speaking of adolescent males, it is so *easy* to generalize, particularly in the wake of the Columbine shootings. Boys are isolated, lonely, prone to violence, oppressed by a "boy code," addicted to the visual media, and incapable of the sustained attention that reading requires. There's, to be sure, an element of nostalgia at work; we, of course, were different, more attuned to schoolwork, more willing readers. At least, that's the way we remember it.

The great strength of this book is the way it takes us beyond these stereotypes. We can listen to the young men in this study speak at length about their passions for professional wrestling, sports, computer games, comics, trade magazines—and their deep pleasure in social interaction with friends. We also can enter into the logic of their resistance to much that school, and English classes, ask of them. Smith and Wilhelm are careful to stress the individual differences among the boys. Some for example, resisted introspective literature, but not all; some disliked most school reading but loved *Hamlet*. While acknowledging this variability, Smith and Wilhelm carefully and scrupulously come to insights that raise powerful questions about the ways in which reading is taught in secondary schools. I can only briefly preview two of what I consider the most significant findings.

First, literacy, as these young men practice it, is intensely social—"literacies grow out of relationships." These boys are likely to read material that can be transported into conversations with their friends. Literate activities are centered around shared interests. The mantra for the boys they interviewed was, "it's always better with friends, always." The school activities that worked for them drew on this social energy, but often the boys found schoolwork, including reading, to be disconnected from their social networks.

This conclusion contrasts starkly with popular works like William Pollacks' *Real Boys: Rescuing Our Sons from the Myths of Boyhood* in which the boys are described as victims of a "boy code," which precludes intimate friendships among boys. According to Pollack school problems stem from a masculine code that endorses individualistic, self-reliant, action. The boys Smith and Wilhelm interview reverse this argument. They revel in the intimacy of shared interests, and find school *insufficiently social*, lacking in the camaraderie they experience when speaking and working with each other on projects that they choose.

The study also makes brilliant use of Mihaly Csikszentmihalyi's concept of "flow," a term he uses to describe optimal, and most fully pleasurable, human activity. A key characteristic of flow is the sense of being lost in the activity: we lose sense of time, and the pleasure of involvement is more central than any instrumental advantage we might gain. Paradoxically, many of the boys experience flow in activities the literate public often dismiss as mindless. Smith and Wilhelm cleverly show how computer games often have the characteristics of ideal learning environments—they present interesting and manageable challenges or problems, they have clearly defined levels of difficulty, they build off previous games, and they provide steady feedback to the player. In short, they invite the player into the flow state. By contrast, boys tend to view school reading as purely instrumental, as a means to a grade, graduation—something they have to do.

Smith and Wilhelm raise unsettling questions about what counts as literature in high school classes. If, for example, *The Scarlet Letter* fails, year after year, to draw students into an engaged reading experience (as I think it does, even with committed teachers), why should we continue to teach it? They show convincingly that these boys are regularly "overmatched" when they are confronted with these books. No book, after all, should hold its place in the curriculum without regard to the experiences students have with it. Schools will be more successful if they know students well enough to recognize what

Smith and Wilhelm call "identity markers," passions and interests that distinguish them—and to match books to that interest or taste, broadening the curriculum well beyond classic literature, and beyond narrative fiction.

There is often a considerable lapse of time before a major study is recognized beyond a small group of researchers—if it ever does get that recognition. I hope I can speed that process just a bit. The work you now hold in your hands is profound and compelling. And it is grounded so clearly in a comprehensive theory of learning that I suspect even those skeptical of the this new attention to boys will conclude that the recommendations for change will benefit all students.

It is about more than boys, about more than literacy.

Thomas Newkirk
University of New Hampshire

ACKNOWLEDGMENTS

The study we report here could not have been done without the help of many others. Most especially, we'd like to thank the young men who were willing to spend so much time talking with us about their lives in and out of school. We've tried to honor your participation by preserving and using your words as best we could and by thinking hard about what you had to say.

We'd also like to thank the administrators and teachers who helped us connect with those young men. Confidentiality issues keep us from thanking you by name, but our thanks is great nonetheless.

The Spencer Foundation provided the financial support we needed to do our work. The data presented, the statements made, and the views expressed are solely our responsibility, but without their support the data wouldn't have been collected and the statements and views wouldn't have been written. Tim Jenkins helped us design one of our instruments and Michael Michigami helped us pilot another. Melissa Larson did a wonderful job transcribing, and Diane Eriksen and Liz Kaplan helped with the data analysis we report in Chapter 4. Thanks to all.

Theresa McMannus, administrative assistant at the University of Maine, provided invaluable help organizing and keeping track of various features of the project. Thanks to Tanya Baker for her help of a variety of sorts throughout the project. Thanks go also to Phyl Brazee, Melissa Larson, Liz Kaplan, John Pickering, and Brian White for reading and responding to drafts and to Casey Scott for her help with the index.

We'd also like to thank our editors at Heinemann for their help. Bill Varner supported this project from the beginning, and Lisa Luedeke and Renee LeVerrier have pushed us to make the book better through their skillful editing.

It's never redundant to thank colleagues and friends. Those listed here deserve the highest compliment we can give: They are good friends and teachers in the truest sense. Michael would like to thank the Chicago crew for all of their support over the years, especially George Hillocks, Jr., Steve Gevinson, Larry Johannessen, Betsy Kahn, Steve Littell, and Peter Smagorinsky. He also sends his thanks to his colleagues in the Department of Learning and Teaching at Rutgers, especially to the Literacy Education cluster, Judy Diamondstone, Melanie Kuhn, Lesley Morrow, Dorothy Strickland, and to his dean, Louise Cherry Wilkinson, for creating an atmosphere that supports inquiry and reflection.

Jeff adds his thanks to his own teachers and mentors: Bill Strohm and James Blaser, who inspired his entry into the profession of English teaching, and to friends and teaching colleagues like Brian Ambrosius, Bill Anthony, Jim Artesani, Rosemary Bamford, Erv Barnes, Bill Bedford, Ed Brazee, Jim Chiavacci, Mike Ford, Paul Friedemann, Gail Garthwait, Stuart Greene, Leon Holley, Jr., Bruce Hunter, Jan Kristo, Craig Martin, Paula Moore, Bruce Nelson, Wayne Otto, and Denny Wolfe.

Special thanks go to Dean Robert Cobb and Kay Hyatt of the University of Maine and to Joni Scanlon of Rutgers University for their support in promoting this project.

We'd also like to thank our parents, Cordelia Smith and Jack Wilhelm, for believing in us. And although we wrote about men, our lives are full of amazing women. To them we owe our biggest thanks for all they have given us. Our love goes out to our wonderful wives, Karen Flynn and Peggy Jo Wilhelm, and to our constantly delightful daughters, the Smith girls, Catherine and Rachel, and the Wilhelms, Fiona Luray and Jasmine Marie.

PREFACE

What This Book Is

Simply stated, our impetus for writing this book was understanding and helping the individual boys whom we have taught and will teach and whom our current preservice teaching students will teach well into the future.

The importance of looking hard at individual young men came home to us when we heard the interview Bill Moyers did with the Chicano poet Jimmy Santiago Baca for the *Language of Life* (1995) series televised by PBS, so much so that we drew our title from that interview. In it, Baca tells the story of why he learned to read. It wasn't easy, for Baca experienced trouble in his youth far beyond those of most of our students as he was in jail at seventeen. He couldn't read much then, just some simple words, *man, lake,* and *round.* He tells of stealing a copy of an anthology of the Romantic poets from the jail clerk, a college girl with whom he was flirting. And he tells of reading it, using his words to conjure an image of a man walking around a lake the way his grandfather did. He was filled with a tremendous urge to write about his grandfather. And he was filled with a tremendous need to read more, to find out why "95 percent of the people in prison were Chicano, and 95 percent can't read and write, and 95 percent are killin' for smokes and coffee. . . . I want[ed] to know the answer."

So he decided to teach himself how to read and write. But his decision was met with the jeers of fellow prisoners: " 'You're a coward,' they said. 'You're nothin.' Because books get you nowhere. Books are stupid. Sissies read books. You couldn't do nothin' with a book. You couldn't fix a '57 Chevy with a book. You couldn't take money from some hustler with a book. You couldn't convince or persuade anybody with a book.' "

And not only that, books were "the great enemy," for they contained the lies that "my grandparents had been lazy Mexicans and that I was no good." But he prevailed. And words, he says, "caught me up in the most fierce typhoon I've ever been in and have never exited from—ever."

The title of our book is an allusion to Baca's story because in it we see many of the themes we will be exploring. We see a young man at risk, in part because he cannot read. We see reading dismissed by other young men. We see those young men valuing immediate practical results that they do not see literacy providing. But we see also the potential power of reading and literacy to transform a life and to fight stereotypes and generalizations—a kind of transformative work that Baca does now through his poetry. And we see a young man who defies easy generalizations, a young man whose potential was not tapped by school. He typifies in many ways our concern about the unactualized literate potential of boys across America.

This book details our investigation into the literate lives of boys, both in and out of school, and how those lives relate to the other roles young men play: friend, son, brother, athlete, employee, musician, game player, and on and on and on. We began with two assumptions. First, if we understand what boys are passionate about in general, then we can better understand their feelings about reading in particular. Second, although we are aware that gender is widely considered to be the superordinate category of identity (West and Zimmerman, 1991), and though we recognize that gender is a category that teachers use to think with as they plan, implement, and reflect on teaching, we are also aware that there are many Jimmy Santiago Bacas who defy conventional categorizations, who can be more than they are now, whose possibilities may not be obvious to us or even to themselves.

What This Book Is Not

Our book is not another entry in the gender wars. We want to avoid the highly polarized discussion that keeps us from fully understanding the issues so we can help all of our students. At the most recent NCTE conference Jeff attended, he heard one such discussion. In one session, the speaker began to talk about his experiences as a teacher and single father of boys. He described the way current psychologists feel boys are marginalized in society and school. Suddenly, one of the women behind Jeff could contain herself no longer. She stood up and announced, "Boys are still privileged! They still have a better chance at success than girls! This is all a bunch of—of hooey!" Another woman stood up to add her view that the presentation and the view that boys needed special consideration was "unadulterated baloney!" And they left, along with others in the audience.

The exchange during this conference session reveals just how highly polarized, polemical, and political discussions of boys have become. And with some reason, for a number of books in the popular press point to the inroads of feminism as a major cause of boys' alienation from school. We think it's important to say unequivocally at the outset that this book is not a critique of the impact of feminism. Neither is it an argument that girls are receiving too much attention at the expense of boys.

Another problem made obvious here is that much of the current discussion of boys relies more on anecdotal accounts than on systematic research. We don't want to minimize the importance of personal experience as a contribution to this conversation, but we would argue that such a far-reaching and important problem deserves a systematic look at a wide variety of boys from a wide variety of contexts. We hope that our efforts provide one such careful look.

Introduction

TWO VERY

CONCERNED TEACHERS

When we taught secondary school, both of us regularly taught classes for kids labeled at-risk or lower-track, and without exception they were dominated by boys. A variety of research shows that boys learn to read later than girls and never catch up. They trail girls on almost every literacy measure in every country and culture from which data are available. They are particularly behind when it comes to reading novels and extended forms of narrative fiction—the kind of reading that counts most in language arts classes.

But not all of them. We've always had boys who were excellent students, highly engaged readers, and skilled writers. And now that we educate pre-service teachers, although our classes are dominated by women, we have several young men who are highly literate and very dedicated to becoming English teachers. So the available data haven't struck us as telling the whole story, as giving a full and real picture of how boys feel about and engage with literacy. We have a personal stake in resisting generalizations, for the data in no way represents or explains the two of us, two men who have dedicated our professional lives and much of our personal energies to literate pursuits.

In sum, although research raises intriguing questions about why boys in general don't perform as well in school literacy activities as girls do, we worry that it paints a picture with too broad a brush. We worry, too, that a focus on boys' problems obscures strengths that we can build upon. The available data tell stories of averages, which never really capture the individuals, whom we teach in our classrooms each day.

Take Laurence, for example. Laurence was a conundrum; he never participated in Michael's ninth-grade English class. He only read the assignments under duress. But every week Michael noticed that he carried a new "sword and sorcery" novel. Every day he brought a *Soldier of Fortune* magazine to class. Once during the semester he asked Michael to read a very long and very detailed original story he had worked on at home. And when Michael last heard about him, he was establishing himself as a movie director.

Laurence wouldn't have fared well on many kinds of assessments. But he was a committed reader and writer, perhaps more so than most students who would have achieved far better grades in schools and scores on tests, and who would have fared better in school. The averages of such assessments don't capture Laurence in all of his complexity.

They don't capture Ron either. When Jeff was proposing his dissertation study, which became *You Gotta BE the Book* (Wilhelm, 1997), he wanted to compare more engaged and expert adolescent readers with less engaged and less proficient readers. To do so he thought through the kids in his classes who clearly fit these categories. His initial list of expert readers contained eight girls and no boys. His initial list of poor readers included seven boys and only one girl. However, when his dissertation committee pushed him to select a slate of informants that was more gender-balanced, he started to look below the surface of engagement with school literacy. Ron, a boy he eventually chose as a case study informant, was probably the best and certainly the most engaged reader in Jeff's classes that year. Yet Jeff had missed him completely when he first identified expert readers.

Why? Was the problem that Ron and boys like him were not as literate as the girls in the class? Or was the problem that Ron was just not as overtly literate in the ways that are most visible and valued in school?

When we conducted our literature review for this project, we didn't find studies that we felt captured the boys with whom we have worked in all of their complexity. We care about those boys. And we care about literacy, for we think it offers unique and powerful ways of knowing. If boys are not embracing literacy, we want to think hard about what we can do to help them. Laurence and Ron taught us that to do so, we need to look beyond averages and conventional measures.

So that is what we set out to do in the study we will report on here: to take a close look at a wide variety of adolescent boys, to observe and talk with them about their literate activity in and outside of school. We did this to understand them personally, to understand their literate behaviors, and to come to understand how to teach them in improved ways that will benefit them and society.

Setting Up the Study

Because of our concerns, we wanted to test the commonsense proposition that gender is a category that is useful for teachers to think with. We therefore decided to work with boys who differed from each other on a variety of dimensions: race, class, school experience and achievement, and linguistic background. We thought that asking if there was sufficient similarity among this group of young men to warrant generalizations would provide a more stringent standard than comparing boys to girls. For example, saying on average that boys tend to like video games more than girls doesn't mean that it's safe to say that boys in general like video games. This approach also allowed us to evaluate whether other issues—such as past experience in school, social class, or ethnicity—might be more important categories for teachers to consider.

With that purpose in mind, we worked in four very different sites in three different states: an urban high school made up almost entirely of African American and Puerto Rican students; a diverse comprehensive regional suburban high school; a rural middle school and high school; and a private all-boys middle school and high school.

The schools with which we worked set up different ground rules for selecting our participants. In one school we worked with an entire Department of English. That allowed us to select three boys from each of the four years, one from each of the school's three tracks. A second school had been divided into learning communities, and so the administrator who approved our study suggested we could get the most diverse sample by working with boys from different communities. In that school, we worked with three boys in each of four communities. In our final two districts, we worked with particular teachers who agreed to help us solicit participation from their students. In those two schools we worked with seventh and eleventh graders selected by their teachers to represent the widest possible range of previous school experience and achievement. In total, we worked with thirty-two European American boys, ten African American boys, five Puerto Rican boys, and two Asian American boys. Approximately one-third were regarded as high achievers, one-third average achievers, and one-third low achievers (see page iv *).

We collected four different kinds of data. To understand how the boys in our study valued different kinds of activities, and how literate activities fit in to their overall values, we had each informant rank a series of activities from the ones they most enjoyed to the ones they least enjoyed. We then interviewed the boys about their rankings. This data set is the subject of Chapter 2.

To understand more specifically their attitudes toward different ways of being literate, we wrote short scenes profiling different kinds of males engaged in embracing or resisting various kinds of literate activity. We created these scenes with the help of Tim Jenkins, one of Michael's university students. The boys in the study read the profiles and responded by telling us how the students featured in the profiles were like them and not like them and what they admired or didn't admire about them. We followed up on these responses during an interview session. We wrote the profiles to display not only different literacies and rejections of literacies, but also different character ethnicities, cultural concerns, economic levels, and so on. These data are the basis of Chapter 3.

We were interested in exploring how the boys enacted their attitudes and values, so we asked them to keep track of everything they read, wrote, watched, or listened to in school and at home for three months. We interviewed them every four to six weeks about these literacy logs. As time permitted, we also observed our informants, both in different classes and outside of class, such as in the lunchroom, in the library, on the sports field, and in several cases, at work or at home. We followed up on these observations during the log interviews. We explore the major themes of our analysis in Chapter 4.

In Chapter 5 we turn specifically to the features of texts that our participants seemed to enjoy. To do so, we return to the literacy logs. We also asked our participants to respond to four stories using think-aloud protocol techniques for recording what they were thinking, feeling, and doing as they read two action-oriented stories—one with a female and one with a male protagonist/narrator—and two highly reflective stories about a change in character consciousness—again, one with a female and one with a male protagonist/narrator—so we could assess whether these different features of texts resulted in different kinds of responses.

Our research, therefore, depended largely on the efforts of our participants and their willingness to share with us. We paid the participants who completed the study $100 as a token of our appreciation for the time they invested in this research.

Throughout Chapters 1 through 4 we consider the teaching implications of our findings for us as teachers. We then conclude each chapter by thinking about the implications of a major question that the data raise for us as teachers. During our overall conclusion in Chapter 5, we develop the implications of our work more fully, focusing both on the more global implications of this study for curricular and instructional (and even school level) reform and on how our findings can inform how individual teachers plan and implement instruction in reading and the language arts. And we want to say at the outset that we believe the implications of our data offer a profound challenge to American schooling and the traditional teaching of English.

We'll talk more about the details of the instruments we used and the analysis we did when we present each chapter's findings (with additional information in an appendix for those interested in methodology). But we hope that our summary here makes it clear that we were able to take a very detailed look at the role of literacy in the lives of these boys over a sustained time period. In addition, our methods allowed us to consider directly not only the role of gender, but also many other influences and how those influences interacted with gender. They also let us look at what boys did in and out of school.

Many of our findings are based on the themes we observed across boys. But because our data are based on conversations with the young men, we never lost sight of the fact that we were working with distinct individuals rather than a homogenous group. In fact, as you will see later, we found that our boys were not all "boys" in the same way. Although there were important similarities among our boys, there were significant differences as well. If there is a monolithic "boy code," as William Pollack (1999) would have it in his bestselling book *Real Boys*, our boys weren't party to it.

Therefore, in addition to sharing the themes, we wanted to allow you to meet the young men with whom we worked so closely. On the inside front and back covers, there is a chart, *The Boys in Our Study: Meet the Crew*, to introduce you to them. In addition, we'll present portraits of four boys from the study after each chapter. We hope this helps you keep track of them and come to know and enjoy them as individuals, as we were privileged to do.

What's Going Down

A REVIEW OF THE CURRENT CONCERNS AROUND BOYS AND LITERACY

1

The Issue: Boys Underperform in Literacy

Time after time in our work with inservice teachers, we have heard them describe "problem" classes with statements like, "Of course, that class has sixteen boys and only five girls . . ." The explanation need not continue, for those statements are met with nodding heads and sympathetic glances. If you have lots of boys in an English or language arts class—or so the conventional wisdom goes—you can expect to have problems. We've been fascinated to see teachers who would never link a troubled classroom to their students' racial, ethnic, or social class background feel comfortable linking the problems to the relative proportion of boys and girls. It seems that gender is a category that teachers use to think with. And they're not alone, for a wide variety of research has focused on boys' achievement relative to girls on literacy.

There is a well-established interest in girls, their learning, and meeting their social and achievement needs in school. The work of the American Association of University Women (Bryant, 1993), Gilligan (1982), Finders (1997), and theorists and researchers throughout the United States, United Kingdom, and Commonwealth nations have provided us with valuable data and perspectives that we find very helpful to us as teachers. To take one instance, the issues of girls' relatively low achievement in math and science has received much well-deserved attention, and as a result demonstrable improvement has been achieved in these areas.

Unfortunately, we haven't seen the same improvement in boys' achievement in literacy, despite the growing body of research that documents a significant problem. Without question, the widest current gender gap for learning achievement recorded by standardized measures is in the area of literacy. The Educational Testing Service, for example, reports that the gap in writing between eighth-grade males and females is more than six times greater than the differences in mathematical reasoning (Cole, 1997). In the 1996 National Assessments of Educational Progress (NAEPs), females outperformed males on literacy measures by 25 points on a 500-point scale (Campbell, Voelkl, and Donohue, 1998). The most recent NAEPs, which were conducted in 1998, provide a bit of better news. Boys' scores went up at Grade 4 and Grade 8, though they remained the same in Grade 12. But that same report provides the troubling findings that the lowest-scoring boys performed at a considerably lower level than they had on the 1992 assessment and that the gap between girls and boys in Grade 12 continues to widen. Newkirk (2000) points out that the gap between the girls and boys is "comparable to the difference between Whites and racial/ethnic groups that have suffered systematic social and economic discrimination in this country" (p. 295).

In 1985, the International Association for Evaluation of Educational Achievement (IEA) investigated writing achievement across fourteen countries and found that "gender by itself or in combination with certain home variables was the most powerful predictor of performance, particularly with academic tasks" (Purves, 1992, p. 201). Females outscored males on all writing tasks, both narrative and expository, and this gap was particularly large in persuasive writing. Once again, the differences generally increased with age.

In a later IEA study begun in 1988 and involving thirty-two nations, girls achieved higher total reading scores in all modes. However, by age fourteen in nine countries (28 percent of the sampled countries), boys did overtake girls on expository literacy tasks, and in eighteen countries (56 percent) on workplace literacy tasks such as working with documents. In only one country at any age level did males achieve higher scores for narrative tasks (the kind most often pursued in language classes). In short, research makes it clear that as a group, girls outperform boys on overall reading tasks, though boys' performances do tend to improve when they read for information, or when they read to do or accomplish something beyond the reading (Elley, 1992).

Again, this is not to argue that schools have not "failed at fairness" in their teaching of girls (Sadker and Sadker, 1995), nor to deny the silencing and discrimination suffered by traditionally underrepresented groups, including girls, in our schools and society. In fact, contributors to the volume *Failing Boys?* (Epstein, Elwood, Hey, and Maw, 1998) question the focus on academic achievement and testing as a measure of success in light of males' continued leadership in the job market and earnings. They argue further that boys' underachievement is strongly classed and racialized and that it is sociocultural factors, not gender alone, that determines who fails. Others, such as Cohen (1998), are suspicious of the political motives behind the current concern about boys given that they have underachieved when compared with girls in literacy since the seventeenth century. She believes that men feel they are losing their traditional advantages and that this is what motivates the current move to help boys, not their actual underachievement in terms of school and literacy.

Their arguments are provocative ones, we think, but they don't explain away the statistics. Schools seem to be failing boys in literacy education. And while this failure may be rooted in a complex amalgam of issues, we believe that perceiving a problem of ANY group of students obligates us to try to understand it, so we can do something about it. And in a wider sense, if, as Thomas (1983) once maintained, "language makes us specifically human," then we certainly have another cause for alarm.

Though the importance of literacy is seldom doubted, we think often of how Donalson (1978) demonstrated how reading and language awareness leads to developing intellectual control and disembedded, abstract thought. And of how Bettelheim (1976) demonstrated the importance of story, particularly fairy tales, to healthy psychological development. And of how Inglis (1981) showed the importance of narrative on children's introspection and self-understanding and on their ability to understand and reflect on the experience of others. All of these abilities are clearly important to lives of health and happiness in a democratic society. They are central to our own concerns and goals as teachers.

The evidence of boys' relative lack of literacy skills and their continuing loss of ground is consistent across studies and forceful in its accumulated detail. But we worry that the arguments based on this data take for granted that the very tests that document the gaps are not themselves gender-biased, a questionable assumption. For example, in her study of large-scale writing assessments, Peterson (1998) points out that girls' narrative writing was privileged during the assessments. If, say, action stories are a genre that is not rewarded on large-scale assessments and if boys nonetheless write them, poor scores may be a function of evaluation bias and not actual performance. In fact, Jeff has done table reading for state assessments in three different states, and on one occasion much discussion ensued about how a particular piece written by a boy exhibited highly proficient writing but did not fit the scoring rubric. It was subsequently given a non-scorable evaluation.

Barrs (1993) makes a similar argument with regard to reading, wondering if boys only underachieve relative to girls on certain kinds of tasks, like narratives, and excel on others that are not on the assessment radar screen. She argues that

> girls' generally higher levels of achievement in reading may reflect the
> nature of the reading demands made of them, and may in fact mask sub-
> stantial under-achievement in some areas of reading, which, for a complex
> of reasons, are less carefully monitored in schools, such as the reading of
> information texts. (p. 3)

It is well documented that various schooling and testing practices discriminate (consciously or unconsciously) against various groups (e.g., against children from minority groups or lower socioeconomic levels). Children from various groups are also sometimes labeled as deficient because their home communication styles are not understood by teachers. See, for example, Gee (1989) or Michaels (1981). The same may certainly be true of many boys.

To summarize, the available quantitative data establish boys' underachievement in literacy. But there are concerns that the data may be biased and do not tell the full story, at least not a full enough story to help teachers. We believe that our own research design allows us to fill in some of the considerable holes in the existing data and to examine the various issues raised here in ways that can help us think about our teaching, and practice instruction in new and more powerful ways.

During the rest of this chapter, we will review three important strands of the existing research on boys: discussions of boys' psychological health; discussions of their learning in general; and discussions of their literacy learning in particular. In our review we will examine powerful theoretical lenses for approaching and understanding these issues. Though we'll show how this theory and research is important to us as teachers and how it helped us think about our study, some readers might want to skip ahead to the interchapter preceding Chapter 2. By doing so, you can immediately meet some of the boys with whom we worked and immerse yourself in what they revealed, and then go on to our subsequent chapters to see what we learned from them. You can then return to this review later.

Current Framings of the Issues

The "New Boys" Movement: Concerns for Psychological Health

The perception that boys are in trouble, both in school and out, has led to an increased attention in our culture to boys. One manifestation of this concern is the explosion of books in the popular press on the plight of boys and their general psychological health. The general concern is so pervasive that it has been dubbed "The New Boys Movement." The authors of these books generally refer to boys' in-school problems and sometimes to their low literacy scores (without ever exploring these issues, as we will do here), but their focus is more generally on helping boys navigate the tricky waters of adolescence and move into the oceanic challenge of manhood.

Though the authors generally agree that boys are in trouble, they have widely differing explanations for why this is so, and they bring different theoretical orientations to bear. Kimmel (1999), a gender historian, argues that these recent books provide very different understandings of gender. He lays out a continuum that begins on one end with biological determinism. According to Kimmel, books from this perspective argue that the way sex roles are played out in behavior is biologically determined. This view holds that boys' problems stem from individuals' and institutions' inability to understand masculine biology.

On the other end of the continuum are books that offer socially constructed notions of gender. In this view, sex and gender are fundamentally different. Gender is not determined by the biology of one's sex but by social constructions in the social worlds in which we live. In this view, boys' problems stem from society's inability to understand how it has shaped them with various communications about what is expected of them.

Views from Biological Determinism

As we've noted, one side of the debate includes authors who articulate arguments based to some degree on biological determinism. The two most popular authors in this group include Biddulph, author of *Manhood* (1994) and *Raising Boys* (1997), and Gurian, author of *The Wonder of Boys* (1997), *A Fine Young Man* (1999), and *How Boys and Girls Learn Differently!* (2001). Kimmel (1999) also places these two authors on the biological determinism end of the scale, though we personally feel that Gurian makes moves toward recognizing some social influences on the formation of gender.

These authors and others like them have been immensely influential, as are their arguments that males' propensity for many behaviors is genetically influenced (at least to some degree). They argue that the testosterone geysering through boys' bodies propels them toward activity, risk taking, and more overt forms of aggressive behavior. Biology mandates that "boys will be boys," they claim, and those who interfere with boys' natural behaviors are subverting natural male behavior and doing untold damage. Schools, they argue, are among the cultural institutions that contribute most significantly to that damage. These authors propose that society needs to celebrate who boys are (determined as it is by nature) and give them a wide berth to explore their natural inclinations and guide them gently in healthy directions.

We agree that biology does have a role in the development of boys. This makes obvious sense. However, we are compelled by the weighty evidence that gender is a historical and social construct that changes with time, culture, and situation (ideas we'll explore more fully). Just as important, we find this idea and its consequences more powerful for us as teachers.

The Case for Social Constructionism

According to Kimmel (1999), on the other side of the debate are those writers who see gender as a social rather than biological construction. West and Zimmerman (1991) provide a succinct statement of this position:

> Rather than as a property of individuals, we conceive of gender as an emergent feature of social situations: as both an outcome of and a rationale for various social arrangements and as a means of legitimating one of the most fundamental divisions of society. (p. 13)

This position informs many of the most popular books that take up the issue of the trouble with boys. For example, Pollack's *Real Boys* (1999) explores the "boy code" that governs male behavior through culturally created and perpetuated "myths" of masculinity. This socially constructed code, according to Pollack, harms boys, so society, which defines and enforces social definitions of manhood, must actively interrogate and redefine masculinity. Kindlon and Thompson's (1999) *Raising Cain* also talks about the cultures of masculinity, such as the nefarious "culture of cruelty" that is perpetuated through various cultural means, including popular media and peer relationships, and acted out in schools and classrooms.

We think that this second perspective is a more useful one for us as teachers. In the first place, it jibes with our experience. In our own social worlds, we see many ways of being male. Different families, cultural groups, religious affiliations, extracurricular associations, and so forth with which we are familiar all have different expectations and offer different possibilities for being male.

For instance, Jeff has a friend in whose orthodox religious tradition it is expected that the man will be the sole breadwinner in the family, that he will be the first served at dinner, and that he will be the one who makes all decisions of import that affect the family outside of the home, down to arranging and approving the marriages of his daughters. This authority is symbolized quite concretely by the way his family must follow him when they are out and about. Neither his wife nor his children are allowed to walk beside him or in front of him.

However, another friend, from a different ethnic and religious group, stays at home to take care of his children. He jokingly calls himself "The Houseman." His wife is the sole breadwinner. He does the cooking and cleaning, and since he serves the morning and evening meals to fit his family's schedule, he is always the last to eat. His wife earns all of the money, keeps the financial records, and makes all of the major financial decisions.

More personally, both of us have taken on very different gender roles than those of our fathers, and what we found out during this research project itself emphasized to us that boys today experience different cultural expectations than we did as young men thirty years ago. For instance, the boys in this study expressed radically more liberal attitudes toward homosexuality and feminism than we expected and that our social groups possessed in the late sixties and early seventies. Whether we fully believe the authenticity of these attitudes or not, it is clear that the boys in our study feel the weight of different expectations on their attitudes and behaviors.

Overall, the social constructionist position seems more useful to us as teachers. Social constructivism emphasizes that changing instructional environments, methods, and expectations can change the experience of kids. It can also change how they act, behave, learn, and interact. Therefore, focusing on how society and school influence gendered behaviors like literacy seems to us to be a fruitful and promising avenue for educators.

We think that books from this perspective offer more potential for helping boys than those from a biological one. Nonetheless, we would critique both the work of Pollack (1999) and Kindlon and Thompson (1999)—and others like them—because of the data on which they are based. Pollack derives his ideas at least in part from his therapeutic work. It's not surprising that boys in therapy talk about their problems. But we worry that Pollack infers the trouble with boys from troubled boys. Kindlon and Thompson write from data gathered in an elite prep school. The boys with whom they worked do not represent boys in general in terms of class, cultural background, or school experience.

Boys and Violence

Other books that look very specifically at the cultures and definitions of masculinity and how these lead to violence also come from a social constructivist perspective. They are of interest to readers exploring the link of cultural constructions of masculinity to violence.

Though studying violence is not the purpose of this study, it is a growing problem in our schools. And although girls are certainly involved in school violence—both as perpetrators and, perhaps especially, as victims—boys are at the center of the maelstrom. While statistics differ somewhat, available databases suggest that boys are four to six times more likely to commit suicide than girls; more than twice as likely to get into physical fights; three times more likely to be suspended from school; four times as likely to be diagnosed as emotionally disturbed, depressed, emotionally isolated, or suffering from Attention

Deficit Disorder; up to fifteen times more likely to be perpetrators of violent crime (statistics cited variously in Bushweller, 1994; Pollack, 1999; Ravitch, 1994; Silverstein and Rashbaum, 1994).

One well-respected book that explores this issue is James Gilligan's *Violence* (1997). The author, the former mental health director for the Massachusetts state prison system, argues that the socially constructed privileges, status, and social positioning men enjoy can also be the very things that harm them, ultimately frustrating them and encouraging and enabling them to inflict harm on others. He explores the causes of violence and how a failure to meet cultural expectations brings on the shame and humiliation that incites and perpetuates violence. Likewise, Garbarino's (2000) *Lost Boys* explores case studies of "kids who kill" because they are in search of attention and love. Miedzien (1991) takes a feminist perspective on the issue in her *Boys Will Be Boys*. She critiques how males use physical oppression and violence to construct and express their male identities in various venues like gangs, sports, sex, business, and warfare. She argues that the only way to change the cultural landscape significantly enough to modify the pervasive association of masculinity and violence is to adopt a national policy of zero tolerance that condemns all forms of violence and oppression of others.

Miedzien's book lines up with other books from the social constructivist perspective that take issue with biological arguments that see certain male behaviors as natural. These texts express the necessity of culturally redefining masculinity using feminist theory. For example, Kivel's (1999) *Boys Will Be Men* argues that creating sensitive and healthy boys requires parents and significant others (like teachers) to love and care for boys, to come to know them and attend to their needs, to communicate that loving is important, and to help boys deal with their emotional life. He argues further that these significant others must address harmful social and behavioral issues. They must do this by honestly confronting and exploring with boys issues influencing their behaviors and responsibilities, refusing to let boys—or society and social institutions like schools—off the hook to unquestioningly accept cultural conceptions of maleness.

Battle Lines over Boys and Learning

Books like Miedzien's, Kivel's, and others such as Silverstein and Rashbaum's *The Courage to Raise Good Men* (1994) all propose transforming the meanings of manhood by using the principles of feminism. They have therefore drawn a firestorm of the most politicized response.

Perhaps the most famous and vitriolic of these responses is Hoff Sommers' (2000) *The War Against Boys*. This attack from the right argues that boys are so oppressed by feminist ideology, typically expressed through schools, they have in fact become "victims" and "the second sex." Sommers calls into question the research of influential feminist scholars such as Gilligan and calls efforts to "feminize" boys misguided. Echoing many arguments also expressed in Faludi's (1999) *Stiffed*, she argues that boys have become ostracized and marginalized and that this state of affairs, a failed promise of a fair shake, is leading to frustration, depression, and many other obstacles for boys.

As we've already maintained, this "war" between boys and girls is not one that needs to be fought. Though many battle lines have been drawn and skirmishes conducted, we are convinced that school and society can help boys *and* girls at the same time, and that helping boys in the ways we will propose will in fact benefit girls in important ways.

For example, a counterargument to Sommers' comes from school and learning-oriented literature about boys in Australia and the United Kingdom. Using a social constructivist perspective, scholars such as Gilbert and Gilbert (1998), Alloway and Gilbert (1997), and Mac An Ghaill (1994) make powerful research-based arguments that boys are not suffering from feminist initiatives, but are rather suffering from definitions of masculinity that are hegemonic, culturally embedded, and harmful to both boys and girls. According to these authors, existing conceptions of masculinity and alignment with particular male groups undermine attitudes toward many kinds of learning and achievement in school. Gilbert and Gilbert, in *Masculinity Goes to School* (1998), and Salisbury and Jackson, in *Challenging Macho Values* (1996), provide classroom methods for questioning and disrupting the kinds of masculine-defined attitudes and behaviors that Gurian (1997, 1999, 2001), Biddulph (1994, 1997), and authors from a biological orientation believe we should accept and even celebrate.

One reason the battle lines are misdrawn is because there are boys and girls on both sides. Though people often must necessarily think in generalizations and categories, these are always too simple, and this study has led us to believe that the cost of this oversimplification is too high when it comes to boys and literacy. Many girls excel in math; many boys love to read. We categorize for the sake of argument, clarity, and for ease of thinking, but sometimes our categories cause problems and keep us from seeing the students before us.

Boys and Literacy

When we began this study, we found that it was eagerly anticipated by the teachers with whom we work. A Native American teacher who works with Jeff told us that her "prime concern" was "her boys." She asked Jeff, "Who is going to help me with these boys [who won't read]? Who cares enough to help me help them?" A veteran twelfth-grade English teacher echoed her remark: "If you can help these boys, it will be worth more than I can say."

Their concerns are in line with the research documenting the achievement gap between boys and girls. It is also in line with a well-established research tradition that focuses on more specific differences between boys and girls, which is partly why the battle lines are drawn where they are.

A Summary of the Research on Gender and Literacy

We've warned against overgeneralizing, yet we realize that research that identifies characteristics of groups can provide a useful starting point for teachers by alerting us to issues we might encounter in our work with individual students. There is a long tradition in educational research that examines the differences between boys and girls on literacy tasks. Rather than discuss this huge body of research in depth, we'd like to present a quick statement of the findings we believe are most compelling:

ACHIEVEMENT

- Boys take longer to learn to read than girls do.
- Boys read less than girls read.
- Girls tend to comprehend narrative texts and most expository texts significantly better than boys do.
- Boys tend to be better at information retrieval and work-related literacy tasks than girls are.

ATTITUDE

- Boys generally provide lower estimations of their reading abilities than girls do.
- Boys value reading as an activity less than girls do.
- Boys have much less interest in leisure reading and are far more likely to read for utilitarian purposes than girls are.
- Significantly more boys than girls declare themselves "nonreaders."
- Boys spend less time reading and express less enthusiasm for reading than girls do.

- Boys increasingly consider themselves to be "nonreaders" as they get older; very few designate themselves as such early in their schooling, but nearly 50 percent make that designation by high school.

CHOICE

- Boys and girls express interest in reading different things, and they do read different things.
- Boys are more inclined to read informational texts.
- Boys are more inclined to read magazine articles and newspaper articles.
- Boys are more inclined to read graphic novels and comic books.
- Boys tend to resist reading stories about girls, whereas girls do not tend to resist reading stories about boys.
- Boys are more enthusiastic about reading electronic texts than girls are.
- Boys like to read about hobbies, sports, and things they might do or be interested in doing.
- Boys like to collect things and tend to like to collect series of books.
- Poetry is less popular with boys than with girls.
- Girls read more fiction.
- Boys tend to enjoy escapism and humor; some groups of boys are passionate about science fiction or fantasy.

RESPONSE

- The appearance of a book and its cover is important to boys.
- Boys are less likely to talk about or overtly respond to their reading than girls are.
- Boys prefer active responses to reading in which they physically act out responses, do, or make something.
- Boys tend to receive more open and direct criticism for weaknesses in their reading and writing performances.
- Boys require more teacher time in coed settings.

These findings were drawn from the following studies: Abrahamson and Carter, 1984; Barrs, 1993; Children's Literature Research Centre, 1996; Dunne and Khan, 1998; Hall and Coles, 1997; Kelly, 1986; Maybe, 1997; Millard, 1994, 1997; OFSTED, 1993; Equal Opportunities Commission and OFSTED, 1996; Shapiro, 1990; Whitehead, 1977; Wilhelm, 1997; Wilhelm and Edmiston, 1998; Wilhelm and Friedemann, 1998.

As we noted before we presented the summary, we believe that this research is important because of the way it can alert us to some of the issues we might be facing in our work with boys. Yet at the same time, we worry that the tendency to compare boys and girls means the pitting of one gender against the other. Moreover, teachers have been shown to use this research in ways that emphasize traditional socially constructed notions of maleness and to reinforce boys' current general tendencies rather than to expand on or redefine them (Millard, 1997; Telford, 1999).

Literacy and Masculinity
Another issue is that these studies leave the critical question *why* unanswered. Fortunately, other scholars have taken up that question in their research. Among the most provocative is that of Martino, an Australian scholar. Martino's work (1994a, 1994b, 1995a, 1995b, 1995c, 1998) bluntly argues that hegemonic versions of masculinity are not consistent with being literate, and are in fact militant against and undermine literacy and literate behavior. Boys see literacy as feminized, he argues, and since males define their maleness as "not female," literacy must be—and in fact is—rejected.

Martino's work builds on that of Walkerdine (1990), who was among the first to argue that boys are pushed by culture toward certain conceptions of masculinity and associated behaviors that run counter to literacy, which is presented culturally as a passive and private act that is feminized. And it resonates with other research as well. Cherland (1994), for example, studied images of reading presented in various media, including library and reading campaigns, and found that the images were almost entirely of females reading in private situations or with other females. Osmont (1987) found that what children observed adults reading out of school had a far-ranging effect on their conceptions of reading as a gendered act. Millard (1997) cites the case of a boy who suddenly stopped choosing fiction at age ten and began to read exclusively the farm journals that his father read (from Minns, 1993). When he had to read fiction, he began to respond to different features because of his new orientation toward "finding out" and "gathering information," which he had adopted from his father.

Phillips (1993) and Barrs (1993) argue that while most girls arrive at school with a secure sense of gender, most boys do not. As a result, boys are more susceptible to peer pressure as they attempt to ascertain and enact what it means to be male. Clark's (1976) and Bissex's (1980) studies indicate that there is less room in schools for boys to pursue their interests and tastes. Voss

(1996) has gone so far as to suggest that school structures unconsciously discriminate against many boys. They may be denied the very chance to be male *and* literate. This may lead to a poorer attitude, less interest in reading, less time spent reading, and lower achievement.

These commentators and others (Chodorow, 1978; Paley, 1984) have posited that boys will go to great lengths to establish themselves as "not female" and follow what their peer group establishes as gender-specific behavior. If reading or other literate activities are perceived as feminized, then boys will go to great lengths to avoid them. This is particularly true if the activities involve effort and the chance of failure, for incompetence and expending effort are also seen as unmasculine. Achievement, for men, is supposed to be attained with ease. Boys will avoid feminized behaviors or responses as a form of "pollution."

These researchers use this argument to explain why boys are reluctant to respond to reading or talk about feelings. Such discussions go beyond the rule-bound safety of many of their exchanges, are exploratory and tentative, and make them vulnerable to being "shown up" or "laughed at" for breaches of male protocol. It may also expose some of their thinking or feelings as feminine.

The Explanatory Power of Critical Theory: The Work of Millard

Critical theories add an important dimension to the discussion of boys and literacy. These theories provide lenses for examining and critiquing the status quo and for providing alternate visions of social worlds such as schools and classrooms. Critical theories can provide us with perspectives for seeing our social practices in new ways, for making the familiar strange. They can help us see the way our social worlds (family, sports team, book club, classroom) and the ways we act in them are constructed and nonnatural. They give us a vantage point as an outsider who can evaluate underlying purposes, assess intended and unintended effects, and see alternative visions and ways of doing things. Critical theory can therefore make the ways we are gendered, our social attitudes, and how we consider and use literacy as part of our classroom project something to be examined and explored. Specifically, it can help us see three things: (1) how we are positioned (how society, parents, our students, and our school define teaching and learning, our role as teachers, the role of curriculum and testing, the role of students, and the purpose of education); (2) the consequences of this positioning; and (3) the possibilities of a repositioning. As such, critical theories can also help us understand and begin to transform teacher and student attitudes and behaviors that we may find to be limiting or counterproductive.

Millard (1997) demonstrates the power of critical theories in her compelling work. She draws on this perspective to argue that general changes in reading habits occur because of environmental influences (in the home and the school) and media access. She finds that there are "marked differences in access to literacy that are directly related to gender" (p. 156). This access causes boys and girls to construct their ideas about reading, what it is used for, why it is important, what it means to be a reader, and how this all relates to gender in very different ways.

Millard suggests that boys are disadvantaged in academic literacy as a result of current curricular emphases, teacher text and topic choices, and lack of availability of texts that match their interests and needs. She urges teachers to get to know the field of contemporary children's and young adult literature and to get to know their students so that they can help them choose appropriate books and learning projects. She also found that choosing books that match stereotyped views of boys' interests and capacities may perpetuate those stereotypes and deny alternative interests. As well, Millard emphasizes the changing nature of literacy and the role of technology. She suggests that boys' underachievement in literacy may have something to do with the huge mismatch to how they practice literacy with electronic technologies outside of school.

Masculinity in School: The Notion of Gender Regime

One argument that we found especially important for our current study is Millard's use of the notion of "gender regime," an idea so important we think it's worth quoting her at length:

> Harris, Nixon and Rudduck (1993) suggest that the concept of sex role modeling is lacking in sufficient complexity to account for the contradictory aspects of gender relations and the competing views given to adolescents by schools, parents and the wider community. As a way into interpreting their own data relating to schoolwork, homework and gender, they proposed instead adapting the framework of *gender regime* (Kessler, et al., 1985) to describe the ordering of the practices that construct various kinds of masculinity and femininity in schools. They explain that their "data led us to see young people as caught in overlapping gender regimes—

the regime of the community, the regime of the peer culture and the regime of the school" (Harris, Nixon and Rudduck, 1993, p. 5). They further suggest that although challenges were offered to each external regime by the school, to some extent the residual effects of the other influences were still strong. Perhaps the most powerful influence of all was the pressure of peer culture, particularly that of the gender appropriate peer group. Actions performed in similar contexts on a daily basis have the effect of reinforcing the dominant (patriarchal) structures of society and uniformity of gendered behavior. (p. 21)

In other words, the various social influences or "regimes" interact to instill and reinforce unconscious habits of behavior and in turn lead to enduring patterns of conduct and motivation. Also worth noting is the paramount importance of peer culture. Using popular and peer cultures to help us as teachers is a theme we follow up on in later chapters.

Overcoming the Traditional and Accepted: The Challenge of Habitus
The theorist Bourdieu (1990) also accounts for this residual influence of traditional cultural practices with his concept of "habitus." Habitus, according to Bourdieu, uses past historical practices to produce new historical practices:

> It ensures the active presence of past experience, deposited in each organism in the forms of schemes of perception, thought and action, and tends to guarantee the "correctness" of practices and their constancy over time, more reliably than all formal rules and explicit norms. (Bourdieu, 1990, p. 54, cited in Millard, 1997, p. 22)

Millard (1997) writes that "what the habitus creates, in effect, is an unexamined common-sense or practical way of proceeding within any repeated social routine that rules out, as extravagant or unconventional, other kinds of behavior" (p. 22). The concept of habitus helps explain the resilience of masculine attitudes, including those toward literacy, and it offers a challenge to teachers who want to invent more progressive and helpful forms of instruction for students. Given the evidence that Millard presents that boys who act like girls are considered more deviant than girls who act like boys, the challenge to help boys is particularly great.

Millard (1997) also makes use of French psychoanalytic theorists Lacan, Kristeva, and Foucault. She notes that all three of these theorists examine the ways

> in which the gender differences of a particular cultural group are inscribed in its language, so that the "habitus" is reinforced and positions created within discourse appear more "naturally" available to one gender

than to the other. Authority, it is argued, is located within male culture; on the other hand, the creative process may be inscribed within the feminine, particularly in its most expressive and experimental forms. (p. 28)

Since English teaching, and particularly the teaching of reading, is dedicated in large part to the development of the individual through language, boys may be particularly disadvantaged and undermined by cultural attitudes, structures, and institutions that promote the status quo. This may be especially so when the focus is on narrative, emotional response, expressivity, and creativity, as is often the case in English classes, which are, perhaps importantly, most often taught by females. This deprives boys of male models who embrace the life of the mind, the emotions, and the various forms of literate creativity.

How Can We Help Boys: Examining Social Constructions

Millard does an excellent job of setting out the problem facing teachers. Other important research uses critical theory lenses both to examine aspects of the problem and to explore potential ways to address it. Such studies include the research of Young (2000), who worked in a homeschool environment with her two sons and two of their male friends. Her work explores how versions of masculinity can be articulated and interrogated in an alternative environment. She worked with these boys to inquire into the socially constructed nature of their tastes, interests, and masculine identity, and into the constructedness of various popular culture texts, such as magazines. In this way she helped the boys examine how their very sense of maleness was constructed for them by others, including the media. Young, too, found that competing gender regimes impacted on the boys' participation in these critical literacy activities.

Martino (1994a, 1995c, 1998) has also explored how teachers can actively intervene during the use of certain texts and assignments in ways that may help open spaces for examining and debating certain "accepted" attitudes toward masculinity. Martino maintains that this examination and debate is a necessary step toward the awareness and critique that are requisite precursors for changing these actions and their attendant consequences.

Historical Notions of Literacy and Gender

Although habitus creates a common sense that constrains the choices individuals have available, historical studies have established that the common sense can change. The history of literacy and what it means to be literate has changed considerably over time (see, for example, Hunter, 1988; Willinsky, 1990, 1992). Willinsky (1990) argues that literacy was taught and practiced by the working classes of mid-nineteenth-century England as a way to achieve better working conditions and political power, and that this was actively discouraged by the elite. The workers set up their own "Sunday schools" so that workers and their children could learn to read on their one day off, despite the unavailability of public schooling. The elite, worried about the political power the working class was gaining, were able to undermine the political value of literacy by establishing compulsory public schools (a long-time goal of the working class) and then subverting the Sunday school's focus on literacy as power, changing the focus to the study of literature!

According to Willinsky, this is one reason why literature has never been taught as part of socially transformative social projects in school; the tradition of teaching literature since its inception in British and American schools has essentially been a conservative venture in maintaining the status quo. We'll explore how to do otherwise in our final chapter.

Reynolds (1990) describes fears from later in the nineteenth century, when many believed that British working-class boys were reading too much popular fiction and therefore wasting their masters' time and resources. She cites a commentator from 1891 arguing that the libraries were full of "loafing office boys or clerks . . . using their masters' time for devouring all the most trivial literary trash." According to Reynolds, though the purpose of controlling literacy for the ends of the upper class is the same, the perceived problem has changed. Instead of worrying about political danger from a literacy-empowered lower class, the elite expressed anxiety that reading among the working classes was a frivolous waste of time and energy that should have been spent working.

Times and ideologies have continued to change. It is now accepted as a truism that participants in a democracy and a technological era of electronic information must be highly literate, and that they should use their literate power to exercise personal power and choice. Not being literate is unacceptable; not using literacy for personal ends is now the danger.

The History of Gender

Gender also has an evolving history. Gender historians such as Kimmel (1996) and Rotundo (1994) explore the history of manhood in America and how various social forces have shaped what it means to be a man; how males are allowed to relate to each other, to their families, and to women; and how men feel about various tasks like literacy.

It can't be emphasized enough: changing definitions highlight that gender is a socially constructed concept and that the systems of belief and gender roles are susceptible to transformation. If boys are in trouble in the area of literacy because of gender, then our systems of belief both about literacy and about gender can be changed in ways to help them. As McCormick (1999) writes:

> The recognition of historical difference helps us in the present to question the apparent naturalness and universality of our own points of view: We come to see that there are changing beliefs and assumptions behind even such everyday activities as wearing jeans to class. Why, for example, does our manner of dress differ so dramatically from the dress of only one hundred years ago? What larger values and beliefs are revealed by the clothing that we wear? (p. 4)

McCormick recommends explicitly studying with students how the meaning of cultural concepts and texts evolve over time due to shaping by powerful social and cultural forces. Such a project foregrounds the choice and agency of students, which in turn gives them a sense of their agency and an opportunity to see possibilities for choice and transformation since things as they are is not how things must be.

If gender is a powerful social construct, then this is because of habitus. But because gender and other concepts are socially constructed, then they can be examined and transformed in the ways McCormick suggests.

Three Worries

Although all of the research and theory that we've cited has informed our thinking, we have three major related concerns about the existing research base that we wanted to address in our own work.

Essentializing and Oversimplifying Our Students

First, it seems to us that much research simply assumes that gender has an impact. McCarthey (1998) is among those who provide a caution against that way of thinking. She argues convincingly of the danger of essentializing students' performance based either on a conception of stable personality traits (e.g., shyness, aggressiveness) or on the application of categories such as race, class, or gender. In her study, she found that students defined as shy or helpful by their teachers were only that way in certain contexts, when engaged in particular tasks with specific groups of others. In other contexts and situations, the students were often quite different. McCarthey's challenge to researchers studying gender is threefold: to be alert to (1) the influence of context, task, and grouping; (2) the variation within the category; and (3) the possibility that gender is not a category that is useful for teachers and researchers to think with about students.

Losing Sight of Individuals

A related worry we've mentioned is that research that categorizes or groups individuals in order to make comparisons inevitably loses sight of the individuals within the group. Telford (1999), like Millard, argues that teachers use the research findings that aggregate boys into a single group to reinforce boys' general tendencies rather than attend to individual differences or widen possibilities by introducing boys to different kinds of texts and responses.

If teachers and schools use the research in a stereotypical fashion, they may perpetuate boys' tastes and achievement levels. We have a personal stake in this worry, for neither of us have ever fit the portrait of boys and reading offered by the research. And if we address boys as a group defined by averages, then we will not meet the needs of many of our boys.

Narrow Visions of Success

A third worry is that the assessment of boys' literacy achievement is done entirely through their success at tasks in school. Turning again to Telford's (1999) research, we can see why that might be a mistake, for it establishes that the confidence and experience some boys demonstrated in their private home reading was at odds with negative public attitudes they adopted in discussions with peers. Heath and McLaughlin (1993), Mahiri (1998), and Moje (2000) are among the other researchers who have established that various groups of young people employ powerful literacy practices outside school that then go unrecognized, untapped, or unvalued in school.

What This Makes Us Think About: Getting to Know Our Students

As we have noted, our primary interest in doing our research was to help us and other teachers think about better ways to meet the needs of boys. We want this research to affect how things are done in school, so we want to think hard about the implications of our research. We'll discuss these implications at length in our final chapter, but that seems too long to ask readers to wait for what likely matters most to them. So at the end of each chapter we'll talk about some of the practical answers we might offer to the most compelling question each chapter raises for us.

In this chapter we've presented a wealth of research that talks about boys in general, but we've presented it with the caveat that as teachers we need also to look at individual boys in particular. One of our major concerns in doing this research was to get a close qualitative look and understanding of individual boys so we could help and teach them better. The dearth of such research has prompted a question: *How can we get a close look at the individual students in our classes so we can see their strengths both in and outside of school, and so we can get beyond essentialized definitions?*

Personality Profile
One possibility is to ask students to do a personality profile. When Jeff taught middle school, his students came from several different public and religious elementary schools. Since the kids were new to each other and to him, the first assignment was to create a hypermedia stack on the computer, with cards describing their appearance, interests, and favorite quotes, quotes from friends about them, and so forth. They used the scanner and software to edit a photograph, used an audio file to download a favorite song, provided hotlinks to favorite Internet sites, and used the draw tools to create a floor plan of their favorite place. The assignment helped Jeff get to know his kids, and it helped create a classroom community. It also taught the kids about hypermedia design, which was used throughout the year, and about characterization and making character inferences, another set of skills that was built on throughout the year. In addition, it ensured that the first assignment of the year was something they were the world's big expert on: their personal identity. (See Wilhelm and Friedemann, 1998, for a full description of this assignment.)

Information Exchanges: Inventories, Surveys, and Letters
Interest inventories, surveys, and letter exchanges between teacher and student seem to be another set of good ways to exchange information about personal preferences and interests. But, as we will see, caution needs to be taken that students interpret this task as one in which the teacher honestly wants to get to know them, not as a way of perpetuating schoolish values. Letter exchanges, perhaps involving parents, hold the additional value of establishing personal relations and communication.

Daily Student Officer
Especially in blocked or extended classes, another effective technique is to ask a student or a pair of students to be each day's class officer. The class officer

takes attendance and fulfills other chores. The most important chores are providing an Opening Moment and a Closing Moment. These are personal sharings of something related to ideas being explored, or something the student would like to explore in class. The chores also involve writing a class history from the student's perspective of the unplanned and perhaps unnoticed underlife of the class. What things happened today that were not on the official agenda? That may not have been noticed by the teacher? Why are these things important? The role of class officer puts each student on stage for a day every four to six weeks and allows them to share who they are and their perspective on the class. As well, the teacher can get a lot of information about what is really going on in the class.

Sharing Their Music

One of the things we discovered in our study is just how much the boys valued their music. We started to think about the potential benefits of asking one student in each class to share an especially important song each day (or week) by bringing in a CD. Alternately, they could identify an MP3 file for us to download at home. Listening to a few songs might only take us the ride home from school but could pay huge dividends in terms of getting to know students and developing relationships with them.

There are countless other ways to get to know students as individuals: eating lunch in the cafeteria from time to time with different groups of students, attending student concerts and athletic events, featuring students of the week with a bulletin board display that they create themselves. The important thing is to engage in activities with our students that allow us to get to know them and that communicates our care and concern for them as whole people.

Knowing students as people allows us to relate to them and teach them as people. This in turn will assist us in creating classroom contexts that accommodate difference, a topic we will pursue in later chapters.

One of the reasons we feel so strongly about the importance of getting to know students as individuals is how much we enjoyed getting to know and learning from the boys in our study. Because we want our readers to get to know at least some of what is a very memorable cast of characters, as we noted in the Introduction, we present four profiles after each chapter. The first four in the following interchapter, *Meet the Crew*, derived from activity interviews of each of the boys.

Meet the Crew

Ricardo

Bambino

Pablo

Bodey

Ricardo

Ricardo, a European American eleventh-grade student at the private boys' academy, did well in school, which he hugely enjoyed. His English teacher labeled him a "top rate" English student. He was involved in many extracurricular activities in the area of service, sports, and the arts. But his true love was the visual arts and the stories they can tell.

Ricardo followed movie releases both in America and abroad over the Internet. He followed the films of particular producers and directors and could talk at great length about their development, the meaning of their work over time, and the work they currently had in development. He had visited Japan and particularly liked Japanese comics and "Japanimation" movies. Ricardo was a photographer. During the course of the study he was running for a school-wide office and used his photographs in a series of election posters that poked fun at himself and that satirized issues of school life. He hugely enjoyed the satire of *The Simpsons* and the World Wrestling Federation, which he described as "a giant romp of a soap opera, but funny and made for fun!" He was privileged with humor and loved critiquing cartoons, jokes, and humorous scenes from movies and television, often connecting these to his reading. Ricardo helped us understand that a teacher who looked only at his school literacy would miss much of his literate life and much of who he was and wanted to become.

Bambino

Bambino, a Puerto Rican eleventh grader in our urban school, was one of our most enthusiastic participants. He kept a meticulous log and was eager to talk with us about it. We found it somewhat surprising, then, when he told us how much he disliked school. He did his work, though he resented homework for intruding on his time. But he did it in only a perfunctory way, evidencing what Nystrand (1997) calls *procedural* rather than *substantive* engagement.

Outside of school, it was a different story. Bambino was an avid wrestling aficionado. He specialized in Extreme Championship Wrestling, a less popular version of wrestling than the WWF (World Wide Wrestling Federation) or the WCW (World Championship Wrestling), which include popular culture icons such as The Rock and Goldberg. And he did more than that. He kept a notebook of all the wrestling moves he had seen, a list of more than six hundred at the time of our interviews, creating what was in essence his own wrestling encyclopedia. He sometimes offered the latest wrestling news in the form of play-by-play announcing, thereby using forms of oral literacy to relay information and interact with his friends in creative ways. He also elaborated on his interest by keeping a list of wrestling names, including what he, his family members, and his friends might be named if they ever participated in any of the wrestling federations.

In this way, a young man who scraped by doing the absolute minimum of what was required to get by in school did much more than that outside of school, in ways that were entirely voluntary yet very schoolish (e.g., writing summaries and encyclopedia entries). We asked him about what we saw as an interesting contradiction. He explained that he was willing to work on what interested him but that little in school fit the bill. In fact, he was willing to go a step further: to work for a teacher who simply recognized his interests and expertise.

Pablo

Pablo, an eleventh-grade European American, was a student at the rural high school who professed to enjoy school because of its social nature and the opportunities it offered him to actively resist what he considered to be un-ethical or uncreative ways of being. In fact, in the classes Jeff observed, Pablo was almost celebrated by his teachers and many of his peers for his resistant attitudes. He wore an old Army jacket with various pins and patches pro-claiming various causes, such as "Free Tibet" or "Your favorite aunt is a les-bian." He deliberately chose his dress in a way that classmates would code as gay, yet he had a very serious girlfriend with whom he spent nearly every free moment. He considered himself an "activist" whose job it was to "raise peo-ple's awareness and help them be different."

Pablo was active in local political causes, and he was very concerned about the environment, including contamination at a local chemical site. He used his interests in art, quilting, fabric design, drama, and jewelry making not only for great personal pleasure, but to make various political statements that he was happy to propound.

Pablo played in a Christian rock band, which Jeff had the privilege to see perform at a church revival. He enjoyed viewing and critiquing musicals and dramas and traveled to New York City with his church youth group to do so. He was profoundly alive and used various nontraditional forms of literacy to define himself, for pleasure, and to communicate about what he considered to be socially significant issues.

Pablo was very comfortable and in fact seemed to very much enjoy taking on nonhegemonic, alternative male roles. He seemed abetted in this project by many teachers and at least some of his peers. Though he sometimes alluded to people's judgments of him, he professed never to have been hassled about his style or "rebel" activities. Clearly, Pablo does not fit the profile of the male straitjacketed by "habitus" and conventional conceptions of masculinity.

Bodey

Bodey, a European American seventh grader from the rural school, rejected school as a "mind numbing bore." He was failing English, refused to do much of his work, and claimed to have forgotten the rest of it at home. He loved the social nature of school so much that he would excuse himself from our interviews a few minutes early so he could get to lunch to meet his friends. He loved football and looked forward to being on the high school squad. He hung out with friends who also liked to play sports. At the same time, he was reading *Moby Dick* on his own, refusing to write about it in his school-sanctioned reading log or literary letters. "This is for me," he told Jeff. "I'm reading the action and skipping the other stuff [e.g., the cetology sections]. And it's damn good stuff." When Jeff asked if he anticipated reading the whole book, he answered, "As long as I keep liking the story." Bodey also followed favorite sports teams on the Internet and through the media and newspaper, but he refused to write about this as well, despite his teacher's encouragement.

The passion evidenced by these four young men regarding many aspects of their literate lives beyond school and many of their out-of-school activities lay in stark contrast to the much less passionate way they engaged in school in general and school-sanctioned literacy in particular. If that passion could be tapped, school would be revolutionized. But to tap the passion, we must understand its source. Doing so is the purpose of our next chapter.

Going with the Flow

WHAT BOYS LIKE TO
DO AND WHY THEY
LIKE TO DO IT

It was a cold, damp Saturday in March. Just the kind of morning that's perfect for catching up on some much-needed sleep. The window was open a crack, just to let some air in, creating the need to snuggle tightly under the covers. But at 7:30 Michael was awakened by the *skrtch-skrtch* of wheels on pavement. He made his way to the window to see three neighborhood boys practicing their skateboarding, as they had been doing the night before and the night before that. 7:30 A.M.! In the drizzle!

Every day a group of three or four boys in Michael's neighborhood is working on their tricks. They're not very good, no heirs to Tony Hawk yet, but they are improving. They've built a ramp and have arranged with neighbors who have hilly lots to use their driveways. And they practice, practice, practice. Even in the rain. Even when Michael, at least, would rather be sleeping.

The mantra that boys are in trouble has been picked up by the popular press. In our last chapter we explained our reservations about much of the research upon which that mantra has been built. But even if we accept it, it doesn't mean that boys are in trouble in all aspects of their lives. Michael doesn't know how the skateboarders in his neighborhood are doing in school, but he does know that they've displayed diligence, ingenuity, and persistence—all qualities that ought to contribute to their success.

If boys are successful outside of school, then it raises the question of whether it's the context or the kids that are to blame for their problems in school. Like Mahiri (1998), we believe that trying to understand the sources of young men's success and enjoyment outside of school may shed light on how schools can better serve them. In this chapter we'll look at what characterizes the activities that the boys in our study value and see how that relates to their feelings about school in general and reading in particular.

To find out, we asked the boys in our study to rank the activities they most enjoyed, and then talked with them about their rankings and the reasons behind them in interviews that ranged from thirty to sixty minutes. Michael used the ranking sheet illustrated in Figure 2.1. Jeff modified it somewhat, chiefly by specifying other kinds of reading that one might do. (For example, he added *Reading a Magazine* to the ranking sheet.) After transcribing the interviews, we coded them, looking at each of the conversational turns the boys took and identifying its major theme or themes. We tried to understand why each boy liked to do what he liked to do. We then looked at how those themes played out across the interviews. We had technical difficulties with two tapes, so this chapter is drawn from interviews with forty-eight young men, one of whom dropped out of the study after the activity interview. (See Appendix A for the major coding categories that we used.)

As we explained in the last chapter, as we looked at our data, we wanted to be on guard against assuming a homogeneous population and overgeneralizing. The stance we took was a teacher's stance. When we thought about a theme, we asked ourselves whether it sufficiently characterized the group to the degree that it would be a sensible starting point for us as teachers when we planned our curriculum and instruction. We found several such themes. But we also found several important ways in which the data suggest that our boys were different and defied generalization. The implications of both the commonalties and the differences challenged us as teachers and teacher educators. At the end of this chapter, we will highlight the key issues that the data from this activity and interviews raised for us, and we will share how this is causing us to think about our teaching in new ways.

Before we present what we found out, though, we want to turn to the lens that has helped us understand the activity interviews. And interestingly, that lens was not provided by the myriad studies of gender that we discussed in the last chapter. Instead it was provided by Mihaly Csikszentmihalyi (1990a), a psychologist who researches what he calls *flow*, "joy, creativity, the process of total involvement with life" (p. xi).

Csikszentmihalyi (1990a) begins his book with a simple premise: that "more than anything else, men and women seek happiness" (p. 1). Everything else for which we strive, he argues—money, health, prestige, *everything*—is only valued because we expect (sometimes wrongly) that it will bring us happiness. Csikszentmihalyi has spent his professional life studying what makes people happy, more specifically by examining the nature of flow, "the state in which people are so involved in an activity that nothing else seems to matter" (p. 4).

He offers eight characteristics of flow experiences that we think can be usefully collapsed into four main principles:

- A sense of control and competence
- A challenge that requires an appropriate level of skill

FIGURE 2.1   Activity Ranking Sheet

Please rank the following activities in the order that you like them. Put a 1 next to the activity you like most, moving down to a 14 for the activity you like least.

_____   Listening to music

_____   Hanging out with friends

_____   Playing sports

_____   Playing video games

_____   Doing something mechanical, like fixing an engine

_____   Drawing, painting, or cartooning

_____   Reading a good book

_____   Watching a favorite sports team on TV or at the stadium

_____   Surfing the net

_____   Learning something new about a topic that interests me

_____   Working on a hobby (Please specify your hobby _____)

_____   Going to school

_____   Watching television or going to the movies

_____   Other (Please specify _____)

- Clear goals and feedback
- A focus on the immediate experience

These principles resounded throughout all of our data.

What we found in our study is that all of the young men with whom we worked were passionate about some activity. They experienced flow. But, unfortunately, most of them did not experience it in their literate activity, at least not in school. Before we discuss how they talked about their reading, we want to give an idea of how they talked about the other activities that they loved.

A Sense of Competence and Control

According to Csikszentmihalyi (1990a), when people describe flow experiences, they typically talk about a sense of competence and the feeling of control that stems from having developed sufficient skills so that they are able to achieve their goals. He quotes a dancer, who exclaims, "What a powerful and warm feeling it is! I want to expand, to hug the world. I feel enormous power to effect something of grace and beauty." And though chess is a much different activity, a chess player offered a similar description: "I have a general feeling of well-being, and that I am in complete control of my world" (pp. 59–60). The young men in our study shared similar feelings. They gravitated to activities in which they felt sufficient competence to have a feeling of control. What they were good at varied widely, but their feeling of competence was crucial.

Here's Johnny on cooking:

> Um, it's kind of a way I can express myself. I like to cook for my family and friends. They all like to cook. And when they know I'm cooking they say, "Oh, I'm coming over for dinner." And they usually do. I just like cooking. It's really the only thing I'm good at.

And Deuce on rapping:

> Well, music, I've been doing music and art the same amount of years. Since I was young, I was doing music, and music, I just had this talent in music that I know. It's some thing called freestyling or when you have just a person just knock over the song. When people try to battle me, it's like a big thing. You know, different artists try to battle each other. I just look quiet, but everywhere I go, all around town, nobody can beat me. I get respect from everybody. Everybody comes out of their houses to come

listen on the corners and stuff, and I just walk away. I know that I can write because I'm smart. You know what I mean? I'm smart. Plus, I'm street smart so I know I could write about some good, interesting stuff. You know what I mean? So I'm real confident with music, and I'm confident in my team.

And Prinz on hockey:

Well, I think it's just a fast-paced sport, it's just something that, well, I'm small but . . . I have an advantage that I'm fast in hockey and I just like to play hockey because it's one of the things that I'm best at.

Our data also suggest that there may be a cost to this emphasis on competence, for it keeps many of the young men from developing new interests and abilities. Ricardo made this very clear:

Yeah, I can't do snowboarding. I thought I could, my parents got me a snowboard for the first time and I couldn't even stand up on it, so I gave up on that real quick.

As did Clint:

Like I try and do new stuff but I usually stick with what I already know. Like if I try and do something new, and I'm no good at it, like I won't just try something for a minute and then say I don't want to do it because I'm no good at it. I'll try it for a long period of time, but if I don't get better at it, I'll just stop.

Buster felt much the same way. He was a prize-winning mountain biker and he spoke about how he enjoyed the feeling of competence and control his sport gave him:

Just, I don't know, it just gives me a thrill and a sense of accomplishment I guess. I mean it's something that I did, not something you know that someone else did or you know it's all about if I had a good race, then I had a good race, and if I had a bad race, well then that was me.

The same feeling marked his mechanical work:

Um, I guess it's just kind of a sense of accomplishment as far as you know if I actually put something together or take something apart and plus I'm learning while I'm doing it. If, say I'm, say I'm replacing my exhaust and my dad's there teaching me how to do it and that's something I can learn and then I know and I can pass that on to my kids and it's just something, it's kind of like attained knowledge I guess that you can get from, you know, just from doing.

But absent that feeling of competence, Buster did not enjoy pursuing an activity, even if he thought it was important:

> I don't know, something about computers, I'm really not all that, I mean I like the communication aspect of computers, but I'm really not, I don't know, something about them that I'm not—first of all, I'm not all that computer literate, and second of all, there's just something about them that I'd rather, they're too complicated for me I guess.

Buda took it one step further, suggesting that even within an activity in which he felt competence, he focused on his strengths rather than trying to address his weaknesses:

> Stick handling is a hobby for me. I don't have the speed like some people do, but I'm always aware and stick handling is one thing I'm very good at, like most people would say I'm very good at and ah, it's something I always want to work on because I know I'm not the fastest guy. I know I have to work on my speed, but I don't know, stick handling is just fun to improve. It's fun to work on what kind of new moves you can come up with and you can. It's also you can watch professional hockey and see what kind of moves they have and try them out.

Again and again we heard boys talk about how a feeling of competence kept them involved in an activity. Again and again we heard boys exclaim that they would quickly give things up if they did not gain that competence. That's why it was so striking that only two boys made a link between accomplishment and reading.

Pablo talked about how he had enjoyed seeing himself improve as a reader:

> Well, I think it gains a certain, like you gain knowledge from it, from whatever you read, and I like that aspect of it, that I've accomplished reading a book because I used to struggle when I was younger, I didn't like to read at all. I liked to read, like, comic books and that was it. But I've gotten a lot better and I read more for myself and then I'll read the English books and things and I think it's almost a sense of accomplishment as well because—I think in everything you do you learn knowledge.

And Larry was alone in linking his increasing competence to school:

> Um, I haven't started reading until this year pretty much. . . . I have been starting novels this year because of Mrs. _____, kinda like assigns the homework and this is the only time it's really been due so I've been reading pretty good novels now and I like John Steinbeck and stuff. A

lot of novels like that get to me and Mrs. _____'s been kinda showing me the road and the path. I kinda thought reading was dumb, but now I'm kinda getting more into it.

Larry went on to talk about the recognition his teacher had given him and the pride he took in recognizing and naming his own improvement. Several boys, however, reported that reading didn't give them that feeling. Mark explained why he ranked reading so low: "It feels like it is almost a waste of time, because you are not accomplishing anything."

Thus far, we've focused on competence. We've referred to both its importance as a motivator and how its absence might stifle activity. This has powerful implications for literacy instruction.

The boys also discussed the importance of feeling control. This came out clearly in their discussion of school. Csikszentmihalyi (1990a) notes that "knowledge that is seen to be controlled from the outside is acquired with reluctance and it brings no joy" (p. 134). The boys in our study seemed to concur, both in their discussions of reading and of writing.

Here's Chris talking about writing:

> A lot of times with writing I get excited, especially when the teacher doesn't give you a limitation. Like with ———, we did a lot of writing assignments with poems and what not and that really caught my interest because you could write about whatever you wanted to write about.

Guy echoed his point:

> I like writing without having any guidelines to follow, just where you have to do your own thing. I might not mind having a guideline as how long it has to be, but I don't like having a topic to write about, just to make up my own story.

According to some of the boys, what was true for writing was also true for reading. Joe noted the importance of control over his reading:

> I don't like it if I have to read it, but if I read it on my own then it would probably seem a little better.

One indication of the salience of the theme of control is the reaction it provoked from Melissa Larson, a university student of Michael's who did much of the transcribing for this study. Michael began every class with what he called "opening circle." The circle was an invitation to students to discuss anything education-related that was of interest to them. The only time Melissa initiated the opening circle discussion was when she brought up the issue of choice. "Choice is so important to so many of the kids whose transcripts I'm typing. I'm wondering what [my classmates] are going to do to allow choice." From the time we began this study, our data have provoked similar questions for us. In this case, Melissa's question started a long discussion about balancing the desire for choice and the chance to work on common projects with the mandates of curriculum and assessment (cf. Rabinowitz and Smith, 1998; Wilhelm, Baker, and Dube, 2001).

We'll talk about the issue of choice and control at much greater length when we discuss our reading log interviews in Chapter 4. But from the time we began our interviews with the boys, the question that Melissa raised was with us. And so was the warning issued by Newkirk (2001) that sometimes when we think we are offering choices, our students—particularly the boys—may construe the classroom context and what is valued there in such a way that they do not feel they are really being offered a choice.

A Challenge That Requires an Appropriate Level of Skill

As Csikszentmihalyi (1990a) notes, "By far the overwhelming proportion of optimal experiences are reported to occur within sequences of activities that are goal directed and bounded by rules—activities that require the investment of psychic energy, and that could not be done without the appropriate skills" (p. 49). He explains, "Enjoyment comes at a very specific point: whenever the opportunities for action perceived by the individual are equal to his or her capabilities" (p. 52). We found that the young men in our study gravitated to activities that provided the appropriate level of challenge.

Unlike Martino (1995a), who found that sports are used as a way to enforce a particular kind of masculinity, it seemed that the young men in our study spoke instead of sports as a way to provide a particular level of challenge. Geo described it beautifully:

> Because when I get the ball—people draw things and stuff like that— that's my art, get the ball, I like to run, make moves, and like if they make good blocks, I just read the blocks, it's like, I don't know, it's a challenge every time and I like challenges. So, I'm just going to go up there hard. If people are big, I'm going to run there anyway.

But the boys didn't have to be starting on varsity teams as tenth graders as Geo was to have similar feelings. Wolf played on a club hockey team, and his remarks resonated with Geo's:

I don't know, I just enjoy it. I think I like it because what other sport can you play on ice, you know. There is a lot more skill involved than playing football or basketball or baseball. Not to say that those games are not completely, totally skill oriented, it is just that in hockey there's a lot more going on. That's more of a thinking game than it is a physical game, despite what it looks like. I mean, there is a lot going on. I mean, yeah, there is a lot of hitting and checking and elbowing and sticking and things like that, but that is just like minor stuff. That's like low level, you don't have to think about that. At the same time you got to know where everybody else is on the ice and you've got to put yourself on the court, you need to be in a good position to make a play.

Even when the boys were not involved in team sports, they spoke of the importance of challenge. Deuce, who saw himself primarily as a rapper, reported:

Basketball, I'm not competing that much. Well, you got to compete, but I just like playing basketball, just like playing it. It seems like everything I like doing is proving a point to myself: How good can I do this? Do you know what I mean? I don't never do nothing to lose. I don't ever do nothing to lose.

We wrote earlier about the boys' feeling of the importance of control and competence. But control did not mean domination. Challenge had to remain. Aaron suggested that absent an appropriate level of challenge, sports lose their interest:

Well gym is, we're playing badminton in gym and my partner and I are like 9 and 0 in badminton games and I think we had—when we were both there—a total of 6 points scored on us in the 7 games that we were both there for. So it's kind of, gym is kind of boring.

Not every boy was involved in sport. But challenge was important for them nonetheless. Our data suggest that one of the primary attractions for the boys who enjoyed video games was that the games provided the kind of challenge they found compelling. And once again, if that was not the case, the boys rejected the game.

Maurice talked about why he liked Lara Croft video games:

Yeah, they're more of a challenge. Like you have to search here, kill animals, find keys, and find codes, and door latches, and everything. It's an adventure. Something like Indiana Jones but she's a girl, and it's real good.

And Fred talked about why he liked Zelda: "The video game, like Zelda, that causes you to think a lot . . ."

The fact that video games contain different levels means that the level of challenge will always be appropriate. That, Bodey explained, is what makes them so compelling:

> James Bond, when you first play, um it's OK and then I think the thing that really sucks you into it is there is a lot of hard levels and there are a lot of things that you can do. In terms of finding cheat codes, um to make yourself invincible. Therefore, you feel the urge to keep playing.

Without that sort of challenge, the games lose their luster, as Barnabas, the most passionate devotee of video games, acknowledged. The best games, he said, are

> games that take a long time to beat. Where you can finally beat it [after a long time]. Like fighting games, like they are OK but they get really old. Like if you play with every character it is like five times [before you master it] so it gets old. I mean if you can do all of the finishing moves, you do them all like ten times and it gets pretty old.

The importance of an appropriate level of challenge extended into schooling. As we noted earlier, Johnny loved to cook. So he tried to sign up for his school's cooking elective. He was unsuccessful, but in the end he thought that was OK:

> Yeah, I cook good. I never took the cooking class here. I mean, I signed up for it every year, but I never got it. So, but the things they cook are like, so easy to cook, I think it just wouldn't be any fun. It's just the fundamentals they're probably teaching in there.

The emphasis on an appropriate level of challenge extended beyond their favorite sports and hobbies. It also marked their discussions of reading in interesting ways. Some of the boys wistfully recalled reading *Goosebumps* books that they had found interesting but that were now too easy. But more often the boys talked about feeling overmatched by reading. Haywood put it this way:

> Ah, well I like a book that isn't, isn't easy but not so difficult that you don't understand what is going on. Ah, because if you are reading a book that doesn't make sense to you then you just, you know, "Well I don't know how to read this" and then you have negative attitude and you don't concentrate and you don't really gain anything from the experience.

Ricardo provided a specific example:

Ah, I don't like reading plays because it's hard, it's just everything is talk-ing and . . . when you've done a page you have to look back and say OK, this person is talking to that person.

The potential impact of feeling "overmatched" is clear as we recall the comments in our discussions with the boys about the importance of compe-tence and control. The young men in our study wanted to be challenged, but they wanted to be challenged in contexts in which they felt confident of im-provement, if not success. If the challenge seemed too great, they tended to avoid it, instead returning to a domain in which they felt more competent.

Maybe this should not be surprising. After all, it jibes with very established research literature on self-efficacy. Bandura (1993) is a leading researcher in that field. He critiques psychology for its "austere cognitivism," for its neglect of the impact of motivation and affect. Bandura is especially interested in the ways that people's perceptions of their capabilities affect their courses of ac-tion. He puts it simply: "It is difficult to achieve much while fighting self-doubt" (p. 118).

Hundreds of studies have concurred. In fact, when we did an ERIC search on self-efficacy, calling for journal articles published after 1995, we found 619 entries exploring the impact of self-efficacy in a myriad of arenas—from per-formance in various school subjects, to health, to career choice, and so on. As Pajares (1996) points out in a comprehensive review, the area of research is abundant and thriving. Pajares also makes what we think is a significant point: "Particularized judgments of capability are better predictors of related outcomes than are more generalized self-beliefs" (p. 563). This means that self-efficacy beliefs don't extend from one context to another, especially if those contexts aren't clearly related. For example, Haywood's self-efficacy beliefs about basketball seem to have transferred to his beliefs about his abil-ity in football and lacrosse, but they didn't extend to his reading. Our findings suggest that there may not be a generalized self-esteem that teachers can mine. Rather, the boys in our study developed self-efficacy beliefs that emerged from experiencing success in particular domains. This offers a clear challenge to teachers to work toward ensuring success with particular kinds of literacy tasks and texts, an idea we will follow up on in later chapters.

The work on self-efficacy and our findings here clearly relate to Vygotskian views of teaching. Vygotskian theorists (e.g., Tharp and Gallimore, 1988) emphasize that teaching is assisting learners to more competent performances. In other words, teachers need to provide students with a repertoire of expert strategies for approaching and completing particular tasks. This is a break with other views and models of learning that see teaching as transmitting information or allowing for student discovery. The sociocultural model based on Vygotsky's work instead argues that teaching is providing the procedural means for a student's participation in a community task so that the student can move from being a novice to being an expert. This occurs by helping students understand the specific procedures that are required to complete particular tasks in particular contexts and by helping them name and employ their understandings. Unfortunately, the boys in our study did not report receiving such help. Instead, they reported being assigned texts that were beyond them and working (or not working) to muddle through them.

Clear Goals and Feedback

The importance of clear goals and feedback is intimately associated with the two characteristics of flow experiences that we have discussed so far. First, without a clear sense of a goal, it seems impossible to have a sense of competence. Second, it is impossible to identify an appropriate level of challenge. As Csikszentmihalyi (1990a) points out, sports and games provide goals and feedback by their very nature: a tennis player wins or loses a point, a lacrosse player scores a goal or is scored upon, a video game player moves up to a new level or loses the game.

Though the activities the boys most enjoyed were different, they all valued clear goals and feedback in the activities they enjoyed. Gohan talked about his love for taking photographs of sunsets. Marcel wrote poems. Hasan mixed raps. Mike was learning to play bass guitar. Rev played Dungeons and Dragons. Joe created hyperstudio stacks. Stan had taken up painting. In every case, the activity provided the kind of feedback of which Csikszentmihalyi (1990a) speaks. Gohan, for example, only had to look at his photograph to see what he had accomplished. Johnny, who loved cooking, provided perhaps the most succinct statement of the importance of clear goals and feedback when he talked about another of his loves—weightlifting:

> Yeah, like, I mean, no pain, no gain. There has been times when I work out so hard that I can barely pick up an apple to eat. I'm in so much pain, but I like the way I look at the end. I look all pumped up and everything, and uh, I feel good. And actually, I feel, I look bigger. I like that.

This emphasis on immediate feedback has important consequences for reading. Reading extended texts such as novels is not likely to provide quick and clean feedback, but reading short informational texts, such as magazines and newspapers, does.

For example, in the activity interviews, when boys spoke of their enjoyment of reading, most spoke about how they valued it as a tool they used to address an immediate interest or need. Here's Timmy talking about what he read on the Internet:

> Well, I like to go to the sports and stuff cause I like to see, I like sports a lot . . . I like to see what is going on and what's, like, who won the games and . . . I like to go to NASCAR and I like NASCAR a lot so. I like to see what is happening and they are like [mumble] it is just fun to ah, find out.

And Mark talking about reading a golfing magazine:

> 'Cause ah, it's probably the best golf magazine out there and it, I mean it just tells you ways and shows you pictures on how you can improve your swing and if you slice the ball, it teaches you how to hook the ball so it goes straight and it ah shows you what new balls come out that are fit for you and new clubs that would fit you and just different things like that.

And Bam on reading the newspaper:

> Like, if you find something that happened around your neighborhood, "Oh, I didn't know that happened. I should read it." Stuff like that. I didn't know my friend went to jail because he tried to rob somebody. I didn't know that until I read the paper. They put his name there in the paper.

And Maurice on reading his driver's education book:

> That was something that I thought was interesting because it helps me. It helps me to put my seatbelt on because before, if they see me without a seatbelt on, they couldn't do anything about it unless you were actually stopped and they saw you without a seatbelt on. But now, if they see you, they can just stop you like that. So that's helping me put my seatbelt on at all times, and it's keeping me out of ticket trouble, keeping points off my license.

And Barnabas on reading about video games:

> Some of the stuff be frustrating. All the magazines I read, they say how they made the game too hard. It's true. They made the game too hard. And, sometimes, I beat the game already and I want to see what all the secret stuff was. I mean, it tells you where all the secret stuff is, but I still got to find them myself. That's all. I'm just asking for a little map.

The boys we cite here could be described as taking an efferent stance (Rosenblatt, 1978) in their reading. Or perhaps it's more accurate to say that they choose texts that reward an efferent reading. Csikszentmihalyi (1990a) provides a lens through which to understand that choice. Efferent reading by its nature provides an opportunity for clear and immediate feedback that aesthetic reading does not. If you're looking for information and you find it, you know that your reading is successful: You can beat the game, fix the electrical problem, or hit the ball straighter. Aesthetic reading, the kind that most teachers (us included) want to cultivate, is a much more nebulous thing. The focus in aesthetic reading is not what can be learned but what is experienced. As such it is consonant with the final characteristic of flow experience that we'll discuss in this chapter, a focus on the immediate. But it is at odds with the way most of the boys in our study spoke about reading. (At the end of Chapter 4 we will explore some ways of cultivating more competent and informed aesthetic reading.)

Perhaps that's why Larry's comment stayed with us:

> [My teacher's] been kinda showing me the road and the path. I kinda thought reading was dumb, but now I'm kinda getting more into it.

Not only does this inspire us as teachers, but it was the only comment of its sort that appeared in any of the interviews. Notice that Larry went beyond saying the teacher took a personal interest in him, though that was important. Even more important was that his teacher shared her reading expertise with him, showing him how to approach and read particular texts in a way Vygotskian theory would endorse.

Larry helps us understand that there is a social dimension to competence, a point famously made by Vygotsky (1978) in his discussion of the zone of proximal development (ZPD), which stresses that learning can only occur when the learner is challenged and is able to perform with assistance what he or she would be unable to do alone. Teaching, then, should precede development, leading the learner into uncharted and challenging waters that can be navigated with assistance.

Our data suggest that many of our boys did not feel they received that kind of assistance. Our reading of Csikszentmihalyi (1990a) gives another lens through which to see the experience Larry's teacher provided him. Larry developed a feeling of control and competence in his reading because he wasn't overmatched by the challenge of school reading, in part because his teacher made the road to reading visible. Both lenses suggest that teachers need to do more work to assist learners to develop the competence of experts.

A Focus on the Immediate Experience

The implications of the way that boys valued reading become even clearer in light of the final characteristic of flow experiences. The *sine qua non* of flow experiences is that people are so focused on what they are doing they lose awareness of anything outside the activity. Csikszentmihalyi (1990a) speaks of this quality in a number of ways: the merging of action and awareness, concentration on the task at hand, the loss of self-consciousness, and the transformation of time. In his study, a young basketball player provides testimony: "Kids my age, they think a lot . . . but when you are playing basketball, that's all there is on your mind—just basketball. . . . Everything seems to follow right along" (p. 58).

The young men in our study spoke in ways that resonate with the words of this basketball player. They valued their favorite activities for the enjoyment they took from the immediate engagement in those activities, not for their instrumental value. The boys played sports because they enjoyed them, not to win a scholarship or to impress others. They played music or rapped because they enjoyed being engaged in that way. And when they engaged with other media, they did so because it made them laugh or kept them on the edge of their seats. Unlike their experience with reading, their focus was on the moment, not on the instrumental value of the activity. Stan developed this idea when we talked about listening to music:

> Lately I've been listening to a couple hard-core bands, *Vision of Disorder*, and um *Machine Head* and stuff like that. I like listening to *Vision of Disorder* when I'm really mad because it helps me just, like, feel what I'm actually feeling.

Maurice's description of his video game involvement also showed his focus on the moment:

> Say you're having a problem with someone or whatever. You play a video game or it's like a shooting game or airplane flying game. You have to take the mission. That helps you take your mind off the stuff that's going on in your life, and you just, for that ten or twenty—for however long you play the game—it helps you forget that. It helps you relieve your mind from that and focus yourself on the game.

To these boys, the immediate experience was key. And as we'll see later, when the boys who were engaged readers talked about reading—at least, the reading they did outside of school—they had the same emphasis.

The Importance of the Social

Although Csikszentmihalyi's (1990a) work helped us understand our boys' activity rankings, it wasn't fully explanatory. Csikszentmihalyi notes that "Another universally enjoyable activity is being with other people" (p. 50), yet as he admits, socializing appears to be an exception to the rules for flow that he posits. What wasn't an exception was how important socializing was to the young men in our study.

Mike provided what could be a mantra for the whole group: "It's always better with friends, always." One of the most striking findings of our study was that virtually all of the boys reported having a small close–knit group of male friends. Only five boys reported having girls in that friendship circle. These friendships were absolutely central to the boys' lives. That centrality was manifested in a number of behaviors that challenge conventional images. The boys talked about needing a place where they could be themselves. And all of them had that place. In short, all of our boys spoke of having intimate connections with others in a way not recognized by popular psychology accounts of boys' experience.

Larry and Chris shared a sentiment echoed by many. Chris said:

> I don't know. I guess just because it's the most fun, and it's easy to relax around friends. And, you can be yourself. That's why I put [hanging out with friends] first.

Larry noted:

> There's only like a couple good friends you know I really have. Um, one good friend—it's just fun to, you know, go places. One friend, I go over to his house pretty much every day or whatnot, we're with each other and um, but yeah, I like hanging out. Usually we talk about what's going on with our life and stuff. Usually once you can find a best friend, you can talk to him and stuff, it's usually how you want to spend your time I guess, that's what I do. We always do stuff together, which makes it more fun. Watch a movie or just sit around, watch TV, play basketball, or swim or do something.

The boys talked about how their friendships allowed them to be themselves. What they seemed to mean was that they could talk more intimately with friends. Only two of them alluded to friends as a protection against the pressure of being male in a specified way. Both of those who did were very involved with the arts, and they seemed to see girls as more accepting of their artistic inclinations. Pablo put it this way:

I guess boys are more—they judge you. They think you have to be a big macho man in order for you to hang out with them. I mean, not all boys, but a lot of 'em, and I guess girls accept you more, for who you are, and I guess it depends on person to person, but that's what I've found.

But this was decidedly a minority opinion. The rest of the boys had found friends who supported them. The "boy code" that Pollack (1999) describes as making intimate relationships taboo was not supported by the evidence in our interviews.

What was in evidence, as Larry suggests, is how the emphasis on the social extended to the boys' discussion of other activities, sometimes in surprising ways. Chris, who used a wheelchair to help him get around after a battle with a childhood illness, was one of the few boys who watched much television. But when he did, he often did so with others. He would arrange with friends to watch a show and to be on the phone together as they watched so they could talk about what they were seeing.

Music, too, was a point of contact, as Zach explained:

That's another thing. Like all the friends, we kinda listen to all the same music and we go to the concerts together and we go in the mosh pits and we do all that. And it's hard for adults to comprehend sometimes.

We noted earlier how important feeling competent was to the young men in our study. In fact, only one of our participants talked about liking to do something he wasn't good at. Jamaal continued to play video games because of his friends:

We play a bunch of them. We got one that's like Tony Hawk's pro skater or something. It's like a skateboarding game and I, to tell you the truth, really stink at video games and they always make fun of me when I play it but I just . . . it's just funny trying to do good.

The friendships occasionally affected the boys' literate lives. Gohan had two friends with whom he shared poetry. Mark checked the Internet or the newspaper to keep up with the hockey scores not because of his interest but because his friends would expect him to know. Neil's friendship circle was characterized by long discussions of movies by favorite directors.

The importance of having a closely knit friendship circle also affected the way the boys engaged with technology, especially the emailing and messaging they did. Although some boys spoke of how they enjoyed meeting people from different areas through the Internet, many more talked about how they used the Internet to continue conversations with the same friends they hung out with at school.

Their friendships also affected their attitudes toward school. Of the twenty-one who talked about liking school, nineteen said they did so because of the social dimension of schooling. Buster's sentiments provide a summary of this viewpoint:

> Probably my favorite part of going to school is the social aspect. I don't know, I guess I just like interacting with my friends and stuff. I mean, that's probably my favorite part about school. As far as classes go, there's certain classes I really don't like and some that are OK, but . . . probably my favorite part of school is seeing my friends.

In contrast, only two boys talked about valuing school because they loved to learn. If, as Vygotsky maintains, all learning occurs in social situations where expertise is shared between people, then the boys' desire to be social could be used to great advantage, as we'll explore at the end of Chapter 4.

Not only did the boys have friendship circles to which they were closely tied, but they also spoke of their strong relationships to their families. We did not see the alienation from family that is often depicted in the popular press or popular psychology accounts. Fred, for example, talked of a family connection through sports:

> I like to [watch football] because that gives me time to sit down with my stepfather and we, like, spend time, we sit there, cheer on the team, like if we're on opposite teams, we still have fun. A family thing in my house is like the Superbowl. He'll cook up some chicken wings, and some stuff, and I'm allowed to stay up and watch the entire game, and, like, we all sit there and cheer on the team we want to win. And it's just a fun night.

The importance of socializing and friendship and the way all our boys were able to achieve healthy and supportive relationships belies the current psychological concerns. However, we recognize that our population may be skewed in the opposite direction from those of the psychologists whose works dominate the discussion in the popular press. We asked teachers to nominate a wide variety of boys, boys from diverse backgrounds and with different histories of school success. Some of those boys needed a little persuading before they agreed to participate. Though we'd like to think we achieved a representative sample of American boys, it's not surprising that boys in therapy talk more about alienation than those who feel sufficiently comfortable with adults to agree to participate in a project that would require them to meet with a stranger for six interview sessions.

The Importance of Getting Away

One way that our data do relate to the arguments of those who argue that boys are in trouble is the number of young men in our study who reported feeling stress and the need to get way from it somehow. Nineteen boys made comments of this sort in their activity interviews. School was a source of pressure for some, as Brandon explained:

> I watch comedies, like *The Simpsons*, *Malcolm in the Middle*, *Married with Children*, those kind of sitcom programs. *Seinfeld* is another one of my favorites. I just feel after a long day of school, I really try hard at school, I really bust my hump, and after I finish all my homework and take a shower, to relax, TV is the best thing to go to. I got a nice large TV up in my room, so I crawl in my bed and just put it on sleep timer and watch that until I fall asleep.

Liam sought his escape by being with friends:

> Ah, I just enjoy really relaxing with my friends, getting out of the whole school mind-set and just kicking back. I go over to their houses, watch movies, um, other activities, I play lacrosse with my friends, I play sports with my friends, ah, but mainly just stuff that's relaxing that I like to do. I do it to just relieve stress.

Bam was among those who used music to escape stress:

> That's when I like to just come home from school, I just want to sit down, just be myself. I'll go in my room and turn on the radio.

Even those activities that brought boys joy occasionally brought pressure as well. Geo was an accomplished athlete, in both football and wrestling, and he felt pressure to do what was necessary to continue his accomplishment:

> Because they don't like—after that class, I go to a different class and then you know I do whatever, then after school I got wrestling and then I got to concentrate on that, then after that I got to take a shower and try to unwind a little and I'm a little tired and I got to still look over all my work. Usually I don't do my homework at home, but if I got something important then I'm gonna look over it, but once I get home, I usually just watch the TV and unwind because you know sports is like real pressure like. I don't want all that pressure to get to my head so I think about it too much. I'll just watch a little TV.

All of the boys we've cited in this section were successful at something important to them, yet their success didn't reduce the pressure they felt. Not all of the boys spoke about such a feeling, but the number and intensity of those who did surprised us.

The Importance of Activity

Other themes that emerged in our analysis were less salient but, we think, worthy of attention. More than half of the boys in the study talked about the importance of physical activity, the drive to be doing something at all times. None were as adamant as Robert. Here he is talking about watching a movie:

> No. I can't really sit down and watch no movie, just sit there and watch it. I got to be up, walking around or moving or talking or something. I can't really sit down and watch no movie for a long period of time.

And playing a video game:

> I just can't sit down and play no video games. I'll play, like, every once in a while. I can't play it on a regular basis.

Wolf voiced a similar understanding:

> One, I can't sit down to a board game. Either my attention span isn't long enough, or I don't have enough patience. I can't sit still. I'm always on the go. I mean, my parents can't understand how I can always keep going 'cause, I mean, I'll go to bed at 1 A.M. and I'll have to get up and ref a hockey game at 7 A.M., don't go back to sleep after I get done with that, go right to a friend's house after that, and go to the movies and then go sledding or skiing and then go out somewhere that night and then wake up early again. I'm always on the go.

Though the majority of the boys in the study were less insistent on the need to always be moving, many talked about their desire to avoid having nothing to do, a much-dreaded occurrence. In fact, many of the boys talked about the lower-ranked activities on their lists as activities of last resort, picked up only to ward off boredom. For some of the boys, this meant browsing to see what was on television. On occasion it meant picking up a book, as we'll explore in greater detail later.

The Importance of Avoiding the Routine

A number of the boys spoke of their desire to avoid routines and to do things in new and different ways. As we'll see in Chapter 4, one of the fundamental criticisms boys had of school was its sameness. Eleven of the boys spoke of their enjoyment of variety. Scotty, for example, enjoyed snorkeling for just that reason:

> When I started snorkeling when I was probably in fourth grade or fifth grade in the Bahamas, um, I just thought—I just had so much fun and thought it was really cool. Like I've been to Cancun snorkeling, uh, Hawaii, um, like scuba diving and snorkeling and different stuff, like probably every island, British Virgin Islands. I've been to the Bahamas. I've been to Florida. I've just been to different places where I'm able to scuba dive and snorkel and, like, each time is different. Like there is never two things that are the same. So I mean, every time you go down, a coral is going to be different.

Bodey enjoyed going to his family's wilderness cabin for a similar reason:

> Well, what I like to do is, see, when I'm here like now, I know what time lunch is, I know what time I'm going to go home, I know what time I have to wake up. Up there at [the cabin], let's say, I have no idea what time I'm going to go to bed, I have no idea what time I'm going to wake up, I have no idea what I'm going to do the next day, if it's going to be hunting, if it's going to be snowshoeing, or if it's going to be staying inside playing cards, and that's I think what I like, and that's what I like to feel, you know, once a year.

Of course, not all of the boys were able to get away from their routines in such a dramatic fashion. Rev offered a related view of a more mundane activity, game playing: "I play anything that's not really repetitive." School meant routine activity for many of the boys, and some of them emphasized the importance of the unexpected as an antidote to that routine.

Two Issues

Thus far, we've argued that our data resonate with the work of Csikszentmihalyi (1990a). The young men in our study sought out flow experiences and described them in ways similar to the participants in Csikszentmihalyi's work. Though we found these similarities compelling, we realize that discussing them to characterize the young men in our study is problematic for two reasons. First, if Csikszentmihalyi is right, then what we are saying about boys would be equally true of girls. That is, we realize that our analysis cannot be used to make a comparison. Second, we are wary of overgeneralizing, for we also identified important differences among our participants. We discussed some of these differences when we explored the range of the boys' interests. Even more compelling was the patterns we noticed within two smaller groups that distinguished them from their colleagues.

Significant Departures

The Readers

As we noted previously, virtually all of the boys noted that reading played a part in their lives outside school, but only seven spoke of the enjoyment they received from reading extended text outside of school, which seems to us to be the conventional understanding of what it means to be a reader. Of these seven, two were primarily readers of history and five of novels, though two of the novel readers talked especially of their interest in historical fiction.

These seven boys provided a number of reasons for their enjoyment of books. Stan worked the hardest to articulate his feelings:

> I like reading books because they let you think about certain things that have happened or they . . . I wouldn't say I want to get away from the world, but it's kind of an escape, like watching TV but it's better than TV. You can't really—like reading a book is—watching TV is, like, no comparison to reading a book because reading a book you can get right into it and all that stuff, and I'm not quite sure what makes a book good, just it has to be sort of interesting. I mean it's different for, you know, certain people. Certain people like certain things. I like a lot of books, I like books that sort of keep you on your toes, books that make you think, controversial books, just a little bit of everything I think.

Stan's last statement resonates with previous ones we've cited on the importance of challenge. Suspense and the drive to figure out the "puzzle" a book provides were important. He raises other key points as well, including the need to be able to enter a book. We took this to mean that he was able both to visualize the story world and to see things from the perspectives of others. Like Stan, the boys who were readers spoke of a desire to be engaged in the big ideas they encountered in reading. Stan, in fact, distinguished the "pie and cake kind of reading" he does during the summer from the more serious reading he undertakes at other times of the year. They also talked about using books to get away.

For Neil, the engagement in these serious ideas were major markers of his identity. He spoke of how he and his friends thought and talked about things of little interest to most of his classmates. He asserted his difference from those classmates through his reading, making a show of carrying complex adult books to class and reading them there.

The Urban Young Men

As we exchanged ideas about what we were hearing as we collected data, it became clear to us that what boys needed to get away from varied considerably. While boys in all four schools spoke of the pressure of school or sport, only the urban boys felt a pressure to make a success of themselves. This feeling was most clearly manifested in the elaborate plans for the future that many of the urban young men had. Jigg, a student in the learning community designed for students who could not make it in a traditional setting, detailed his future plans at a level of specificity far beyond any of the boys in the private, rural, or suburban school:

> After I graduate? I want to do this. This is my plan when I got out of high school. To go to barber school . . . but I said I want to try to go to college. I'm going to go to college first. I was looking at _____ University. They've been sending me letters. My grades are OK. My [test] scores are OK so they're probably good enough to get into that college. I was probably going to go to college for Computer Programming and Business Administration. That was just next year. Five years from then, I was planning on owning a barbershop because I know how to cut hair right. Five years from then, I was planning on a nail salon.

Hasan diplayed similar kind of planning:

> Yeah, I just want to have a better life. I ain't really had to go to public school. I chose to go to public schools because I just wanted that experience because I wanted to be a counselor and I wanted to counsel urban area kids to encourage them to do better and let them know that they can do it. I don't want them to say, "Well, you went to private schools, and, if I go to private schools, I could do the same." So, yeah, I knew what I wanted to do in the future. I always wanted to do it.

The sense of an impending future that would require careful planning and preparation was largely absent from the interviews of the boys outside the urban area.

But that does not mean that the feeling of pressure was absent for the working-class boys from other settings. When Michael read the interviews Jeff had done at the private boys academy, he was able to pick out the two scholarship boys, not because they referred to money pressures but rather because of a feeling of pressure that permeated their entire interviews. One of our worries about the emphasis on gender as a superordinate category is that it may bring with it a lack of emphasis on other structures that affect an individual's experience. Our data strongly suggest that social class is one of those structures.

What This Makes Us Think About: Where Do We Start?

When we talked about the way that we approached making thematic generalizations from our data, we noted that we tried to do so in a teacherly way. We asked ourselves whether the understandings that we gained across our participants was sufficiently similar to provide us with a sensible starting point for us as teachers in thinking about how to teach them. The most compelling question our generalizations in this chapter raised for us is a very basic one: *Where do we start when we plan instruction?* We think our data fundamentally challenge the starting point from which many teachers, ourselves included, proceed.

In planning instruction, most teachers start by asking, "What am I preparing my students for?" The answers to this question vary: for the unit test, for college, for the upcoming state assessment, for next year's class, for success in the world of work. And each answer is undoubtedly important. But if we want our students to bring something of the passion to our classes that they bring to the activities in which they engage outside of school, our data suggest that we have to start by asking another question right along with it: "What is the quality of the experience I want them to have today?"

This isn't a question educators are used to asking. Our friend Brian White, who read a draft of our book, told us that our analysis reminded him of a metaphor he heard in a curriculum theory class taught by Herbert Kliebard at the University of Wisconsin. "In the education-as-preparation view," Kliebard argued, "life is a concert—and education is the bus that takes you there." In such a view, as long as students ultimately hear the music, it doesn't matter how long or bumpy the ride is for them.

How much changes when teachers ask "What is the quality of the experience I want them to have today?" instead of—or along with—"What am I preparing them for?" A lot, we think. When we apply this new question to our own teaching of preservice teachers, we see that it makes us more immediately accountable for our curricular and instructional decisions. For example, it means we can't select a difficult text for our reading list and say simply "This is important for them to know in the future." It means we have to think about the kind of instruction that will make their engagement with that book immediately rewarding.

Doing this kind of thinking has caused us to look for inspiration in unlikely places. For example, we suspect that many teachers regard video games with suspicion or even contempt, as symptomatic of our students' need for flashy visuals and instant gratification, which are at odds with what they get in our classes. But our study has convinced us that thinking about video games can be a useful guide, or heuristic, for us as teachers. By their very nature, video games are designed to hook their players by providing flow experiences. Because they get more difficult as players become more accomplished, they provide both a feeling of competence and an appropriate level of challenge. Because the goals are clear, they provide unambiguous feedback. It's no wonder that many of our boys could lose themselves in video games.

Sequencing Curricula

The attraction of video games resides at least in part on the fact that they provide players with a careful sequence of experiences. But a similar sort of careful sequencing characterizes too few classrooms. When Applebee, Burroughs, and Stevens (2000) examined the curricular structure of the classes of a group of experienced and highly regarded literature teachers, they found that in the vast majority of them, teachers did not sequence texts in such a way that students could make connections and build understandings from text to text.

Unless curricula are structured so that the understandings students gain in one text or activity can be brought forward to the next one, they can't develop a sense of competence. Instead, as our respondents told us, they're likely to feel overmatched and then resistant. But if students can bring their learning from one text to the next, they can feel equipped to meet the challenges they encounter in their new reading. Moreover, they'll be more likely to understand why they're doing it.

In Chapter 6, we explore in greater depth the idea of sequencing assignments so that students develop strategic knowledge in one activity or assignment that they can then apply in the next activity or assignment. Right now, though, we want to stress that we think the notion of carefully sequencing experiences with texts challenges many common practices in language arts classrooms. When you play a video game you know the rules and get better at abiding by them and using them to your advantage. When you read a certain kind of text like a satire or an editorial, the same thing happens. But the genre divisions that inform textbooks and curricula are simply too broad to provide the same kind of experience. Are short stories sufficiently similar that one reads them all in similar ways? Poetry? In many American literature anthologies, Dickinson and Whitman appear close to each other. The fact that both wrote poems in the same country at about the same time doesn't mean that they have the same expectations of their readers. In fact, what it takes to read the free verse of Whitman is very different from what is required to read the lyric poetry of Dickinson.

While short stories might not be a useful category, short stories with unreliable first-person narrators might be. Accepting the invitation to read such stories requires one to identify what might make a narrator reliable or unreliable in certain circumstances. It requires identifying the facts of the story that are beyond question. It requires applying standards from outside the story to the interpretation of those facts. (See Smith, 1991b, for a more complete discussion of judging narrator reliability.)

Other sets of stories that share the same expectations of readers might also be usefully grouped. Stories told through letters and diaries, for example, require attention to dates in a way that other stories don't. However, more than using strategies is typically involved in responding to a genre or a particular kind of theme. Stories told through diaries can also require assessing how and why a character changes. And if the diary is by an adolescent, it often means thinking about what it means to grow up and whether the character is making positive progress in that direction. As another example: survival stories usually need special attention paid to the setting and how people relate to nature.

Our object here is not to make exhaustive lists, for slicing genres so thinly would involve teaching a virtually limitless number of rules that had very limited application. Rather, it seems to us that we can help our students feel competent in playing the game by identifying relatively broad genres that invite the application of similar interpretive strategies. Thinking of poetry as a genre probably does not work, so putting Whitman and Dickinson together might not be sensible. But maybe grouping Whitman with some Sandberg and some Ginsberg and some rap in a unit on what might be called oratorical poetry would.

Ricardo didn't like reading plays because he was baffled by them. We wonder how much experience he had reading them. If his experience is like most students, the answer is likely one a year. We wonder how he would have felt if he had experienced reading short dialogues and then one-act plays as a way to gain experience in understanding the subtext of dialogue, and of imagining the scenes in which that dialogue takes place. We wonder how he would have felt if his teachers had shown him "the road and the path" and had given him repeated practice in traveling. We think he would have felt more competence and as a consequence his attitude about reading plays and his performance both would have been much better.

We want to stress that when we look to video games for inspiration, we're doing more than saying study has to be leavened with a bit of fun. If, say, we were faced with the requirement of teaching *Twelfth Night* (as was one group of teachers we observed) or another text that we felt would be too difficult for our students, creating the conditions of a flow experience would have to involve far more than tossing in an occasional wordsearch or *Jeopardy* game. Instead it would have to involve setting up a sequence of texts and instruction so that students would understand why they are reading, how they ought to be reading, and that they're able to do the reading.

We want to stress as well that our attention to students' likes and dislikes in this chapter doesn't mean that we are simply saying, "Just give them reading that relates to their interests." The boys' interests were sufficiently different that doing so would mean a class could never read a common text. Rather, we are saying that if we understand why they like what they like, we can work to create the conditions that will make students more inclined to engage in learning what they need to know. These conditions are those of "flow" experiences: a sense of control and competence, an appropriate challenge, clear goals and feedback, and a focus on the immediate. Sensible sequencing can help us to do just that.

Meet the Crew

Zach

Gohan

Haywood

Yuri

Zach

In many ways, Zach, a European American eleventh grader, was an English teacher's dream. He was in an honors class and was consistently engaged in the classroom activities. He worked hard to excel in school. He went out for the school plays, often winning the lead. He planned to become an English teacher himself. However, the activities he most enjoyed, and on which his literate life revolved, centered not on school but on the complex role-playing game he and his friends played. The movies he watched, the books he most enjoyed, the music that he listened to all related to the game. The game provided him a chance to enter an alternate world—one, he explained, that involved taking on multiple identities. He told us:

> I have a definitive taste for books. I do. Quite narrow. I mean, don't get me wrong I appreciate Thoreau, Emerson, Dickens. And there's nothing wrong with them. And I love English class, but I'm more of . . . like I read novels associated with my game. And Dungeons and Dragons. Sci-fi. And, um, people like Tolkien and, um, occasionally someone like H. G. Wells. Kinda like science fiction a little bit.

For Zach, the game's the thing.

Gohan

Gohan, a Puerto Rican twelfth grader who was also the father of a young daughter, attended the same alternative school as Jigg. He had been unsuccessful at the district's traditional high school, which he left after a year with only two credits. A facile description would label Gohan as "at risk" of failure, and indeed he had experienced failure in school. Yet when he talked about the activities he most enjoyed, his intellectual curiosity was clear. Listening to music was his favorite activity, one to which he devoted his undivided attention. He loved the complex rhymes of his favorite hip-hop artists. And he wrote himself, though he wrote poetry and not raps, because of the freedom it gave him:

> Poetry, it don't have to rhyme. You could write anything on the poetry. You could write about the sunset or about how you're failing in school, but won't nobody know what you're talking about and it doesn't have to rhyme. Rap is more complicated because if you want to write raps, you're going to have to write it for other people so they will like it, and they have to rhyme and it's hard to rhyme sometimes. But poetry, it's just free, more free. It's freestyle writing.

Unlike most of the boys in our sample, Gohan described two friendship circles, one with whom he played basketball and one with whom he shared his poetry. He noted that he never got a chance to use his poetic ability in school, but if the subject ever came up, he'd be the first with his hand up. His reading interests were also schoolish. Like many of the boys in our study, Gohan enjoyed magazines. But rather than use magazines to find out specific information, Gohan like to browse through news magazines, looking for stories on the latest technological developments. Gohan may have experienced failure in school, but his interests led us to wonder why he wasn't more clearly at risk of success.

Haywood

Haywood, a European American eleventh grader at the private boys academy, appeared in many ways to be a stereotypical man's man. He loved sports, especially physical sports in which he could "hit." In his words, he enjoyed "dominating" others, both through his size and his skill. And he used sports as a way to get out his frustrations and escape the stress of his work at school. He put it this way:

> Well, the thing that I like about sports is that, ah, you know, school is very hard. There is a lot of time put forth into your work and stuff and after going through a six-hour day of classes and, you know, using your brain and stuff, sports kind of relaxes you. It is kind of a way of, like, meditating, I guess you could say.

When we spoke about his favorite activities, he said he enjoyed challenge and competition both on the field and off, such as when he played video games. Haywood explained how he read little outside class, using the newspaper, the Internet, and magazines to do assignments or to read brief articles about his interests. But as he continued, the stereotypes seemed to fail away. He had lots of friends, most of them athletes, and had a group of four with whom he was especially close and could share "anything." Though he talked about the action and horror movies that he enjoyed watching, he talked at much greater length about historical movies, in which he could vicariously experience something that he had never gone through. He talked about *Amistad* and *Schindler's List*, and his empathy was clear. And he talked about books he had read for school, texts such as *Black Like Me* and even *Hamlet*, and how much he enjoyed them (though he felt overmatched by *Beloved*). Haywood never did extended reading outside of class; he didn't have the time. But the seeds for a lifelong engagement in reading seem to us to be planted.

Yuri

Yuri was a European American eleventh grader from the same school. He described himself as a "loser" and "nerd" because he didn't like sports in a very sports-conscious school. Yuri deliberately set himself apart from what he saw as the mainstream, both by his dress (he favored all-black, goth-style clothing) and by the attitudes he espoused. He was especially concerned about how men objectify women, something he actively worked against in his interactions with girls. Those interactions were almost exclusively electronic, for the center of Yuri's out-of-school life was the computer. He used it to converse, and he had a website on which he posted his latest writing. And he devoted countless hours to simultaneously playing various role-playing games, text-based games that require extensive reading and writing. Yuri lost himself playing the games. As he explained:

> I get a lot of stress out because, you know, sometimes it is like something hypnotizes me and I can just set there for hours and then by that time I've forgotten what I am mad at. I have forgotten what I have been stressed about.

Yuri loved to read fantasy. He explained that reading *Ender's Game* by Orson Scott Card helped him think through some of the problems he had to confront in middle school. Despite this love of reading, Yuri didn't enjoy much of the reading he did in school, believing the school "pounded" away at multicultural issues until they were not longer interesting.

As the portraits reveal, there is much that the boys share. They all have intense interests they actively pursue and lose themselves in. They all have arenas in which they are accomplished. They all have close friends with whom they share their accomplishments. But they are very different too. And each defies conventional expectations. For teachers, generalizations are comforting. They give us something to go on when we devise curricula and instruction. But the complexity of the portraits provides a warning. We have to be alert for differences too. Surfaces can be deceiving.

Do the Right Thing

3

Every night, both of us engage in the same ritual with our daughters. "So, how was school today?" we'll ask. And the wealth of information we hope for never materializes. To find out about our kids' experience in school, we have to piece together an understanding from a variety of sources: watching them doing homework, looking over their assignments, reading with them, talking to them about their report cards, going to Parents' Night, and looking for patterns in the very short answers we typically receive from them when we ask about school directly.

The boys we've taught and the boys who participated in our study are like our daughters in that way. We knew that if we wanted to discover their feelings about school and literacy, we'd have to try a variety of ways to do so and check them against each other. This is called *triangulation* in research methodology. In our activity interview, we used both direct and indirect methods. When we talked about why they ranked school where they did, we asked them directly. And when we asked them about other activities, they sometimes discussed school indirectly, though rarely with the passion or in the kind of detail that they talked about other interests.

We wanted to find out more about both the boys' feelings about school and different ways of being literate, but we were worried about the utility of asking them directly. We were concerned that they might not talk much and that they might say what they thought we expected them to say.

Martino's (1998) research suggested another tact to take. In his study, Martino asked his participants to respond to a set of profiles that he developed to portray different ways boys engaged with school. As deBeer (2001) points out, Martino's research is consistent with the premises of narrative inquiry, which is becoming an increasingly important method of educational research. Connelly and Clandinin (1990) argue that "Learners are storytellers and characters in their own and others' stories" (p. 2), so researching their experience requires eliciting their stories. The very rich data that Martino shares in his research suggests that having participants respond to stories is an effective way of doing just that.

Working with Timothy Jenkins, a graduate student of Michael's, we developed eight profiles (see Figure 3.1). The first five profiles (rapper, techie,

FIGURE 3.1   Profiles

Eric

Eric is a fifteen-year-old student at Central High School who loves music, especially doing raps. Because of his skills, his friends call him "The Poet." However, Eric does not particularly like school. He does not think learning in school will help him achieve his goals. Every day at lunch, Eric grabs his radio and starts rhyming. Sometimes he does his own raps and other times he'll do the raps of popular artists. Occasionally, small crowds gather to watch and hear him display his skills. Eric learns everything he can about the music industry in general and rap in particular. He has a subscription to *Vibe*, and as soon as he gets it, he reads it cover to cover. Unfortunately, no one takes Eric and his desire to become a rapper seriously. Girls stay away from him because they feel he is too preoccupied with his music, his male friends think he is wasting his time, and his teachers think his interest in music is interfering with his academic progress. Eric feels alienated because he thinks that everyone is against him. However, he is certain that he has the ability to succeed in the music industry.

Allen

Allen can't understand why his teachers and his school are so old-fashioned. He can't understand why they keep insisting that he read books and stories when technology is going to make books a thing of the past. Allen spends most of his free time on-line or playing the latest video game. Sure, he might have to read a computer manual or instructions for a game, but even then he really learns by doing. School, he thinks, would be much more interesting if it caught up with the times.

Jason

Jason is a very creative person, and he is good with his hands. When he is at home or in electronics class, he seems to be able to fix anything. If someone tells Jason he or she has a problem and gives Jason a manual, he can read it and solve the problem. Instead of being current with the latest stories in *Sports Illustrated*, he spends his free time reading fix-it books. Many people at school think he is weird because he loves spending a lot of time in his industrial classes rather than joining a club, playing a sport, or hanging out with friends. Though Jason is not sure what profession he wants to enter, he is certain that after high school he wants to go to a trade or technical school to enhance his skills. However, his parents have other plans for his life. They are insisting that Jason go to college and obtain a degree.

Andre

Andre is a sixteen-year-old junior in high school. Occasionally, Andre feels overwhelmed by family pressures. However, reading puts his mind at ease. When Andre reads a book, his mind is completely absorbed by the characters and the story. His passion for reading developed at the age of six from reading Bible parables in church. Whenever his Sunday school teacher needed someone to read, Andre was always the first to volunteer. Instead of spending his free time playing sports or video games, Andre chooses to go to the library to read to have fun. He goes to the library at least three days a week so he can browse through the latest best-sellers. Consequently, he is not as popular as the other boys in his school are. But his grades and SAT scores are significantly higher than average. After hearing a librarian speak at the city's annual career day, Andre is considering a career as a librarian or teacher.

Jermaine

Jermaine is the most popular person and the best athlete in his high school. One might say that he is "the big man on campus." As a fifteen-year-old freshman in high school, Jermaine played varsity basketball and was considered one of the best high school players in his state. Many people seem to be showing interest in his ability to play basketball. Now Jermaine feels that he has to maintain the image of a "jock," and he loves it. Since Jermaine expects to receive a full scholarship to attend the college of his choice, he rarely attends class and is pushed through his classes by many of his teachers. All he reads are the sports section of the paper and sports magazines. He's not that much of a fan, but he wants to keep up with the competition. Consequently, his reading and writing skills are below par. He has so much confidence in his athletic potential that he does not place much emphasis in his schoolwork.

Brian

When teachers at George Washington High think of their most memorable student, Brian Johnson's name is almost always mentioned. Why? Brian is known for being a disruptive student and a troublemaker. He never causes any physical harm to any of his peers; however, Brian always finds ways to agitate his teachers and interrupt instruction. Whether he tells jokes, passes notes, or makes funny gestures behind his teachers' backs, he has definitely earned his "class clown" title. He knows that in order to get a job he needs to get a diploma. Nothing, or no one, seems to motivate him to get beyond that way of thinking. He is determined to do only what is necessary for him not to get expelled and to receive his diploma.

James

James has almost completed his sophomore year in high school. He has maintained a "B" average throughout high school. James' teachers feel that he has the ability to succeed at a university. However, James is beginning to feel out of place when he is in English class. Initially, he didn't voice his concerns to anyone, but he does not feel comfortable with the material he is reading in class. James' teacher began to notice changes in James' attitude toward reading. In a one-on-one after-school conference with his teacher, James reveals that he is losing interest in reading because he cannot relate to any of the stories that he is asked to read. He said, "Who cares about Shakespeare? Sometimes I don't mind reading things like Shakespeare, but I want to read things that I can understand and relate to. The stuff we read makes me feel White!"

Other ending: He said, "Who cares about Shakespeare? Sometimes I don't mind reading things like Shakespeare, but I want to read things that I can understand and relate to. I'm no English major."

Chris

Due to financial problems within his family, Chris has not been able to concentrate on his schoolwork. Unfortunately, Chris has never been the student he aspired to be because he has always been burdened by family obligations. Chris is good in math and enjoys reading, but he cannot seem to focus on his academics. To help relieve his family's burden, he is considering getting a part-time job that will help his mother pay bills. Chris' mother feels bad about the situation but there is nothing she can do. Being a single mother with an associate's degree has not left her with many options. Though she encourages Chris to excel in his academics, she appreciates and accepts the assistance Chris gives. For Chris, school is his second priority. He puts his family's well-being before anything.

fix-it man, reader, and basketball player) were designed to suggest different ways of being literate, ways that involve different relationships with different kinds of texts (e.g., song lyrics, websites, etc.). The sixth profile, a class clown, attempts to get the boys' reactions to a particular attitude toward school. The final two profiles, one about an African American student losing interest in reading because he cannot relate to what is being read in class, and the other about a young man who is struggling to balance school with helping his family escape financial difficulties, were designed to elicit talk about race and class (socioeconomic status) and their impact on reading and school performance. At the suggestion of one of the schools, we wrote an alternative ending to the profile on race for the White students at that school.

We worked with each boy individually in a private room. After reading each profile aloud to them, we asked the boys three questions:

1. What, if anything, do you admire about the character in the profile?
2. What, if anything, don't you admire about the character in the profile?
3. Where, if anywhere, do you see yourself in the profile?

We have forty-five profile interviews. We analyzed them using the same coding scheme as we used for the activity interviews in Chapter 2. We think that our analysis establishes interesting relationships to the work we reported in the last chapter and to the research we reviewed in Chapter 1.

The Instrumental Versus the Immediate

In our last chapter, we talked about four primary characteristics of what Csikszentmihalyi (1990a) calls flow experiences, and we argued that our respondents' descriptions of the activities they most loved in large measure shared these characteristics. Two of the four characteristics had a clear temporal element: clear goals and feedback, and focus on the immediate experience. That is, the boys valued activities in which they could immediately get a sense of how they were doing. When they talked about the activities they most enjoyed, they focused on how they valued the time they spent doing them rather than on what the activities might mean for them in the future. Our analysis of the profile interviews pointed out a striking disjuncture between how the boys talked about the activities they loved and how they talked about school in terms of these two characteristics.

By far the most striking theme of the profile interviews was the boys' belief in the instrumental value of school. Every one of the respondents talked about how important school was for the future. In conversation with Michael, Mick said he hated school but he valued it, at least theoretically, at the same time:

> Yeah, but you need it anyway. I need to graduate to get to my goal. Even my mom told me that. I'm not getting out of school. This school sucks. No other schools don't suck like this school.

Mick's last two sentences seem to reach for an understanding of the conflict Michael pointed out. "School," Mick seems to be saying, "is really important. That must mean that other schools are different from and better than this one."

Like many of the boys, Mick talked about personal goals. Stan extended his discussion of the value of school to the nation at large:

> Yeah it, it seems that America in general is just being dumbed down. You look at China and Japan and just countries like that where they have a strong, strong schooling environment where people have to go to school. You know they can't [slack off], you know, things like that and they excel in a lot of things, just because of that. And they probably look at us and see a bunch of slobs eating greasy potato chips, watching Sunday football or something, 'cause we are pretty low as far as academically strong countries I think.

Stan expressed a strong value about the importance of school and doing schoolwork, in part, it seems, because he bought the rhetoric of school reform that is often based on international comparisons.

The strength of the boys' belief in school was manifested in their responses to all of the profiles. We will put the names of boys from the profiles in italics throughout to differentiate them from the boys in the study. Here's Larry on *Eric*, the rapper:

> Exactly, I mean, yeah he's, he's a good rapper and stuff and that's awesome. I mean if he wants to know, like that's what he wants to do that's great. I mean, I sort of know what I want to do with my life but, why not go to school and stuff because what happens if he goes into a trial later in life? He gets sued or something. He won't know what to do. Or if he gets an award or something, what's he going to say? He's not smart enough to defend himself, you know, he just—. Education is power, I guess, and he's not going to win many awards if he's not educated, I guess.

And Fred on *Allen*, the young man who rejects school because it's too old-fashioned:

> I don't think that's very smart. I mean, he may be able to get a job, which could be a good one, working at a computer place, but if he—like in school they teach you how to type faster and better and properly and how to write and do outlines and stories and make you get stuff done better. And, like, if he has to give a report or something, always talking on the Internet and playing video games aren't going to help him with that.

And Chris on *Brian*, the class clown:

> Yeah, because I've seen a lot of people like *Brian* and, from what I hear, it hasn't turned out too well. I won't name any names just in case you may see the person. There was somebody who was my friend in junior high who was just like that. And, now, not only is he apparently not in school, but he's out doing drugs or whatever. It hurts me to see people when they do stuff like that because, it's like, "What's the point of doing it?" Yeah, you'll always be remembered, but at what cost? At the cost of your education, your future life. I don't think reality has really set into him yet, and I wonder what's going through his parents' heads—what they're thinking about.

And Aaron on *Jason*, the fix-it man:

> Personally I would go to college because if you don't have an education beyond the, um, technical and he can always, um, if he doesn't learn the technical stuff he needs in college then a lot of the trade schools aren't really four-year schools, they're a year or so, and so it would be like just a year after college and having a degree in college would probably mean you could make more money, I mean even in a technical field.

We could go on. Suffice it to say that the boys, all of them, evidenced a profound belief in the importance of school. In an age in which athletes of *Jermaine's* caliber can make millions and millions of dollars, some right out of high school, a number of the boys worked to concoct a story that would maintain the importance of school. Scotty provides an example:

> If he goes to college and breaks his knee, he can never play again. Like, let's say that he breaks both knees one night, you know some guy comes up and hits him and he is in a wheelchair for the rest of his life. You know he has got no education to back him up and, like, I think that it is necessary to have an education to back you up.

The boys' emphasis on the instrumentality of school extended to their discussion of the profile of *Andre*, the reader, in an interesting way. That profile begins by emphasizing that *Andre* reads because reading "puts his mind at ease." The profile continues by noting that "when *Andre* reads a book his mind is completely absorbed by the characters and the story." Nonetheless, when the boys talked about *Andre*, their focus was not on his getting lost in a book, the immediate pleasure he took from it, but rather on what his reading would bring him in the future. This tendency was true from boys across schools and ability levels. Once again, we'll provide a sampling of our respondents' comments. And because we think this tendency is an important one, we'll share more of their comments than we typically have done so far.

Here's Drake:

> I admire that he likes to read, so he is going to be able to go somewhere in life because most people that read a lot, they are smarter. Like it says in here he is higher on the SAT's scores. And after hearing the librarian speak, he wanted to become a librarian or teacher so he has already made his mind up, so he is probably going to pursue that goal till he gets there.

And Sisqó:

> I admire the way that ah, he likes to read. That is a good skill that, you know, that will be helpful down the road, especially in college, where you have to read a lot of books.

And Geo:

> Yeah, that's a real good thing, that's where all the information is at. So, I guess you need to know the information. He reads, that's being successful. He goes to school; he does his work. He's like, it seems like you know the way, like, the role model thing takes effect when um, when he seen somebody speak and that's when it clicked for him: Yeah, this is what I want to be. And he's been reading like, you know, since he was little.

And Mike:

> Because when you read it gives you more knowledge. If you have a lot of knowledge it's real good, especially because he wants to be a teacher.

And finally Hasan:

> Yeah. It's a good thing that he read and everything. At least he literate. Because if you don't know how to read and write, you're a lost cause. Anybody can just get over [you] about almost anything.

Bodey devised an entire story that focuses on the instrumentality of reading:

> This all goes back to being in high school. Maybe you get A's and B's and you're a nerd because of that, but when you're thirty or something

and you're grown up, it turns the tables because that smart kid is now in charge of the business and if you want a job, you have to go and ask them for that. So like that, it turns pretty quick.

Perhaps their emphasis on the instrumentality of reading is a function of the fact that they did not find immediate interest in their reading in school. In their responses to the profile of *James*, the student who was losing interest in reading because he could not relate to what was being read in class, 80 percent of the boys expressed sympathy for his desire to read material that was personally relevant. Mark was the most enthusiastic:

> I like *James*—that right there, you can put my name in for *James*. That's pretty much the same way I feel.

Maurice elaborated:

> Yes. Like I said before when I first talked, who wants to read about ancient history, you know? If I can't relate to it, so what's the point of reading the story? Like he said, *James* feels that he's losing interest in reading because he cannot relate to any of the stories that he's reading. I'm coming from the same point as *James*. Me and *James* coming from the same point. Why would you read a book if you cannot relate to the setting, the atmosphere, or the neighborhood or whatever?

On the surface, much of the evidence that we have presented so far ought to be encouraging. The boys clearly valued school in a profound way. And they valued reading as well. Both of these findings hearten us, but, as we pointed out in the last chapter, surfaces can be deceiving. Csikszentmihalyi (1990a) raised our awareness of what might be troublesome here.

As we have discussed, the *sine qua non* of flow experiences is that when you are engaged in them, you lose yourself in the immediate experience. But the boys' discussion of school and of reading is almost entirely future-directed. The pleasure of learning and the pleasure of reading were not something that they focused on.

Maybe the focus on the future is to be expected. But as Dewey (1916) points out, it's unfortunate and it undermines the very purposes of schooling. In *Democracy and Education*, he contrasts his view of education as a continuous process of growth with the view of education as preparation, a conception clearly aligned with the views of the boys in our study. Seeing education as preparation, according to Dewey, creates four fundamental problems. First, he says, it "involves the loss of impetus. . . . Children proverbially live in the present: that is not only a fact not to be evaded, but it is an excellence" (p. 55).

Second, such a conception puts a premium on "shilly-shallying and procrastination" (p. 55). After all, the future is a long way off. Third, it allows teachers to avoid focusing on the students we have before us. What is important is not what those students are in the here and now but what they might be in some remote future. What is important is not a thorough understanding of students' strengths and weaknesses, but rather "a vague and wavering opinion" of what they may be expected to become.

The fourth evil so clearly resonates with Csikszentmihalyi (1990a) that we think it's worth quoting at length:

> Finally, the principle of preparation makes necessary recourse on a large scale to the use of adventitious motives of pleasure and pain. The future having no stimulating and directing power when severed from the possibilities of the present, something must be hitched on to make it work. Promises of reward and threats of pain are employed. Healthy work, done for present reasons and as a factor in living, is largely unconscious. The stimulus resides in the situation with which one is actually confronted. But when this situation is ignored, pupils have to be told that if they do not follow the prescribed course, penalties will accrue; while if they do, they may expect, some time in the future, rewards for their present sacrifices. Everybody knows how largely systems of punishment have had to be resorted to by educational systems which neglect present possibilities in behalf of preparation for the future. (pp. 55–56)

When the boys talked about their music, their sports, their hobbies, their art, they seemed to us to be talking about healthy work. Most of them talked about school and reading in a different way, as a means to an end or as an obstacle to overcome to get where you want to go.

The emphasis on the instrumental was also apparent in the way the boys talked about the dreams of the characters in the profiles. The boys admired the accomplishment of the rapper and the basketball player. Sisqó noted:

> I admire, his, ah, his talent as a rapper. I think that that is something that I want to do, but I don't really have that talent.

Ian had similar feelings:

> I admire that he has this great basketball ability because I think that's great that he likes playing and he's good at it. I think that's good.

This admiration resonates with our discussion of the importance of competence in the previous chapter.

The boys also focused on the determination to succeed that the rapper and fix-it man manifested. Huey provides a representative example:

> The thing I admire the most about *Eric* is that he won't give up on his dream, or he doesn't really care what other people say. He wants to be, like, a rapper when he grows up, and I admire him because he's not a— he's really not letting anything get in his way. That's all he wants to do is just be a rapper.

But the boys worried that the dream of making a success in the world of music was too risky, as Rev explained:

> I think that if you want to get, if you are looking for a career in entertainment, then you should have something else to fall back on. Because it is really hard to do.

To the boys, *Jason* and *Andre*, the prospective fix-it man and the teacher/ librarian, seemed to be taking more sensible routes to success, though some of the boys feared that *Andre* was underselling himself in his career goals.

We found it striking that so many of our respondents put such an emphasis on the practical in discussing dreams. Chris wanted to break into wrestling production. Deuce wanted to be a rapper himself. But they were all developing fallback positions. School, to their minds, did not seem to figure into directly helping them meet their primary dreams, but provided fallback positions or were a means of credentialing them to pursue an end they valued.

Only Pablo, among all the boys, seemed committed to following what he knew was a risky path:

> Ah, I don't know. I guess me and my mom have had some of the same talks as probably [*Jason's*] parents have. I want to go to school in the arts and there is always this story of the starving artist. There is always that, and I guess that you have to do what you like. Because you could spend your life making money being miserable. Wouldn't you rather make just enough money to get by and be happy with your life? I think as far as me, I think that that is more important. I guess that it would be more important to do something that you like to do, than do something that makes you a lot of money. I have talked with my mother and I am going to go to school in the arts and stuff. I have convinced her that that is what I want to do.

And if he didn't make it as an artist, Pablo believed he could move on to something else. The road of the future, in Pablo's eyes, is winding and unpredictable. He was content with that unpredictability in a way that none of the other boys were. The boys' lack of intellectual or creative risk taking connects clearly to their intense need for competence and visible success, which often kept them from trying new things and growing in new ways.

In Chapter 1, we introduced Bordieu's notion of habitus, accepted "schemes of perception" that influence the adoption of conventional behavior. At the same time, we discussed how conventional notions of masculinity might influence a young man's behavior. Here we see habitus operating again. The conventional understanding of school as instrumental, as preparation for the future, seems to affect the way that boys engage in school. It also affects the reading they do for school, as we will see in our next chapter. And though they "buy into" cultural notions of school as preparation, this very notion estranges them from their immediate concerns and the higher purposes of schooling.

Dewey points out that the view of school-as-preparation is not constrained to students but extends to many teachers as well. But if we think of education only as preparation for the future, it lets us off the hook when we devise curricula and instruction. All we have to be able to say to ourselves is that our teaching might be good for our students some time in the future. The profile interviews challenge us to think about teaching in another way. If we are to avoid the four evils that Dewey articulates, we have instead to set up contexts in which our students can lose themselves in the "healthy work" of the present.

What Price Success? The Conflict Between Being Competent and Being Social

As we argued in the last chapter, the importance of competence was one of the most salient themes we found in the activity interviews. Another was the importance of the social. In the activity interviews, these themes were clearly compatible. Because the boys shared interests and activities with their friends, they developed their competence in their favorite activities through their engagement with their friends. For example, this was clearly true for all four of the boys we introduced in the last interchapter: Zach with his role-playing game, Gohan with his basketball and poetry, Haywood with his sports, and Yuri with his computer skills.

But in our profiles, this compatibility was not clear. We tried to isolate particular ways of being literate, so we set *Eric, Jason,* and *Andre* off from the crowd. This created an interesting tension for the boys when they responded to the profiles. While the main characters' competence was universally acclaimed, some of the boys wondered whether the cost of the competence was too high to pay.

Buda put it this way in his discussion of *Eric*, the rapper:

> Well, I admire that he, again, he knows what he wants to do, and I mean, if he likes it, it is his passion, I mean, go for it. But I don't admire, I mean, you don't have to be popular but you have to have friends just, I mean, because it is part of the social life. You won't be a well-rounded person unless you do [have friends]. Unless you get into the world and meet new people and try to make friends. You can't just spend all of your time doing one thing. You have got to have different choices.

His sentiment was echoed by Ricardo:

> I think that it is nice that he has, like, musical talents, but he is getting alienated. He is alienating himself from everybody, it looks like. Because, I mean, all he does is focus on rapping and reading *Vibe*. I mean, he doesn't go out and he doesn't, like, talk to his friends nor do his homework or anything. So he is pretty much like, this big idea that he is going to be a rapper, and if that falls through then he is stuck with nothing. It is just, like, so, I don't know, there is not really much that I admire about *Eric*. I mean, beside the fact, sure he is talented, but he's not really living up to his real potential that he could live up to if he focused on other things not just rapping.

And by Bob:

> Ah, I admire that how he's determined to do well, like he wants to be a rapper and he's trying to make it in the business I guess. But I don't admire how um, he doesn't have a social life, he just works on his rap. He's, he just decludes everyone from everything and I think he should be more social.

This emphasis on socialness seems to be related to an emphasis on well-roundedness, another way that some of the boys' discussion of the profiles differed from their discussions of their favorite activities. In the activity interviews, the boys described themselves as engaging in specific and sometimes quite narrow areas of interest, and they thought this was OK. It seems, though, that the boys expected the profiled students to be more well-rounded than they were themselves. Mark made this conflict clear when he talked about *Eric* in relation to himself:

> I like the way he sets himself to a goal—he's working on his trade and he's not letting a lot of other things get in his way. I'm sort of the same way with golf in a way. I like the way he's reading *Vibe* and he's doing what he has to do to make himself better at that skill. But what I don't like

is he still should be working on his academics and he shouldn't be so overfocused with it that that's the only thing in his life. That's sort of the same thing that goes along with what I was saying about the electronics: You need a little variety. . . . When golf season comes around, I'm pretty much like this guy. I'm constantly working on it, but you can't do that all the time. You're going to—eventually, it's just going to get monotonous and you need to do other things.

Mark seems to be holding *Eric* to a standard that he didn't hold himself. To us, the root of his discomfort seems to be the suggestion in the story that *Eric* is willing to sacrifice friends to pursue his dream, something none of the boys in the study endorsed.

The Question of Hegemonic Masculinities: Andre

The importance of the social also marked the boys' responses to *Andre*, the profile we think is most important. We wrote *Andre*'s profile to allow the boys to talk about literacy as a feminized practice. As we explained in Chapter 1, sociocultural theorists and scholars from Australia and the United Kingdom have led the way in arguing that boys' problems with literacy in school stem from a resistance rooted in the belief that reading isn't appropriately masculine. We crafted *Andre*'s profile to include a number of details that might mark him as feminine—or, at least, unconventionally masculine. He's a reader. He's a churchgoer. He is interested in pursuing occupations that have traditionally been dominated by women. We tried to make him appear sensitive and emotional.

We fully expected that some of the boys would dismiss him as a "faggot," duplicating the reaction of some of the boys in Martino's (1995a, 1998) studies to profiles of males who were not conventionally male. But only one of them did, and he did so because, as we'll explain later, he saw *Andre* as insufficiently social.

In general, many of the boys admired *Andre* for what his reading had brought (the high SAT scores) and might bring him (a good job). Instead of seeing *Andre* as a figure worthy of ridicule, Gohan sees him as a model:

He does a lot of good things. There's no negativity in him. He's not that popular so he couldn't get distracted by other people. He goes to the library all the time, and I don't see no TV anywhere in here nowhere. So that's good. There's nothing to dislike about him. He's the dream son.

What seemed to make him an attractive figure for some of the boys is that he follows his own path. Jigg and Larry were most outspoken in their admiration. Jigg notes,

Because you got to be comfortable with yourself to be comfortable with everybody else. You can't not like yourself and like everything everybody else likes about you. You can't wear sneakers that you don't like, but everybody else's wearing them so you wear them. I'm not too fond about that. I like that about him. I also like that he was a volunteer and everything. He was always there to help, always there to go. Always. An outgoing person, I like that. The library, I didn't do too much of that. "His SAT scores were significantly higher than average." That's only right because he put more practice in his studying than everybody else.

Larry offers similar praise:

That's great, I found myself that reading is a great thing. I mean, I just, like, last month I was like, well, I guess that I can go to the library or something. I really haven't gone. It's just a place that you can sit down and stuff books that you can read. I mean, if he wants to become a librarian or teacher, I mean, that's basically every workshop and stuff that comes to this high school. People say, like, that you have to have fun with your job because, like, it doesn't matter how much money you make if you stay in the shower fifteen minutes longer because you don't want to go to work and you're not happy. This kid, it seems like, I mean, he seems like he likes to read and stuff. I know that even if kids make fun of him he can still go to the bookstore and be happy and stuff. So that is his way out. And if that is his, looks like what he wants to do with his life and he has a career aim, then that's great. He wants to be a librarian or teacher 'cause then he can share his knowledge and passion for reading and stuff with other kids. Which I think is great.

Larry's admiration is perhaps understandable; as he noted, he had recently begun to see himself as a reader. But it was striking that even some of the boys who were not readers shared that admiration. Take Clint, for example:

I like that. He has developed reading at age six and he followed through with it, just like I do some things, like, long-term. I don't read that much, but if somebody reads and they really get into it and it's the one thing that they really like, I respect 'em for it because that's their thing, they like to read. I just don't like to read, but I like that he followed through with it and that he's gonna go for a career as a teacher or librarian because that's what he knows what to do.

Marcel had the following discussion with Michael:

Michael: Anything about *Andre* that you don't like?
Marcel: No, he's straight. He's all right.

Michael: Do you see yourself in him in any way?

Marcel: Not really, because I don't go to the library too much. I do play sports and video games and kinda the opposite.

Michael: But you admire him anyway.

Marcel: Yeah.

Michael: Would you advise him to sort of loosen up, to have some more fun?

Marcel: I mean, I can't tell him what to do, he's his own person. I'm no one to tell him how to be or whatever. If he's comfortable the way he is, then let him be.

Some of our respondents' admiration even took on a wistful quality. Far from criticizing *Andre*, Buster wished he could be more like him:

> I admire that. I mean, he enjoys something that is really critical to, you know, how to do in life. I mean, that is really good. That is something that, I wish that I had a love for reading. You know that is something, if you have a love for reading, it is real easy to obtain information and read a lot.

Bambino offered a similar sentiment:

> The fact that he reads a lot, that's good. I have no problem with people reading. I always wanted to be like that, to read that much, but I could never do that.

This wistfulness was especially poignant in the case of Mick, who was reading at an early elementary level. Here's the exchange that Michael had with Mick immediately after Michael finished reading *Andre*'s profile:

Michael: OK. Next guy is *Andre*. [Reads *Andre* profile.] What do you think about *Andre*?

Mick: He's doing better than I am.

Michael: Yeah, why is that?

Mick: He can read better than me. I can't read that good, but that's good that he's staying in classes and all that. His SATs scores are high. That's good.

Yuri also manifested a wistfulness about reading. Interestingly, he complained that what kept him from reading was school: "I wish I could read more, but schoolwork takes time out of my life." We'll explore this tension more fully in the next chapter.

The admiration, though, wasn't unadulterated. Some of the boys who admired *Andre* tempered their enthusiasm with a critique of his lack of socialness. That was the case with Bob:

> I admire how *Andre* is ah, he likes reading and he's doing what he likes to do no matter what other people say. They call him weird and names, and I think it's really hard to overcome peer pressure. And I also admire how he wants to do well because if he's really smart, then he'll do well in the long run, so that's good. And then, but I don't admire, I don't think he has much of a social life. I think he should, but he has to do what he likes. I think he should find some people who like to do, who like to read as much as him.

Hasan was more outspoken:

> *Andre*. He's good. He's positive and everything. He going to be able to take care of himself because he's smart, but I don't feel—he's corny. All he do is read, read, read. I mean, he got to have some type of fun. You're a sixteen-year-old boy. Go to a party once in a while. I know you read about parties. Go somewhere. Don't just sit around the house and read all day. You're going to go to college—you've been to college, right? All them good-looking girls, but he's sitting there just reading. It's good to do that, but it's a time and place for everything. Sometimes, you just got to. A sixteen-year-old boy, it's good that he's on his reading thing, all his grades and stuff is high, but he don't have no fun. If he's happy like that, I'm all for it. I won't put him down. If you're happy the way you live, go ahead. Do your thing. I don't want you to be not happy, whatever, but I couldn't be like that. I couldn't see myself like that. I like to have fun. It's like he's not having no fun. To him, he's having fun. But to me, I wouldn't have fun doing that all the time.

Hasan claimed not to want to put *Andre* down, but put him down he did. It seems to us that his critique was informed by his belief in the importance of activity and socialness and by his suspicion that reading can't be all that much fun.

Even devoted readers critiqued *Andre*, as was the case with Liam:

> Well, I like, I enjoy reading a lot like *Andre*. It says that he enjoys reading best-sellers. I think oftentimes the best-sellers aren't the best books out there and you have to, you can't limit your field to just what's popular and what's known. I admire his desire to pursue a career as a librarian or a teacher. I think if, choosing a career, like a service career, I guess you could put it that way, is admirable. Doing something for the benefit of others, especially as a teacher. I think that is definitely something to be admired. I think it says that reading is a very important part of his life and that his social skills have suffered and that his popularity has suf-

fered. I don't think anything is wrong with being unpopular, but I think you do need to know how to have a discussion with various different types of people and I think that is important. And I think people who are able to deal with all walks of life are more able to succeed and more able to relate to different people. I think putting yourself into a situation where you have to deal with diversity, it will prepare you, 'cause life is diverse.

Liam stressed the instrumentality of social connections, and he revealed a belief in the limits of what one can learn from books.

Rudy took a similar line of argument in an extended exchange with Jeff:

Rudy: So I admire his commitment to his work even with his family pressures. Um, he's kinda like me 'cause I have an older sister who's basically like a genius. She has, like, a 4.0, probably above that at the girls' school. She's a junior right now and ah, I kinda feel like I have to live up to her standards. So, to feel that pressure and to still be committed and do his best and get high SAT scores, read in the library, that kind of stuff, I admire that. But ah, I don't really feel that just reading is that fun. You know I like to get out, you know, socialize with people. You kind of learn lessons and learn life, like, you know, out in the real world socializing with people and not, like, maybe reading a book or sitting in a library.

Jeff: So is he missing something because he reads so much?

Rudy: I think he is, yeah. He's not out there, you know, making mistakes and learning something.

Jeff: So there's certain things you just can't learn from reading?

Rudy: Yeah.

Jeff: What kind of things, would you say?

Rudy: Ah, just like street-smart kind of things, like ah, what to do in certain situations, how to hold yourself, how to act, you know, in a group, that kind of stuff.

Both the reader and the nonreader drew a distinction between what one can learn in a book and what one can learn from being engaged in social situations. Clearly they both saw a limit to bookish knowledge. While expressing admiration for *Andre*, their admiration was much qualified.

Bam took it a step further. He too admired *Andre*, noting:

Well, even though he's not as popular in school, he continues to read. He already knows what he's going to be, and he's getting an education, so I totally agree with him.

But despite his admiration, Bam worried about *Andre*, at least about how he would fare at his urban school. Here's more of his conversation with Michael:

Bam: He'd get picked with. They'd pick with him all day like raw meat.

Michael: Do you get fussed with because you care about school? I mean, I know that you're a serious student. You know what I mean? Do you ever get fussed with because of that?

Bam: Nah.

Michael: How is *Andre* different?

Bam: Well, he don't socialize with people, I guess. I socialize with a lot of people, so everybody know me, so it don't matter.

Michael: What advice would you give *Andre* if you were a friend of his?

Bam: At least have some friends. Books can't be your friends for the rest of your life. It would drive you crazy in the end.

Michael: But you admire him?

Bam: Yeah.

Bam revealed complex attitudes about school. He valued school, believing it's essential for his success in life. But he also suggested that being school-ish is met with suspicion unless, by socializing, you can prove you're OK.

Deuce made a similar point, not in reference to *Andre* but in speaking of himself:

I do everything else outside. Everything. Everything, man. Whatever. People see me. I mean, everything. I come back to school, but I was smart. I just so happened to be smart, but the whole thing is that I was raised in a rough environment, all that stuff. Hung out with students, but I always was smart. I always did my work in class so I come home from school and my friends say, "Yeah, Deuce, let's go do this." [I'd say,] "Hold up. Let me go home and do my homework. I'll be right back out after that, though. Let me do my work. I'll be out after that." Come out, still do what we was going to do anyway, but I got my work done. And they respect that. They respect that. If I would be like, "Yeah, I'm going to get this work done." Like from the age sixteen and up—like as soon as you hit, as a matter of fact, fifteen and up, when you start being like, "Yeah, I'm going to just go get my work done. I'll be out," they'll be like, "Yeah, that's good. Go handle that." You know what I mean? They respect that. But if you just all the time, "Nah. No, I'm not coming out. Not coming out," being corny with people, you're supposed to be their friend. So you still got to show your friends some time. You can't just be like, "Yeah, you're my friend in school" because I told everybody; a lot of people I met, I said, "Look, if I only know you in school, you're not my friend." You're just a part of school, a part of my school entertainment. If I don't hang with you outside school or I just know you as high school, you're a part of this school, period.

Deuce drew a firm line between school and what's outside. Deuce and his friends respected school; Deuce was preparing a portfolio for college admission during the time that Michael interviewed him. However, they did not respect being narrowly academic. Like Bam, Deuce had to show that he could do more than school. He had to show that he wasn't "corny," a term that remains somewhat elusive for us but that we take to mean "nerdy."

During the profile interview, Michael discovered that the microphone was malfunctioning, so he asked Barnabas to summarize his views:

> Michael: So next we have *Andre*, and *Andre* is the guy, as soon as you read it, you said, "He's gay." Tell me about that.
>
> Barnabas: I don't know. It's just he spends too much time not doing nothing. I mean, he goes to church. Nothing wrong with that. Ain't nothing wrong with church at all. God bless us all. I mean, I'm just saying that he never goes out with anybody. He goes to the library at least three times a week. He's not popular at all. Then, his grades are all doing good, and he wants to be a librarian or a teacher. He doesn't want to do nothing exciting for his job.

Barnabas, Deuce, and Bam were from the same city school, but though their language was different, the norms of behavior they invoked resonated with those of Rudy and Liam, boys who attended a privileged private school. "You have to be able to do more than school," all of them seem to be saying.

Our data, then, differ from what's been reported by many others. In fact, they are so different that we thought hard about whether the boys were masking their feelings and telling us something socially acceptable. We wondered whether the boys would speak differently about *Andre* to their friends. When we were teaching in secondary schools, and in our visits to them now, we have heard boys who would never dream of using offensive racial or ethnic slurs call someone (or something) "gay" or a "faggot." And we agree with Martino (1998) that they do so to criticize those "who don't measure up to the macho norm" (p. 31).

Although we can't know how the boys adjusted their responses because they were talking to us, we want to stress two points. First, as we have noted, many of the boys in our study applauded *Andre*. Their reluctance to use words they thought we would find offensive does not explain the support that these boys offered for his effort. Second, when they critiqued him, they did so not because of his reading, but because they didn't find him appropriately social. If there is a macho norm involved in this critique, it would hold that boys need to get away from school and the things of school in order to be with friends, not that reading is "sissy" stuff. Those who criticized *Andre* did so not because they saw reading as he practiced it as a feminine behavior. Rather, their critique suggested that they saw it instead as a schoolish and insufficiently social behavior.

The Impact of Race and Class

As we've noted, one of the questions we kept foremost in our minds as we did this research was whether the category of gender was useful to think with. We noted in Chapter 1 our worries about research and theory that essentializes gender, a tendency that's clearly seen in research that argues for a kind of biological determinism. We wrote the profiles of *James* and *Chris* to give the boys a chance to talk about the interaction between gender, on the one hand, and race and social class, on the other.

The Issue of Acting White: James

James' complaint to his teacher that "The stuff we read makes me feel White!" was informed by the case made by Fordham and Ogbu (1986) that African American students link the culture of school with acting White and reject it as violating their cultural norms. We wanted to give the African American boys in our study a chance to discuss whether their attitude toward reading was informed at all by this rejection.

The answer, simply, is that they did not. None of the African American respondents reported feeling the tension that *James* felt. Or if they did, it was overcome by their profound belief in school as the engine that drives future success.

Chris, for example, was offended by the suggestion that anyone would link school success with being White. Here's part of his conversation with Michael:

> Chris: If I was there and he said it to me, I would be like, "What'd you mean by that?" because, for some reason, he has that set in his mind that only White people are supposed to like that and that's not true because, like Shakespeare, he wrote a lot of stories like *Othello* where the main character was Black, right? So, there is no stereotype when it comes to writing in my opinion, and that would really make me get thinking about what's going through *James'* head, and then I would end

up reevaluating his whole attitude, you know? Like if I was his counselor and he said that to me, I would be like, "What did you mean by that?" and "Do you think that just to enjoy it you have to be White?" I would give questions on him to really break down—

Michael: You'd press him on that.

Chris: Right. I'd keep pushing him until he really said the whole reason of why he said that. Stereotypes or race-related stereotypes really annoy me. I don't know. They just do.

Geo explained that no one he knew made that kind of link:

You know, it ain't being White; it's just having an education. Nobody looks at it as being White. I mean, you don't want your kid to be a punk or nothing like that. Maybe that's because they start acting like a White boy, punks and stuff like that. You know, like, you just got to do what you got to do. At the end, you know, everybody wants to have a nice life.

Johnny claimed a color-blind attitude that led him to reject *James'* formulation:

No, that's never made me think something like that. Um, so to me everybody's the same. I don't see color, I don't see race, I don't see religion, anything. And, um, it's if you want to learn, it's if you want to learn, it doesn't matter what race you want to be or what race somebody's trying to make you. If that's what somebody thinks, honestly I think it's stupid to think that if you go to school, you're going to turn more White or any other race. And, um, I can never think of anything like that. It just makes no sense that going to school can make you more White or more Black.

Hasan also made a claim for a universal, in his case, discouragingly, a universal rejection of reading:

I don't know. I ain't never been through nothing like that. It's not whether you're White or Black. Everybody feel the same about it. I don't really know no human being who like reading. I know some, but the majority of them—Black, White, Puerto Rican—not too many of them like reading.

In an extended exchange with Michael, Bam explained that while he had not experienced rejecting school as somehow related to whiteness, he had seen others reject it because of a lack of interest:

Bam: No. I haven't heard of it. Well, if it does, I haven't heard it so I can't relate to the topic.

Michael: Bam, when you were reading *James*—you must have seen people like this before because you really had a strong feeling about him.

Bam: Yup. I've seen a lot of people like that.

Michael: Do you have any idea what happens to make them turn off like you think of *James*?

Bam: They get influenced by the street. Go out to the street. I have a friend just like him. He's in jail right now, ten to twenty years.

Michael: And it happens sort of sudden?

Bam: Yeah.

Michael: Is it stuff that happens that they don't trust school anymore or is it stuff that—

Bam: Something has to catch their interest.

Michael: Yeah?

Bam: Yup.

Michael: So what advice would you give *James*? If you saw this happening, what would you say?

Bam: Stay in school. Read Shakespeare. Act White as you would say it. Get what you got to get and then you can think about relaxing and not reading and getting a good job.

Here again we see a belief in the instrumental value of school, especially for students in the urban school who expressed a belief in school as a foundation for their future. But Bam's story also provides a challenge, for his friend's experience suggests that a belief in the importance of school may not be enough. Even with that belief—school and the reading done in school—has to catch a student's interest.

We'll explore this issue more fully in our remaining chapters. But it seems that our data challenge Fordham and Ogbu's (1986) argument that African American students resist the culture of school for its association with acting White. Instead, Bam's story is more in line with Mahiri's (1998) argument that resistance is situational. That is, Mahiri, drawing on Alpert's (1991) research as well as his own, argues that resistance is linked to teaching behaviors, and that teachers can avoid or overcome resistance with teaching that builds on students' interests and abilities. He argues that African American males, often seen as at-risk for school failure, sustained engagement with a variety of written texts "when they were motivated by the content" (p. 52).

Unfortunately, many of the boys in our study, regardless of their race or ethnicity, did not find or experience this motivation in school. Interestingly, Chris seemed to take this lack of motivation as given, and he put it on the characters in the profiles to find links between their interest and school. For example, he said the rapper should devise raps to help him study for tests. Here's the advice he would give *James*:

> OK, it's good that he eventually did speak up because I think you have to always speak up for yourself. But I think that since they are reading stuff like Shakespeare, and somewhat he may want to read things that he can relate to, he should go out for himself and see if there is anything that he may be able to relate to, like whatever he's into—like if he's into horror, go there to a bookstore and see whatever horrors they have or whatever may interest him, because once he gets that need fulfilled in his head for that certain thing, he may not mind the Shakespeare as much.

Mike, an Asian American, offered similar advice:

> And this part about where he says that he can't relate to any of the stories: I think he should try a little harder to interpret the story and see if there is or to see if he can find anyone in the story that is like him, or an event that happened to him that happens in the story.

While acknowledging the potential for the kind of motivation about which Mahiri (1998) writes, the boys offered little hope that schools will adopt the kind of *mutable* curricula that Mahiri endorses—that is, curricula responsive both to the needs of a diverse student population and to the rapid production of new knowledge and new text forms that characterizes our age. And so, Chris and Mike seem to be arguing, it's up to students. We would argue instead that it is part of *our* responsibility as teachers to create contexts that develop and sustain the interest of our students.

Before we move on, we want to stress that we realize that the profile of *James* emphasizes reading and not writing or speaking, and that the stakes of the game might be higher in those two arenas. Fecho (2000), for example, writes of the complex and emotional set of issues his African American and Caribbean American students faced when they studied the relationships between language and identity and power, a study that was occasioned by one of his student's decision to use ebonics in a school presentation. Their passionate discussions reveal just how intimately language use is tied up with identity. Reading White, therefore, may not be as costly as talking White.

Comments on Socioeconomic Class: Chris

In Chapter 2 we noted how social class seemed to mark the boys' interviews. It's hard to pull a single quote or even a series of them to make this point, but when we read the interviews of boys we took to be upper-middle-class and upper-class (inferences we made on the basis of their talk about their homes, their parents' jobs, their vacations, and so on), we agreed that there was an easiness about them, a sense of their awareness that their future success was guaranteed. Although they saw school as an essential element in that success, it was something they took for granted.

We wrote the profile for *Chris* because we were aware that confronting issues related to social class might affect students' achievement in school, and we wanted to give our respondents a chance to talk about that. We found that *Chris* was by far the most admired character in the profiles. Bob put it this way:

> I admire how he—'cause I think family does come first before anything, and I admire his trying to help his family, and because it doesn't look like they're that well-off, and um, I don't really not admire anything about him. I think he's doing the right thing.

The vast majority of the boys admired *Chris'* devotion to his family, his responsibility, and his selflessness.

But for some of the boys, their admiration was tempered by their worry that *Chris* was making the wrong decision. And once again, this worry seemed especially intense in the urban school. Alucard identified with *Chris*, but advised him to do what he could to keep up with school:

> Do the best you could do because it's understandable. Your family has problems right now. Just try to keep at it in school. Do what you could do in school. Try to keep the grades high.

Bam was more outspoken. Here's part of his conversation with Michael:

> Bam: School is number one priority because if you get an education you going to be able to take care of your family. There's going to be hard times and good times because I understand he wants to help his mom a bit. That's why I got my first job at first, to help my brother with the bills, but then my brother got a better job. He says I wouldn't have to keep my job but if I wanted it, so I kept it.
>
> Michael: What would your brother have said if your job would have started interfering with school?
>
> Bam: He would have made me quit. If I start messing up in school, I was going to have to quit.
>
> Michael: So what advice would you give *Chris*?
>
> Bam: Keep the job. See how the job and schoolwork out together, but, if it don't, quit the job.
>
> Michael: Even if it means sucking it up through some hard times?

Bam: Get a paper route or something. Get a paper route or something where he can wake up early and be ready for school. Get a paper route.

Deuce identified with *Chris'* problems. But despite this identification, he was harsh in his judgment:

Deuce: My situation is just like *Chris'* situation, but I'm just not that much like *Chris*. *Chris* is just dropping everything for his family. Sometimes, you got to drop some stuff just for yourself. That's all right. I wouldn't drop everything for my family because everything, including your schoolwork, is going to help you be somebody to take care of your family. So why would you drop that off?

Michael: So what advice would you give to *Chris*?

Deuce: *Chris*, he said he got a part-time job. That's nothing. I had a part-time job since seventh grade and was still able to keep my grades up. Talking to *Chris*, just tell him to focus on his schoolwork because that's what's going to have him end up to be somebody. I mean, even though he has a part-time job, he can't just drop everything. His family got to handle some stuff on their own, just like he has to handle stuff on his own. Even if they are your family, you can't make all the problems yours.

Deuce's remarks suggest that he sees the problems that *Chris* faces as what's to be expected, as what has to be overcome. He doesn't see them as an excuse for failure.

In short, the boys in the urban school recognize that class issues can have a major impact on school achievement. But their belief in school is so great, they feel strongly that these issues have to be confronted and overcome.

In summary, like the activity interviews, the profile interviews offer both hope and a challenge. The boys' profound belief in the importance of school is something that we ought to be able to tap, as is their recognition of the importance of reading. The fact that they did not see reading as a feminized activity is encouraging. But their view of reading as schoolish appears to have negative consequences. And it poses a dilemma: How can schools make reading seem less schoolish?

What This Makes Us Think About:
How to Make Reading Less Schoolish

Our data convince us that the reason boys reject schoolish forms of literacy is not that they see such literacy as feminized, but because of its very schoolishness—that is, its future orientation, its separation from immediate uses and functions, its emphasis on knowledge that is not valued outside school. The good news here is that the boys in our study did not reject school as a concept; they saw it as a means to an end, a credentialing agency that would allow them to do the real, meaningful, and healthy work they saw for themselves in the future. Further good news is that the boys did not reject reading or other forms of literacy; what our boys rejected about literacy is within the power of teachers and schools to transform. This offers the possibility that reframing literate practices in schools as "healthy work" could lead boys to embrace the very literacies and strategic knowledge they now reject, or at least find uncompelling.

Our boys demonstrated, at least in theory, a willingness to do what has to be done in order to get the credentials they feel they need to secure their future. But if we want literacy to be part of that future, then it seems to us that we have to show them that literacy can be the "healthy work of the present."

Doing so places new expectations on teachers. The expectations are reminiscent of Brown, Collins, and DuGuid's (1989) work on situated cognition:

> Recent investigations of learning challenge the separating of what is learned from how it is learned and used. The activity in which knowledge is developed and deployed, it is now argued, is not separable from or ancillary to learning and cognition. Nor is it neutral. Rather, it is an integral part of what is learned. Situations might be said to co-produce knowledge through activity. Learning and cognition are fundamentally situated. (p. 32)

These researchers argue that people learn more successfully outside of school than they do in school. Learning pursued by JPFs (Just Plain Folks) includes the following characteristics:

- It is personally purposeful.
- It takes place in a real context.
- Assistance is provided by others within that context to meet a shared goal.
- The learning will be immediately applied in that real context.

Competence, control, clear goals: the stuff of the flow experiences students reported having outside school.

Our data have helped us think through the teaching we have done, both to account for some of our successes and to suggest what more we need to do. We'd like to illustrate this by taking a look at a unit Jeff developed before our study.

Jeff was once teaching an American Literature class of eleventh graders in a middle/lower track (track 4 of 6 tracks). The curriculum required that the class read Arthur Miller's *Death of a Salesman*, and despite Jeff's arguments to his department chair that his students would not find it relevant, there was no getting out of teaching it. In an effort to engage his students, Jeff reframed the curriculum. Instead of studying particular required texts like *Death of a Salesman* as artifacts, they studied them as part of an inquiry project based on the question "What are the costs and benefits of the American emphasis on sports?"

He chose this organizing question only after carefully considering his students. Many were athletes or were very interested in sports, including two girls. Those who didn't share this interest could engage with the topic because they felt sports were overemphasized in the school culture. Three of the girls, in fact, had been vigorously objecting to having a Fall Football Homecoming, arguing that it privileged athletes and cheerleaders over other kinds of students with different interests (they were Goths). So they too had a preexisting, albeit negative interest in the topic.

Because Jeff did not know the answer to the question, the inquiry was real and not a "guess what the teacher knows" task. It also provided many chances for argument and social critique.

To start, Jeff used a frontloading activity called an opinionnaire. Students had to explain whether they agreed or disagreed with each statement, and why. They then had to interview several other people about their responses: an adult, an athlete, an artistic person, people of different ages, and so on. Here are the statements:

1. Serious athletes care greatly about their physical health and would never do anything to endanger it.
2. Serious athletes will risk their health and even premature death to use performance-enhancing drugs if they think these will help them win.
3. Participation in sports builds character.
4. Participation in sports reveals character.
5. Participation in sports makes people self-absorbed and care only about personal accomplishment and winning.
6. An overemphasis on winning and competition robs us of the true value of sports and exercise.
7. Winning is what sports (and life) are really about.

8. Sports are better at building character and values than any other kind of activity.

9. The values learned in sports are the values of the competitive free enterprise business system, and that's a good thing.

10. Athletes are not held to the same standards for behavior and academics. They are given unfair preferential treatment.

11. Sports keep some kids in school, and they should be given a break to keep them there.

12. Sports offer important opportunities to minority athletes that they would not otherwise have.

13. Minority athletes are more often than not used and taken advantage of by unscrupulous coaches and owners.

The frontloading asked students to articulate their own opinions and access their own background experience. Right from the start, then, Jeff challenged the school/life divide that so many students see. The activity also challenged them to see that there were other perspectives beyond their own, which helped them build a wider understanding of the issue. It also organized the class and established the terms for the ongoing debate. As well, it set a purpose for future reading: to focus their learning, to clarify what they were coming to know, to monitor their learning progress, and to plan for and engage in the final project.

The importance of such frontloading cannot be overemphasized. Schema theory has shown that there can be little comprehension without activating prior knowledge and possessing a clear purpose, both of which allow the reader to interpret ambiguous words; to make inferences, predictions, and elaborations; and to make meaning and use that meaning for thinking (cf. Rogoff and Lave [1984]).

The students read a wide variety of material in service of the conversation about the values of sport. They read the collection of *Athletic Shorts*, Chris Crutcher stories (and a few students picked up his *Ironman* and *Staying Fat for Sarah Byrnes*); they also read *Sports Illustrated* and various articles on drug use in sports. They read John Updike's poem "Superman," which comments on how advertising manipulates us through sporting values. They studied and critiqued endorsement advertising. They read the newspaper and compared the length and content of the sports section to other sections, and the coverage of school sports to school arts activities. And when they read *Death of a Salesman*, they considered the impact that the place of sports and the values of sports had on Willy and Biff. So while some of the texts they read were the traditional fare of school, many were not.

For a final project the students were challenged to create a video documentary or display that expressed an argument about some issue around sports that intrigued them. Every student completed the final project with uncharacteristic energy and passion. The three Goth girls started a campaign to get rid of football homecoming and succeeded in convincing the student council to change the name of the event to Student Activities Fall Homecoming, in which various groups were featured and celebrated. For these girls, the project was clearly a transformative project.

When we think about the principles of flow that we've discussed, we can see why the unit was successful. Because students pursued their own arguments in their own ways, they had an element of control over their work that they didn't get in much of their schoolwork. Because the texts were not read as artifacts or objects of study for some future or opaque purpose, but as conversants in the ongoing debates, the purpose for reading them was both clear and immediate.

But our data also help us see how the unit could have been more successful still, for we see that more could have been done to make the students feel a sense of competence. We think back to Ricardo's comment quoted in Chapter 2—plays are hard to read—and we realize that Jeff could have done more to help students feel competent in understanding the conventions that dramatists use to convey meaning (cf. Esslin, 1987). We wonder whether the students put up with *Death of a Salesman* because they had the opportunity to read other kinds of texts. We think they would be more apt to see dramatic literature as part of the healthy work of the present if they felt fully equipped to handle the interpretive challenges it presents.

Knowing that students conceive reading as a schoolish activity suggests the need to devise instruction that challenges that conception. Placing schoolish texts in new contexts is one way of meeting that challenge.

In the following interchapter, *Meet the Crew*, we introduce each boy through his responses to the profile interview (see Figure 3.1). Not only do their responses provide another glimpse at memorable individuals, they touch on the importance of relating to texts and feeling a sense of competence.

Meet the Crew

Buster

Ian

Alucard

Geo

Buster

Buster, a European American eleventh grader from the rural district, was a champion mountain biker, one of the best in the entire region. But he said that this accomplishment was not key to his identity. He explained that biking was what he did, not what he was—a people person. It's not surprising, then, that though he applauded the accomplishment of the characters in the profiles, he would have identified with them more if they were more social. The profile that resonated most for Buster was *Allen*, the techie. Buster connected immediately with him because he too liked to learn things by doing, often skipping the directions to gain a greater sense of accomplishment.

Buster called himself a "tactile learner," and the extent of his use of that label suggested to us that he had taken a learning styles inventory at some time in the past. He was also aware that his preferred mode of learning is not one that is privileged in schools but instead falls into the vocational track. He wanted to pursue a degree in mechanical engineering, a degree that would give him something to fall back on if he couldn't achieve his dream of designing bike frames, and he had been told that the kind of work they do in the vocational track is not compatible with getting a four-year degree.

Buster wanted that degree, and he was willing to endure school without questioning in order to do so. He made apologies for school: "I mean, I guess maybe it is just too hard to accommodate everyone's needs." As he explained in response to the profile of *James*, he disliked school reading but was willing to put up with it: "I mean, I definitely know where he is coming from as far as some of the stuff that we read is boring, but I guess that we just have to put up with it to get through." School for Buster was a bitter pill. But he was willing to swallow it.

Ian

Ian was a European American seventh grader from the rural school. An accomplished pianist who had been playing for nine years, he was also very interested in sports, though he was less expert in sports than in musical activities. He played sports anyway because of the fun he had playing with friends. In his profile interview he strongly endorsed all forms of achievement and expressed a very strong belief in the instrumental value of school. Not a reader himself, he admired the imagination reading fiction requires, and he valued what he could take from informational texts.

Though not a reader, he saw a connection between himself and *Andre*, in that he was able to lose himself in his music the way that *Andre* loses himself in his reading. In his discussion of *Brian*, the class clown, he noted that sometimes students get made fun of for being either too good or too poor at school or sports or other activities, but he seemed immune from peer pressure. In fact, in his activity interview, he announced:

> I think the most important thing about me is that I'm not afraid to be different. I mean, I'm not swayed to one thing. I mean, it's important you know to fit in, but I'm really not afraid to take that extra step to just be different from everybody else.

Alucard

Alucard, a Puerto Rican tenth grader from the urban school, chose the name of a cartoon character for a pseudonym, a choice that reflected his interest in cartoon art. He brought a sketchbook of wonderfully detailed drawings of superheroes, some established and some that he created, to the profile interview. He knew that he wanted to do something creative with his life. He and his friends were talking about forming a band, though none of them played an instrument, and during the course of the study, Alucard began to try to write some songs. They saw themselves as different from the crowd. Alucard wore a ponytail and avoided the clothing that was most popular at his city school. But he did not take a radically different position on the profiles. His mantra of the importance of balance resonated with what many of the boys said.

Alucard identified with *Andre*, the reader, and would himself spend time in the library if it had books on the supernatural and on drawing, two topics he was especially interested in. He also identified with *Chris*, whose family is having money problems. Alucard had sold his bike, which he loved, to help pay the bills, and like *Chris*, he was looking for a job to help out further. Alucard spoke of the importance of balance. Sadly, there was a lot that he had to balance.

Geo

Geo, an African American tenth grader from the suburban school, was the starting tailback for his large suburban school, and football was the lens through which he saw the characters in the profile. He wanted to be a success, and football was the way he planned to do it. According to Geo, anyone who pursued success in any way was worthy of admiration: "I always think to myself that I'm going to do something, like I'm going to BE somebody, you know, 'like, 'cause, just me being me, I ain't going to settle for nothing else . . . If he likes fixing cars, that may be his football game like mine."

Geo kept careful track of his grades and was working to bring them up to help attract the interest of college recruiters, but he was in sympathy with the characters who complained about school. He said that teachers were getting paid enough tax money, so the least they should do was try to find out what interested students. If they didn't, Geo admitted, he'd just do the minimum. He wouldn't complain, but he wouldn't work to excel the way he worked in football.

All of these young men valued school. All of them were inquisitive and enthusiastic. None of them were readers. They were willing to do what needed to be done. But we can't help wondering how different they would have sounded if they had regarded school and reading as healthy work.

Mostly Outside, Rarely Inside

4

In one English class we observed during our study, we saw two of our boys with their heads down on their desks, apparently sleeping. They made a mock show of trying to wake up when asked by the teacher to start their assigned reading. As the bell rang, though, they sprang to life, and Jeff could not keep up with them as they jostled through the crowded hallway to the lunchroom. One of the boys did not even bother to buy lunch, hurrying to his favorite lunch table, already occupied by his waiting friends.

"Hey, have you guys seen this yet?" he exulted, as he pulled out the latest issue of *Maxim*. Though the boys did pause over several of the photographs, their real interest was in an article on the history of warfare. "This is one hot magazine," he told Jeff when he observed him looking on.

When the second boy arrived with his lunch tray, his plate was perched atop a wrestling magazine that was so quickly grabbed by a friend, his plate nearly overturned. "Hey, hey, hey! Careful with the merchandise!" he joked, holding the magazine protectively to his chest.

In the next two chapters, we take up a magnifying glass to look more closely at the literate activity of the boys in our study. If we are going to understand these activities, we have to include how they practice and respond to literacy both inside and outside of classrooms. As the opening story makes clear, boys' attitudes toward literacy in the lunchroom or at home might be very different from their attitudes toward literacy during fourth-period English.

Reading Logs

The data we will use to take this fine-grained look at literacy center around daily literacy logs that the boys kept of all of their literate activities, widely construed to include television and movie viewing, video game playing, magazine reading, music listening and concert attendance, Internet surfing, and the like. (See Appendix B for the log directions we provided.) Through these logs, we hoped to see not only how boys engaged and disengaged with varieties of literate activity, but also how these activities were embedded in and how they played out in their daily lives.

Each boy was interviewed every four to six weeks about the contents of his log. We analyzed log interviews from forty-six of the boys. We also observed the boys as often as possible in their classrooms and sometimes on informal occasions outside of class or school.

In an article in which he focuses explicitly on the connections between flow and literacy, Csikszentmihalyi (1990b) provides a justification for our approach when he asks, "If literacy is for the sake of the children, how come we so rarely bother to find out what they want to use it for?" (p. 136). When we bothered to find out, the boys provided fascinating answers.

The central finding from this data set is the sharp difference between the literate practices inside and outside of school. As was true for the magazine readers in the lunchroom, the literate lives of all the boys outside of school were surprisingly varied and rich, but this home/outside/real-world literacy was practiced in ways that looked quite different from the literacy they were asked to practice in school. While the boys were often passionate about the literate activities they pursued outside of school, they usually saw school literacy as a tool, not as something to be passionate about. (There were limited occasions when school literacy mirrored the features of home literacy in ways that motivated and assisted the boys, and we'll be examining those carefully.)

Even though the boys believed in the importance of school literacy in theory, as we discussed in the last chapter, they often rejected and resisted it in actual practice because it was not related to immediate interests and needs. Jamaal, who was serving several detentions for skipping school, provides a perfect illustration. Like most of the boys, he articulated a belief that you had to go to school and do your work: "I noticed that I had a really hard time learning everything after I'd been out. You need to be in school to, you know, learn everything and so you'll be ready for life." When Jeff confronted Jamaal with his chronic tardiness, school skipping, and failure to do homework, he replied, "I know, I know. My actions don't match my words." He expressed that school was important but that it just didn't work for him.

As we saw in the previous two chapters, school literacy was related in the boys' minds to the far-off future; home literacy was about immediate interests in the here and now. School literacy was a means to an often unrecognized and ambiguous end; home literacy was a concrete and immediately satisfying end in itself.

For example, Fred was grounded by his parents for his entire eighth-grade school year because he refused to do homework. He maintained that school is school and home is home. He explained, "It was boring staying in my room, but homework is even more boring, so I would rather stare at the wall."

Though Fred was an unenthusiastic reader, he did read to pass the time while he was grounded, especially the *Star Wars* books he got from his best friend. Ironically, he even wrote book reports on them for extra credit.

Then there is Mick, who was functionally illiterate but who subscribed to car magazines. He flipped through the pages to find articles of interest based on the photos and graphics, and looked for someone to read them to him when he thought they were especially important.

Another student, Zach, named himself as a reader, yet he refused to read on vacations. He cited his need to "get away" from school—clearly perceiving "reading" as a school activity not to be pursued when not in school.

The fact that many of the boys saw their home and school literacies as entirely unconnected was also apparent in the way some of them omitted experiences from their logs. For example, on one fortuitous occasion, Jeff was at the same movie theater as two of the boys. They did not see him, but he heard them excitedly discussing the upcoming movie, talking about reviews they had accessed on the Internet and had heard from friends. They said they could not wait to weigh in on current discussions about the movie. Afterward, Jeff found them in the lobby laughing and arguing about "the flick." However, the boys did not record this activity in their logs.

Similarly, on another occasion, Jeff was working in the school library when one of the boys came in, began to read the sports page of the local paper, and then shared various game situations, statistics, and predictions about the NCAA basketball tournament with a friend. But he did not record this reading in his log.

We had been very explicit with the boys, stating we wanted a regular record of their daily activity from the time they awakened until they went to sleep, so we could get a sense of the rhythms and experiences that occupied them each day. We emphasized that they should record any activity that could be considered engaging with or composing a text—ideas expressed in any form that engaged them.

The boys in our study were generally very good and complete about recalling and recording in-class forms of reading. They cited videos watched for class and political cartoons and photographs used in class; most recorded that they read notes from the chalkboard or from their notebook; almost all of them talked about reading math problems. So they construed literacy quite widely, as we had suggested to them, when they were in the classroom.

Yet as we've noted, some of the boys initially failed to record literate activities we had observed when these fell outside of classroom situations. When Jeff asked the boys why they had not included these activities in their logs, they generally indicated surprise that we were "interested in that kind of stuff." Ricardo explained, "I thought you wanted to know about reading, you know, to learn and stuff." In other words, he thought we defined literacy solely as "schoolish literacy." Once we emphasized again to the boys that we were interested in the widest possible range of literate activity, this problem was largely resolved in the subsequent logs.

In Chapter 2 we saw how our boys had many interests and passions that gave them great pleasure, and we discussed how the reasons underlying those interests and passions seldom extended to their literate activity in school. In Chapter 3 we looked at their attitudes toward different ways of being literate and at various influences on literacy, including the influence of ethnicity and class. In this chapter, we take a close look at how school and life literacies are perceived and practiced in mostly different ways, how our boys valued and devalued certain kinds of literate activity, and the connection of these attitudes to specific ideas about how people should be and behave. We conclude the chapter by considering how these findings challenge us as teachers to assist boys in becoming more competent in their literate activity.

Though we analyzed the logs and log interviews by looking for new codes and themes (that is—open coding), we quickly found that the same major codes we had used for the activity ranking and profile data also worked with this data set. Though we did identify and use nearly one hundred additional subcodes, we found that all of these could still be clustered around the four major principles we've identified from the work of Csikzimihalyi (1990a).

We'll discuss three of those themes in this chapter, saving the final theme for the next chapter, in which we focus on the reading materials that boys found most appealing.

Findings: A Sense of Competence, Control, and Challenge

Exercising a measure of control over literate activities—and appearing and being competent in them—were overwhelmingly important to the boys in the study.

Competence

Research has demonstrated that people who consider themselves to be competent enact very particular social practices to mark their identity as competent member of a particular *community of practice*. For example, kayakers prepare their kayaks, use particular kinds of language, and interact in various ways to announce and maintain a sense of competence. The same is true for waitresses, librarians, tailors, game players, and all other communities of practice. As Lave and Wenger (1991) assert:

> Learning . . . is a process of becoming a member of a sustained community of practice. Developing an identity as a member of a community and becoming knowledgeably skillful are part of the same process. (p. 65)

One of the ways the boys demonstrated the importance of competence was through their admiration for the literate work of others and their expressed desire to enter into that community of competence. Robert, for example, loved the facility of the rapper Cannabis; Ricardo loved the movies of Quentin Tarantino. Most of the boys revered some sports figures or musical artists for their skill and competence.

Robert spoke this way about Cannabis:

> He on a different level than all them rappers because most of his stuff he don't write down. He just say it right off his head. What goes through his head, he just come out with it. That's what I like about him. And, he don't always talk about running around killing people, how much money he got and all of this different types of cars and houses. He talks about what he go through in real life. He talk about real-life stuff because he went to college. Because he said the way he raps, it's like he's mathematical.

Maurice brought the same belief in the importance of competence to his writing that Robert brought to his listening. He told Michael he reads his poems over and over:

> Just to make sure if it makes sense or not, because who wants to hand in something that doesn't make any sense. They're going to look at you like, "This kid doesn't know what he's doing. He doesn't know what he's talking about."

But as we saw in Chapter 2, the downside of this emphasis on competence was the boys' reluctance to take on tasks in which they did not feel competent. Aaron, for example, asserted that he avoids his work for English "because I'm not good at it." Fred extended the argument by describing to Michael how he feels when he is engaged in a literate activity in which he does not feel competent:

Fred: I think that I told you about this before about my comprehension.
Michael: Yeah, you said that you had trouble with that.
Fred: I don't know why. If I am, it is weird if I, I feel that I have a lot of pressure on me. And when I have a lot of pressure I get real nervous

because I have lived a life where I am real nervous. And when I get nervous I get real hot and I get real sweaty, and sometimes I felt real lightheaded like I am going to drop. And I get nervous during some tests and, I don't know, I guess that that could be why I can't concentrate that well.

Michael: But you didn't get nervous in your math test?

Fred: Math—that's fun to do; I enjoy math.

The importance of competence was also affirmed by Ricardo. He maintained that you "better be competent" because "what you do is who you are . . . like a lot of people know me as a good photographer. So I guess that is a thing that I would identify with."

Huey seemed to be following Ricardo's advice. He explained that he avoids certain topics to deepen his knowledge in areas in which he is already something of an expert:

> I'd rather be real good at something than know a lot—well, I'd rather be real good at something than have a little bit of knowledge about a lot of stuff. . . . I feel it's better to be the best at something than to be average and know a little bit of everything.

This notion of a circumscribed area of competence was echoed by many of the boys. And when the boys felt competent in literate activity, they found it fun as well, whether it was playing video games; being able to talk about and critique wrestling shows on television; designing a virtual role-playing game home, hypermedia stacks, or websites; or even learning something new.

At home, the boys engaged in literate activities in which they already felt some competence, and they did so in situations with friends who could help them be more competent and who encouraged them to work through challenges. They were rewarded by the immediate payoffs in being able to apply or export what they had learned (e.g., use it in conversation). In contrast, the chances to build on competence in supportive social situations in school were much more limited, and the boys often felt that school put them in a position of being incompetent or feeling incompetent. Some of the boys indicated that they would rather avoid work that made them feel incompetent and suffer the consequences, expressing the attitude that "it's better to say the reading assignment is stupid than to admit or look like you are stupid."

The Role of Teachers

On the surface, the boys' emphasis on competence would seem to bode well for their relationships with teachers. Just as their friends helped them become increasingly competent in their out-of-school activities, teachers, it would seem, would assist them in becoming increasingly competent in their in-school activities.

The young men, in fact, saw providing this assistance as a teacher's role. Marcel, for example, talked about what good teachers do: "They will help you any time that you need it." Sisqó argued that a good teacher is "One who sees your trouble and helps you." Haywood revealed that he was "willing to read really hard stuff if the teacher is willing to help me." But unfortunately, the boys reported that they did not feel they regularly received that kind of assistance from teachers, at least not in a form in which they were willing to accept it.

Again and again we heard the boys talk about what we came to regard as an implicit social contract that the boys felt teachers generally reneged upon. This implicit contract appeared to have several regular features:

1. A teacher should try to get to know me personally.
2. A teacher should care about me as an individual.
3. A teacher should attend to my interests in some way.
4. A teacher should help me learn and work to make sure that I have learned.
5. A teacher should be passionate, committed, work hard, and know his or her stuff.

If a teacher met even one of these conditions in the eyes of the students, the boys tended to respond positively and to learn from and work hard for that teacher. When teachers failed to hold up their end of the bargain, the students echoed Herb Kohl's famous book title: "I won't learn from you."

Bambino was a case in point. We've earlier pointed out that he was a wrestling aficionado. While he realized that his wrestling expertise was not something he could bring easily to class, he wanted it to be noticed. He refused to do anything more than perfunctory work for many of his teachers. But he indicated that if teachers simply talked with him from time to time about wrestling, even for a quick minute in the hallway, he would be happy to do their work. That's all it would take: a recognition that he brought interests and expertise from outside of school to the table. Rev made a very similar contractual argument: "The teachers don't know you, care about you, recognize you. So why should you care about them or the work they want you to do?"

The boys wanted to be appreciated and known as individuals, and they were cynical in general about the teachers' desire to know or deal with them as individuals. Wolf provides a representative example

> Michael: You sort of have an adversarial relationship to school.
> Wolf: Yeah. I really don't like it. I don't like it only because I think for the most part, at this level anyway, it wants to make you into part of the collective.
> Michael: Tell me what you mean by that.
> Wolf: Ah, teachers don't want an individualistic child; they don't want that one kid that has got all of the energy, that is always hyper, that is a real individual. They want everybody to be in a seat listening to what they say so that they don't have any problems, no worries, no troubles. They want a collective. They want everybody to be that one model student that just sits there, asks the right questions at the right time, things like that.

Jigg advised teachers, "If you want me to learn from you, then be friendly, relate to me as a person, help me." Echoing the theme of needing assistance, Marcel said it is a teacher's responsibility to help him. Though he resists school, he said he would learn from a thinking, committed, and action-oriented teacher.

Neil described his favorite teacher as one who

> teaches and, you know, kind of gets with each individual student if he needs it and explains things over and over until you kind of get it. And it is a very helpful environment.

He further argued that this "good" teacher only gives the homework "you need, to freshen things up" and does not give busywork, as she recognizes the difficulty and busyness of the students' lives. Busywork was mentioned by twenty-four of the boys in connection with school, and they described it with disdain as a form of disrespect to them and their lives.

When teachers or other adults did express interest in students and their lives, the students responded with tremendously positive emotion. The boys in the rural public school, for example, loved their principal, as Timmy said, "because he knows your name and what you do. And he's happy for you if you do something good. He knows about it and he mentions it." One teacher was embraced by the boys in her school because she gave them birthday cards on their birthdays and attended their sporting and artistic events. Mark worked in the library of his school because he liked the librarian. Larry signed up to work on the literary magazine and Junior Exhibition because he liked the teacher coordinating it.

All of the boys in the private school spoke of their relationships with teachers there as a primary reason they valued the school. Liam made this clear to Jeff:

> Jeff: OK. Now you mentioned the teachers, what's so special about the teachers here?
>
> Liam: That they are willing to take the time to get to know you, ah, if you have a problem then you can always come to them. Gradually you get to know those people and you start to like them a lot. I know Mr. _____ is one of my favorite teachers, not necessarily as a teacher but as a person. I think that I have gotten to know him and he's gotten to know me this past year, and it has been important to me.
>
> Jeff: Do you think that it is different at other schools?
>
> Liam: Yeah. I know teachers still want to help, but they are not given the environment to help; they may have thirty students to a class. And it is much harder to deal with the student on an individual basis.

Liam went on to praise his school's class trips, community projects, mentor-mentee program, and other endeavors that he thinks helps teachers and students know and support each other:

> So all that encourages community and helping others so that you come to someone and say, "Hey, you are kind of slipping up in class; do you need any help with anything?"

Ricardo, also a student at the private school, repeated this idea:

> Teachers are supposed to care about you as an individual here. School here is about the whole person, not just Ricardo the math student or whatever.

Activities as Assistance

While most of the boys sought some kind of relationship with their teachers as a precondition for their learning, they also identified other features of learning activities and environments that would help teachers build upon those relationships. The most enjoyable and powerful form of assistance and support for reading that the boys identified were activities that involved active, participatory, hands-on response to the reading.

Jeff personally observed a striking contrast between a classroom that was not engaging students in activity and one that was. First, he observed one ninth-grade class in which some of our boys were reading *Twelfth Night*. The teacher assigned several scenes each night and spent the next class period valiantly reviewing and helping the kids understand the assigned scenes. It became apparent to Jeff that none of the boys were doing the reading, and he confirmed this by asking the boys.

The boys revealed that they knew they could "get by" without doing the reading because the teacher was going to tell them the next day what the assigned scenes were about. Buda complained, "It's in a foreign language anyway! . . . It's too hard." The boys all agreed that they wanted to do well in the class, but they were unwilling to read the text. They had many strategies for "getting by," including asking questions of the teacher that showed confusion early in the class period; articulating expressions like "Oh, I get it now!" when the teacher explained something; thanking the teacher profusely; renting video versions of the text; reading Cliff's Notes; asking girls in the class for help; and so on. Jamaal shared a list of "get by strategies" that he kept along with his Cliff's Notes and Monarch Notes. When Jeff suggested that Jamaal was spending more energy on getting by then on actually reading, he just laughed.

This theme of getting by was obvious in many other situations as well. Lax professed to avoid reading in any situation where he could. Jeff and Yuri had an extended exchange about getting by:

> Jeff: You say that you really BS your way through school. Man, I am seeing and hearing this almost every day.
>
> Yuri: Yeah, just fix the teachers some BS. Everyone does it. I mean, there is, like, not one person in this school who does their reading. Even the kids that get 4.0 GPA, they BS.
>
> Jeff: Um, um.
>
> Yuri: My BS just isn't that good so I don't have a 4.0.

After Jeff observed the unified front of twelve boys who refused to read *Twelfth Night* but found ways to succeed in class nonetheless, he then observed a class from the same school reading *Romeo and Juliet*. In that class, everyone was obviously reading and enjoying the play. The students were performing various scenes, and they were also involved as "documentary producers," inquiring into issues like "family feuds," "the historical basis of *Romeo and Juliet*," "rules of dueling," and many other topics that came up during their reading of the play. They used digital video cameras to make and then edit scenes that were knitted together in an iMovie called *Looking for Romeo and Juliet*, based on the *Looking for Richard* movie with Al Pacino.

The experience in this second class indicates that even difficult texts can be made accessible by instruction. In fact, thirty-six of the boys indicated that when teachers created contexts that allowed them to pursue active responses and projects, they felt better able to meet the challenge provided by their reading.

The boys' favorite kind of assistance was various forms of dramatic activity, something that was mentioned as helpful by over half the boys. The most cited drama activity consisted of reenacting various scenes from the reading so that these could be shared, discussed, and reviewed. Another common kind of drama activity was trials of characters like Hamlet, Macbeth, Tom Sawyer, and others. Huey particularly lauded the trial project of Brutus in *Julius Caesar*, maintaining that he learned a lot not only about the play, but "about different legal systems and the courts."

Unfortunately, however, the boys seldom engaged in this kind of dramatic activity. In some ways this is understandable, for performing such elaborate dramas requires a good deal of instructional time. Given the boy's interest in drama, however, it seems that exploring other dramatic alternatives would make sense. For example, some of the boys talked about how much they enjoyed doing in-role writing, in which they wrote from the perspective of a character. Pablo talked about how much he enjoyed "hotseating," taking on the persona of a character and being interviewed by his classmates. Dramatic activities that are scriptless and short have the potential to involve more boys more regularly in drama. (See Wilhelm and Edmiston, 1998, for a discussion of a variety of alternatives.)

The boys' endorsement of teaching through activity matches Vygotskian and neo-Vygotskian notions of instruction, especially Vygotsky's idea of the zone of proximal development (ZPD). The assistance that is necessary to learning in the ZPD allows the learner to appropriate the problem-solving language and strategies of the more expert person who is lending the learner assistance. When the expert's knowledge has been internalized and used by the learner, then competence is visibly enhanced.

This idea of learning only when challenged to go just beyond current abilities also nicely matches Csikszentmihalyi's (1990a) ideas about flow and is reminiscent of Robert Browning's "A man's reach should exceed his grasp / or what's a heaven for?" Csikszentmihalyi (1990b) argues that "one of the most important tasks for a teacher is to make sure that students are neither too overwhelmed nor too bored by the material they must master" (p. 134). Our data challenge us to think about various ways to assist students. This might involve using drama, visual art, debates, and design projects, as well as techniques such as think-alouds, symbolic story representation, and assignment sequences. These techniques make expert strategies visible and available to students in the context of real reading, and they help students practice and master these strategies over time.

Purpose

For the boys in our study, home literacy always had a clear and immediate purpose, whether it was to enjoy themselves with friends, find out about the latest dirt bikes or movie releases, or use a chat room to explore religious ideas. School literacy often did not have this obvious and pointed kind of purpose, but when it did, the effects could be powerful. Haywood, for instance, talked about how his Spanish teacher focused on speaking and communicating in Spanish and on the many ways this would be useful in travel, business, and a future in which many Americans will be Spanish-speaking. Haywood discussed the struggle to learn Spanish, but he also noted how satisfying it was when he could finally converse and use it: "It is good to learn and once I learn, you know it is kinda fun." Having a purpose aids the struggle; using your developed competence is the reward.

More than that, purposefulness seemed to be part of competence. As Joe expressed, "People who know what they are doing know WHY they are doing it."

Problem-Oriented Work

The boys' desire to have a clear purpose for their literate activity was manifested in the way they pursued problem-centered work. Wolf, for example, described to Michael how his nonschool reading agenda was organized around problems or questions:

> Wolf: I just like to know stuff. If I don't know something, I will just sit there and listen to people and just kind of ask a lot of questions, I mean, I just look at little kids and they ask questions like, "Why is the sky blue?" and then some parent will just sit there like "eerrrwww." I try to ask questions like that, just real simple questions that some little kid would ask, that seem idiotic, they're so simple, but they have complex answers. I like to ask questions like that, especially if I don't know anything. I like to go from know nothing to having a base from which to work from. Because you don't know anything, you don't even know where to start, that's the problem.
>
> Michael: Once you have the base, do you then do the work? Do you see what I'm saying?

Wolf: Once I have a base, I go out and I try to get some information. Especially if I like it. If I don't like it so much, I'm not too worried about it. I'll ask a lot of questions, and maybe I'll read the pamphlets or something if they have them, but if I really like it, I'll just try to get as much information as I can.

Michael: Give me the last time you really liked something and went out and got that information.

Wolf: Well, I liked the medieval events and stuff, so I got a lot of information on that the last time.

Wolf continued to discuss how he attends Renaissance fairs with his girlfriend and how doing so posed a problem to him. He wanted to know how he should dress, act, speak, and interact as a person living during the Renaissance. Notice too how Wolf likes to learn about something he already knows a little about and will learn about something in great depth if it grabs his attention, dropping it altogether if it does not.

Wolf was one of the committed readers in our study. As we have noted, Mick was not. Yet he too was willing to read to solve a problem, especially if it related to making or building cars.

Many of the boys expressed a willingness to read to inquire into an issue that would lead to designing a visible product that could be shared or used. For example, the boys were happy to read for school projects such as making video or hypermedia documentaries, completing a bridge-building project, doing a zoo project, creating dramas, preparing public presentations or exhibitions, and even doing I-Search papers in a history class.

The intense enthusiasm the boys expressed for these projects was as notable as the dearth of such projects. The boys were grateful for such activities but saw them as anomalies. They considered participating in such projects "good luck" and did not expect school to offer more such activities. Outside of school, however, they were always in situations in which they were using, applying, or making something that required literate knowledge and competence: playing video games, using the Internet, fixing a dirt bike, discussing issues they had learned about with friends.

Self-Expression
The boys were generally much more willing to put in the effort needed to gain competence when they had the chance to express themselves in ways that marked their identity. Maurice, for example, spoke about his graphic artwork: "You have to put your personal stamp on your work. You don't do it like everybody else. Have your own way."

The emphasis on expressing themselves also informed the boys' enjoyment of their discussion with friends. Ricardo loved to watch movies with friends so they could critique and express opinions about them. He said, "After a movie I definitely, like if I'm with somebody, I definitely discuss parts of it with them, usually, like, on the way home, the drive home, it's usually like, talk time." This talk time provided a chance to "vent" their opinions.

The important of self-expression extended to in-school discussions as well, as Neil told Michael:

Neil: With Algebra and German II we take a lot of notes on those classes because they are basically the ones that don't harvest from your mind. It is not stuff that ah, you produce. It is stuff that you have to learn and then repeat back to them, so it is really two different types of learning.

Michael: So in English you do the harvesting. I love that metaphor. And then in the other ones you do—

Neil: You are taught it and you have to, just, kind of tell it back to them.

Johnny admired his English teacher and enjoyed the class:

I like the way he teaches more than any other teacher. He likes to get our opinion on what we do in class. All my other teachers—they don't care what we say. They just do their own thing.

As a result, Johnny claimed he was more invested and willing to work in this class. He felt more control, competence, and respect in a class where he had a voice.

The desire to express themselves extended to assignments and tests. Sisqó, for example, enjoyed his world religion class because he was encouraged to compare and contrast different views and to make decisions for himself. Wolf enjoyed "Problems in History" questions because they allowed him some choice and the chance to express his opinion:

We have the opinion type where they ask you something. They ask you, like, what do you think about it, and then we have one that we can go in the book to look for that answer, like it was a set answer already. [I like the opinion ones] because the opinion one, you got more options. You could put whatever you want, basically, whatever you feel is the answer as to what the question is.

Unfortunately, the chance to express an opinion was not something most of the students felt was encouraged by school. Yuri put it this way: "School is not a place where I can express my feelings or be myself. School is just something that can keep me away from doing that." Their perception jibes with the research of Nystrand and his colleagues (1997), who found that teachers ask very few questions for which they don't have specific answers in mind. Interestingly, the boys in the private school felt more encouraged to express themselves, something those students attributed to small class sizes, teacher-student relationships, an atmosphere of mutual respect, and an emphasis on educating the whole person.

Powerful Ideas and Depth

Understanding something of interest in great depth was another motivation to develop competence. Rudy, Neil, Buster, and several other boys all rejected computer research as being "too easy." As Rudy put it, "You can do the research, but you don't really understand it with any depth or anything." The importance of depth of learning resonated throughout the interviews. In fact, the boys as a group critiqued school learning as being superficial: a code related to their critique of "insufficient depth" was used for data from twenty-nine of the boys. These boys argued that school leaps from topic to topic, and that textbooks in particular do not provide the basis for the deep understanding that was important to a sense of competence and control. They indicated that in school they just went through and did unconnected assignments; at home they worked over time to develop very particular sets of understandings and skills that could be used in new situations.

In his discussion with Michael, Robert provided a specific example of the wider attitude:

> Michael: Of all the reading that you do in school, what's your least favorite, would you say?
> Robert: English.
> Michael: And why is that?
> Robert: Because after we finish reading, we just go on to something else. We go on to something else to do. Like, she'll give us some different work. After we read, we just close the book and do different work.
> Michael: And you would rather do what?
> Robert: Do work, like, responding to the story, like that.

Control

In Chapter 1 we quoted Csikszentmihalyi (1990a), who wrote that acquiring knowledge controlled from the outside brings no joy. Morimoto, Gregory, and Butler (1973) make a similar point:

> When change is advocated or demanded by another person, we feel threatened, defensive and perhaps rushed. We are then without the

freedom and the time to understand and affirm the new learning as something desirable, and as something of our own choosing. Pressure to change, without an opportunity for exploration and choice, seldom results in experiences of joy and excitement in learning. (p. 255)

The reading logs made it clear that the boys wanted to control the knowledge they acquired. They wanted choice.

Choice and Interests

Throughout our study, it was clear that the boys wanted to do reading that fed preexisting interests. The data contained no direct statements that interests were developed through reading; instead, the boys felt that interests were developed before reading and then could be fed and nurtured through reading. This was one reason choice was so important to them.

As Greene (1988) maintains, exercising choice allows a person to "choose oneself" and consciously mark his or her identity. Robert, for example, chose himself through the magazines he subscribed to for free by filling out "special offer" coupons and then declining a paid subscription when the free issues ran out (at which point he would subscribe to other magazines). At the time of the study he subscribed to and read *Slam, Vibe, Source,* and *East Bay,* magazines that fed his interests in sports, music, and fashion.

Similarly, Ian chose himself in his hyper-studio project. He discussed this with Jeff:

Jeff: What do you think that you will choose to research for this hyper-studio project?

Ian: I'll do piano because I play the piano, or I might do football because I like football.

Jeff: So you are going to learn more about something that you already know something about?

Ian: Yeah.

Jeff: OK. Great. Do you have questions about football or piano that you want to pursue?

Ian: Not really, I mean, I just like to learn about stuff that, you know, I kinda like to learn a little more about. I already know something, so I want to know more.

When Jeff asked Ian if he had ever developed new interests through school activity or reading, he said no. This was true across the boys (with one notable exception that we will discuss later). Interests were brought to school, not developed in school. If we believe that school has a function in developing and nurturing interests, this is a problem that needs attention. We argue that schools do have such a function, particularly given the evidence here and elsewhere that shows how interests relate to and contribute as a resource for learning. (See, for example, Hidi's, 1990, review of research.)

Whitehead (1961) explains why interest is so important. He asserts that knowledge always begins with interest or what he calls *romance*; pursuing the romance deeply over time leads to *precision*; and precise knowing then leads to *generalization* because it helps one see how the area of interest is like, and unlike, related areas. Generalization, in turn, leads to new romances. Deeply cultivating student interests, according to Whitehead, is the necessary first step toward assisting them to becoming knowledgeable. However, devoting the time necessary to developing precision, generalization, and further romance is antithetical to American schooling's incessant push for the superficial coverage of information.

The desire for choice and the ability to pursue one's interests as an exercise of freedom and possibility was pervasive throughout our study. Ian, like many of the boys, championed the sense of control he got from playing video games and lamented the lack of control he had in school. Drake talked about the control he had working in his garage and how he never experienced this control or sense of competence in school.

In opposition to the boys' general disdain for the superficial way computers were used in school, the boys embraced the use of electronic technologies in their home literacies. Wolf loved using the computer at home, explaining, "It gives me the freedom to learn about what interests me." Ian echoed this, maintaining that "Writing on a computer gives more choice and control to me." Bodey too felt that computers gave him more "freedom and possibility" as a reader and writer, indicating that the hyperlinks on websites helped him see related topics he might be interested in pursuing and noting that he enjoyed exercising choice about whether to do so.

The boys almost universally felt that school denied them choice and control and therefore any sense of personal agency or competence. When Jeff asked two of his groups from the public schools for a metaphor for school, both groups agreed upon *prison*. When Jeff indicated that he thought their choice was cynical, he was met with scornful laughter. "Look," they told him, "from the minute you enter the front door until the minute you get off the bus, you are told exactly what to do. You have no freedom whatsoever."

Similarly, Lax argued that "being a man means controlling your choices." He said that school did not allow for that control: "School just forces you to do things." But like most of the boys, he saw no way to change school.

On those few occasions when they were allowed choice in school, the boys embraced it. Rudy was very pleased to be studying animals in science, saying "I like animals and know something about them" and appreciating the choice "about what animal to study."

It was true across the boys that even very limited forms of choice were greatly appreciated. Bob enjoyed the sense of freedom at the private school because he felt that he was exercising more choice, both inside and outside of class. Like Bob, the private school boys generally indicated that there was "lots of stuff you have to do"—course requirements, required extracurricular sports and arts credits, service projects, school trips, and so forth. However, Bob also indicated that "There's always a choice, so you can do the things you want, or that interest you the most." He explained this further to Jeff:

> Bob: We get to choose what we do in some classes. You can do stuff that interests you more, like in our geography project. You can choose a country you really want to go to, or that you know something about. But I think that they should let you choose your classes too but still have requirements, too.
>
> Jeff: Do you have more choice or less choice here than in public school?
>
> Bob: More. I mean, public school you have to walk in single-file line down the halls. Here you can just walk around outside. 'Cause I just like walking outdoors, I think that it is fun.

Bob later indicated that the private school was much less "like a prison" than his public school had been.

Several of the students articulated how school and the way they were asked to read and respond militated against choice and freedom. Gohan told us that though he was interested in health issues, reading the health text "ain't really my thing [because] the book is like commanding you to do things. It's good to do them, but it's like, 'You got to do this.'"

Yuri expressed the same sentiment. He resisted being told what to read and what to think, as if "I can't make up my own mind." Yuri saw school as denying all his choices, and that's why he spent so much time in role-playing games (RPGs) in multi-user domains (MUDs) on the Internet. "There's freedom to be different in MUDs. . . . You can think for yourself—try things out." Thinking for yourself, inquiring into interests, and experimenting with new ideas were things Yuri felt school actively discouraged. In contrast, his Internet friends and role-playing buddies constantly encouraged him to learn in these engaging ways.

We concluded final log interviews by asking students what advice they would give future English teachers. Aaron began by offering a suggestion made by many of the boys: "Choice would be a big part of it."

The Exception That Proves the Rule

Despite the fact that virtually all of the boys talked about how they developed their interests outside school, it was very striking that nearly all the boys at two of the schools professed an interest in history, but only two boys in the other two schools indicated such an interest.

In the first two schools, we were able to tie the boys' interest directly to particular teachers and school activities. This indicates that new interest, though rarely developed in school and never acknowledged by our boys, could be cultivated under particular conditions, even for an academic subject. In one of the schools, every boy who expressed interest in history to us had been taught by the same middle school social studies teacher, who was "crazy about history" and who connected it to the local culture and history of the town. Most of these boys also took an inquiry-driven history class in high school in which they did I-Search projects. Every boy who had this class designated it as his favorite high school class, explaining that it allowed and encouraged students to make choices and pursue interests, and to make personal presentations of projects based on their findings.

The other school was actually set on a national historic site, which may have contributed to the interest. Outdoor class trips were taken, such as a bicycle tour to follow the routes of the Confederate troops on the way to Gettysburg and to visit the battlefield. Students then read books like *The Killer Angels* that followed the characters through places the students had visited. The students at this school roundly lauded their history teachers, one of whom is a regular contributor to national newspapers and magazines. One student at the school confided to Jeff that "We do history here at XXX."

This finding is particularly powerful. It demonstrates that passionate teaching and creative activities can develop and nurture interests and expertise in school subjects. Although individual interest is crucially important, this example suggests that situational interest, which "focuses on how the learning environment can capture or create interest" also must be attended to (Worthy, Moorman, and Turner, 1999, p. 13).

We'll discuss this idea in greater depth later, but it's important to note that the history teachers cultivated an interest in history in part by making history personally relevant, by giving some measure of control over learning history to the students, and by engaging them in meaningful social activity. The importance of competence and the importance of the social were two themes that resonated in the boys' discussion of their favorite activities. It seems that our participants could develop interests in new academic content if the context in which they encountered that content resembled the context in which they developed their out-of-school interests.

Our data lead us to argue that ignoring boys' prior interests and skills harms our ability to teach them. But we are going well beyond arguing that schools should simply cater to these interests. The history examples show that teachers can develop and nurture interests if they attend to the conditions of flow experience.

To summarize our argument in this section of the chapter, throughout the reading logs and the related interviews, the boys sang a hallelujah chorus to the doctrine of choice and pursuing interests. Many of the boys professed to realize through the course of this study that they defined reading differently and more widely than school defined it, and that they were doing much more reading and textual reflection than they had previously thought. Bringing students to such a realization can be an important step in helping students to name themselves as readers.

The findings around the themes of choice and interests challenge us to offer more choices to our students in terms of texts, assignments, and projects in our classrooms. They challenge us to negotiate curricula organized around topics, themes, and problems of interest to the kids in the here and now instead of around mandated historical periods or canonical texts. They encourage us to move to more workshop-like settings as students pursue and design usable artifacts around projects of interest. At the same time, as will be seen in the next section, we will have to be careful to keep the challenge appropriate and to continually "up the ante," providing additional challenges as earlier ones are met and to explicitly offer our expertise during this process.

On the strength of these data, we'd argue that reading can be usefully embedded in and proceed from an activity with which the kids already feel comfortable. This is particularly important for resistant and reluctant readers. For these kids, reading about hunting or four wheelers is not reading *qua* reading, but rather an extension of their interest in hunting or four wheelers. But again, even more important is that the conditions of flow experience are part of the reading situation.

According to our boys, school is so defined, regular, and routinized that kids are starved for choice and a sense of personal agency. When Pressley, Schuder, and Bergman (1992) reviewed the cumulative findings regarding seven years of trying to implement strategy-oriented instruction into classrooms, they cited "control" as the biggest challenge. They argued that the success of strategy instruction requires that teachers let go of old patterns of traditional instruction, most significantly that they relinquish some of their control in order to support the growth of self-regulated, autonomous readers. Exclusive teacher control, they argue, works against student learning. A measure of student control works for student learning. Teachers need to see themselves as teachers of strategies that help students independently engage with content, and of processes—not teachers of the content itself.

However, choice can be complicated. Newkirk (2001) reminds us that simply telling students they have a choice may not work if the structures of the classroom communicate that only particular kinds of choices are valued.

As we argued in the last chapter, despite the boys' consistent criticism of the lack of choices available in school, they nonetheless believed in the importance of school. This means that teachers have much less of an obstacle facing them as they might have believed as they try to reach boys. If teachers can tap in to existing student interests, tap the conditions of flow to develop and sustain new ones, and show students the connection of learning to their lives, the data here suggest that even resistant students can become engaged learners.

A Challenge That Requires an Appropriate Level of Skill

One way to tap the conditions of flow is to provide appropriate challenges. For example, Robert spoke about the competence and satisfaction he felt and the control he held when writing raps in a way that he did not speak about school activity:

> I wrote a rap. I think it was yesterday, the day before yesterday. I wrote a rap because my cousin said he wanted to hear a little something from me because he got a singing group and he got a album coming out and stuff like that. He just wanted to hear a little something. He asked me can I rap. I was like, "Yeah, I can. I can write stuff." It's not really hard. But before you start off writing, you got to really think, like think how to start off. You just can't start off any different kind of way. It's like a certain way you got to put everything, like, in different orders. Like, you got to have one verse. You got to have a certain amount of lines.

Robert made it clear that having an appropriate level of challenge is important. Writing a rap provides a challenge, but it's a challenge he can meet.

The boys' desire for a learning/reading challenge that requires an appropriate level of skill echoes the findings about other activities stated in Chapter

2. It also builds on the insights offered in this chapter about their attitudes toward competence and control and how challenges are more attractive if related to preexisting interests.

We found it especially interesting that so many of the boys talked about their school experience as being insufficiently challenging. Twenty-nine of the boys mentioned that they thought their teachers expected too little of them. Here's Brandon, speaking with Jeff:

> Brandon: My feeling is we go way too slow. We have a lot of people at different levels, so I end up getting bored in that class and don't pay much attention.
>
> Jeff: So you want to move; you want a challenge.
>
> Brandon: I don't want a huge challenge, something that's impossible and keeps me up at night, but I want something that's faster than what we're doing right now and gives a challenge.

Wolf made a similar point. After describing how his psychology teacher made assignments easier and summarized texts for students instead of asking them to read, Wolf described the work he was asked to do as "mind numbing." Yet at the same time, he was enthusiastically reading a tome entitled *Evil*, a complex psychological study of the roots of evil, on his own.

The boys commented often about the lack of stimulating and challenging class work. Some, like Marcel, went so far as to say that work that was too easy led to failure:

> I don't know why I am just slacking off but my worse subject I am messing up in is Spanish. I am slacking it because, I don't know. I find it is not challenging enough, that is the thing, and if I am not challenged, you know, especially with something that I know. If I am not challenged, then I am going to get bored real quick. I am going to get bored real quick and then I am going to be like, I already learned this like in . . . When I was one years old my father already taught me all of this stuff, you know.

Marcel's failing Spanish was especially striking because he spoke Spanish at home.

On the one hand, many of them complained that their schoolwork was teaching them what they already knew. On the other hand, we sometimes also heard complaints when work was too challenging. But when the boys perceived a challenge as appropriate and interesting, they enjoyed taking it on.

Liam, for example, described the best reading experiences as game-like challenges, when "reading is a mental sport" for which he knows the rules and moves. Pablo liked texts that posed a human problem or an issue to figure out. He reported that on a trip to New York City, he "really enjoyed *Miss Saigon* [the Broadway musical] because it gives you a problem to figure out. A challenge to meet."

But often the boys didn't feel they could meet the challenges posed by school, and so they avoided them. This feeling was rooted in a number of more specific concerns, including ambiguity, length, style, and unfamiliarity.

Ambiguity

Maurice was among the boys who disliked the ambiguity of tasks in English that made it difficult for him to know if he had achieved success. Here's part of his conversation with Michael:

> Maurice: Yeah, I'm good in math. I like math a lot. That is a challenge, but sometimes, with word problems, I can't stand them. We had this problem in math called the coin problem. Oh, man! He put it on the board one day. We'll get it out, and I'd be close. I'd be like this much from the answer or one step away, and then the next day he'll have another one on the board so I'll think about using the procedure from yesterday to get the answer and it would be different. It would be totally way off. I like the challenge of them, but they're real hard though.
>
> Michael: You're smiling. You were liking the challenge in math class, but your creative writing class, you weren't liking that challenge so much. You know what I'm saying? I'm sort of interested in how they're different.
>
> Maurice: Because with math, it's like numbers and money involved, and you can look at the example and learn how to figure it out. It's a different way to do both things, to do math and creative writing. With poetry, you're reading someone's poem. You don't know how they feel. You're just reading their words, but they can mean something else.

Like Maurice, the boys welcomed challenges they could meet, especially when they felt they could monitor their success.

Length

This was an issue articulated by more than half of the boys, particularly the poorer readers. When we gave them the stories on which we asked them to do think-aloud protocols (data we'll address next chapter), most of them flipped through to see how many pages the stories were. Many made faces and commented on length before they made any attempt to see what the stories would be about. In fact, thirty of the boys complained that reading took too much of their time, and an additional ten complained that they did not have enough time to read what was assigned in school.

Most of the boys, in contrast, enjoyed reading short pieces. Jamaal said he "loved cartoons. They are short, to the point, and funny." Brandon read *Newsweek* because "the articles are short and you can get informed quickly." He would sometimes read a news magazine instead of doing school reading. Marcel professed to love poetry because "it is short and to the point. No messing around." Bodey said that he only read "in short bursts. Five minutes at a time. That's all the time I can sit there." Reading short, to-the-point pieces kept their attention and gave them a quick sense of accomplishment. In contrast, many of the boys saw the longer texts required in school as beyond them.

Style

Boys also had difficulty with the style of some of what they were asked to read in school, especially if they found the language too old-fashioned or too descriptive. Brandon, for example, complained that he often had problems with "the writing style that it's in. It's kind of hard to read; if it's not really modern English." Neil made a similar argument when he explained his problem reading *Cyrano de Bergerac*:

> It is kind of a lot different because the play was written in, like, the early nineteen hundreds and a lot of the things I don't think, were, as you know, right. Like humor. (Laughs.) I don't think that they all had it together with that. It was written in like, nineteen hundred, ten. Too dated. They didn't have it together around then.

Lax, like the majority of the boys, addressed the issue of what he saw as too much description. He wanted writing "to get to the action and the point." For this reason, he liked "plays . . . I just read what people say. There's no description and you get right to the point."

Fourteen of the boys overtly articulated that they rejected the texture of some texts, including Timmy, who told Jeff, "He should just say it, man!" when he talked about an author he felt used too much description. In contrast, home reading was usually short, to the point, and written in an accessible style. Home reading did not feature the texture and stylized descriptions of the school texts that sometimes frustrated our boys.

Unfamiliarity

The issue of unfamiliarity was raised in two different ways. Twelve students identified problems when they encountered new text structures. For example, Buda had difficulty with plays when his class began to read *Twelfth Night*. He claimed that he did not know how to read the way it was written, which caused "massive confusion." In fact, Esslin (1987) explains how scripts make use of twelve conventions that other texts do not use, and Buda's descriptions made it clear that he did not know the interpretive operations needed to make sense of the conventions dramas employ. Guy also complained about reading scripts.

Haywood had a similar complaint about Italo Calvino's *Invisible Cities*, a text that could not be read "like a story. You have to read it in a different kind of way." As well, several middle school boys complained about the difficulty of reading their textbooks. The textbooks were less storied and much more dense than what the boys had read in elementary school, and they didn't have the appropriate strategies for dealing with them.

The boys also felt overmatched if the ideas in texts were beyond their experience. For instance, Sisqó complained that the worst thing he had read all year was the *Power of Myth*:

> I didn't really understand that too much. It was kind of too philosophical, I guess. Kind of deep and I did not really understand that.

On the other hand, they approved of texts that were appropriately challenging. Marcel maintained that good texts "fit the kids' level." Lax agreed that a book should "Give you something to chew on. Be tough, but not too much."

If we don't provide an appropriate level of challenge, they'll take it upon themselves, for we found that boys who did not feel challenged by school often made up their own challenges. Jamaal is one example. He engaged in various forms of passive resistance so that "school would have some kind of challenge." Every day in English he would put the overhead out of focus while the teacher was in the hallway. He successfully did so for more than thirty straight school days, irritating the teacher each day without being caught. It provided him with "a reason to come to school." Similarly, in science lab, another boy hooked bunsen burners to water spigots. He told us that when lab participants turned the spigot, the water would spray out of the burner, which would "dance around on the table tops. The girls would scream and everything!"

Stan was another boy who resisted school and experienced some difficulties there. In fact, he was told us he repeating English class because "I just didn't do the work," despite the fact that he was one of only seven highly engaged readers in our study. Though he avoided much of his schoolwork, he spent quite a long time planning how to "streak" across the football field during one halftime. He successfully did this and was able to escape in a getaway car. Though he was later arrested, he cited this shenanigan as

> the highlight of my high school career. . . . It was a challenge, it was fun, and I did it. And I made a name for myself. Everyone still talks about it. It will be something everybody in my class will remember when they remember high school.

His prank served as an identity marker for him, one that he was confident would work for him well into the future.

Some of the boys even devised ways to make their reading and viewing more challenging by bringing in the element of competition. Ricardo creatively set up bets on outcomes of books and set up a big pool on the outcomes of Smackdown and Wrestlemania competitions.

The boys in our study needed a challenge. If they didn't find it in traditional school activity, they sometimes found it elsewhere. Their remarks also point to the next theme we'll address, the desire to see visible signs of their accomplishment.

Clear Goals and Feedback

Csikszentmihalyi (1990b) argues that a major problem with the educational system is that "To many children, even if they are dimly aware of the long term goals of education, the purpose of specific drills and lessons remains opaque" (p. 135). The boys' discussion of this issue resounded in our data. Mike complained, "Sometimes I don't understand what I am supposed to do. I just go for a try." Brandon complained that he often didn't understand "the assignment, the purpose, the criteria—nothing! And you still have to try to do it!" More than twenty of the boys made such complaints and contended that the absence of clear goals and feedback interfered with their motivation and homework completion.

The boys in our study wanted to understand the value of the work they were asked to do—and all too often they did not. Robert, for example, contrasted the reading and writing he was asked to do in English to the reading and writing he was asked to do in his health class.

> In English class, we mainly read about stuff like literature, reading over paragraphs and different stuff. We write paragraphs. Like, it would be a paragraph in the book with incorrect punctuation and stuff like that, and we'll have to read over it and make the right corrections. [But] in my other classes, like health class, we read about stuff like AIDS and how AIDS is passed on. Young teens and sex. Drug abuse. Stuff like that.

Robert clearly understood the value of what he was asked to do in health class because of the clear connection to his life. Without such a clear connection, he was baffled by why he was asked to do what he was asked to do.

Rev was even more outspoken in a statement that recalls the taunts of Baca's cell mates when he determined he was going to learn to read and write:

> English is about NOTHING! It doesn't help you DO anything. English is about reading poems and telling about rhythm. It's about commas and crap like that for God's sake. What does that have to DO with DOING anything? It's about NOTHING!

In response to follow-up questions to this passionate comment, Rev explained that he did not think English was about anything important or substantive, personally relevant, or socially significant. Why then, he wondered, did he have to do it?

Many students perceived the readings they were asked to do and the assignments associated with them as purposeless and contrived. "Busywork" was a term or concept used by twenty-four of the boys to describe school assignments, particularly in English. Neil, for example, described the uselessness of a summary assignment:

> It was a paragraph, and imagine trying to describe a movie in a paragraph. And at the same time keeping to the vocabulary of the chapter and what you are studying, like relative pronouns.

Neil described most school assignments as "contrived." Similarly, when asked about the purpose of different reading assignments, Lax professed not to know. Then he said they we are "mostly purposeless, I guess."

Jeff asked Brandon about a Shakespeare assignment few students were completing:

> Jeff: Why do you have to do it? Why do schools make you do it, if everybody's frustrated, and nobody gets it?
>
> Brandon: I really—there's really no answer to that question I can think of right now. They have us do it, but I really have no idea, but they're obviously doing it for a reason; I'm not going to just sit here with a grudge and not do it.
>
> Jeff: So you think there's a reason, but you don't know what it is.
>
> Brandon: I'm sure there has to be a reason because literally, like every school in the area, across the United States is reading Shakespeare. I don't know, he's one of the best classical writers I guess, there ever was, so it doesn't matter if I understand it. I just have to do it.

Most of the boys equated the purpose of assignments with getting a grade. If no grade was awarded, then they saw no purpose in completing the assignment since there was no other relevancy for them. There was no intrinsic value placed on the learning that might occur; in fact, this was rarely if ever mentioned. Even more nefarious, perhaps, is that the boys had no sense of their own critical standards. When asked how well they had understood a text, or how well they had done on an assignment, they almost always replied with their grade on the test, or said, like Buda, "I don't know. I didn't get my grade yet."

The reading the boys enjoyed—most of it outside of school though some inside it—always had a purpose. The boys talked about a variety of purposes or goals that informed the literate activity they enjoyed.

Getting Information/Figuring Out What Happens

The boys liked attending critically to texts in order to figure things out. Johnny, for example, maintained that "the biggest challenge is always to figure things out." He explained to Michael that he loved the movie *Sixth Sense* because he enjoyed the puzzle of figuring out the mystery and the satisfaction of "getting it":

> Johnny: Well, when you get in the movie everybody thought that Mr. Willis is still alive and then at the end he was actually dead. And, like, through the whole movie I was sitting there wondering like, "Whoa, is this guy really alive?" I was starting to catch on and it was a great movie. I love that movie.
>
> Michael: I need to know—tell me more about why?
>
> Johnny: Yeah, the mystery part to it and, like, how it just at the end it was like a big shock, and I love movies like that. The shock at the end of finding out. I hate movies that end and make you want more, like OK, where is the rest of the movie at, and that movie just, it ended right there. It was like the perfect place to end the movie. Most of the time that you go to a movie, they end and you think, can there be a sequel to the movie.

Similarly, Bob told Jeff that he likes

> not knowing and then to know. It's exciting to find out. Because you watch the whole play and you get nothing out of it, don't know what happened, then there is no point to it.

Johnny and Bob enjoyed texts that allowed them to figure things out and that had a definite conclusion. Both they and others voiced their displeasure when texts thwarted that desire. Neil, for example, complained about the movie *Magnolia* because it does not come to a satisfying conclusion. He maintained that the way the movie ended "was pointless." A number of boys complained that the texts they read in school similarly lacked a satisfying conclusion and a clear point.

Classic research on response to literature by Squires (1964) bemoans adolescents' intolerance for ambiguity. Csikszentmihalyi (1990a) helps us understand the source of that intolerance. Figuring something out is a clear goal. And once something has clicked into place, a reader or viewer gets the pleasure of immediate feedback. Ambiguous texts don't offer the same rewards.

Interestingly, the boys in general were willing to learn new strategies that could be used in immediate service for figuring something out, doing, or making something. When they had a need to know something to help them figure something out, they were open and ready to learn, quite a different stance from the resistance we often observed and heard them talk about.

For example, Mark talked about reading *Romeo and Juliet* like a mystery, to find out what would happen. He was satisfied when he understood the story. He described reading it like putting together a puzzle—it was satisfying when the picture came together and he "knew what happened." This was an exception for Mark, who claimed that most assignments in English were ambiguous. "You can't really study for it [English] because it's usually not clear what you have to know or do." This ambiguity of purpose deeply troubled him.

Immediate Function: Fixing Things and Making Things

Many of the boys read to fix things or to figure out how things work. Jeff had the following conversation with Rudy:

> Jeff: [You] spent about thirty minutes reading a calculator manual and computing. Is that something typically that you would do, to read a manual and then do something based on the directions?
>
> Rudy: If I can't figure it out I'll read the instructions, like to a board game or video game. I'll try and figure out all of the controls, but if there is other stuff that I can't figure out, I'll look at the manual.
>
> Jeff: So you first try and do it on your own?
>
> R: Yeah, but if I have any trouble, I'll read about it. I tried to do that in math class to make a program, and I couldn't figure out some of the stuff, so I looked it up in the manual.
>
> Jeff: Great. Now are there other things that you read manuals for, too?
>
> Rudy: Ah, mainly games, maybe like construction like models, building models, folding paper airplanes, stuff like that.

Many other students also used manuals, particularly to figure out video games. The "players" frequently went on to the Internet to "steal code" that could help enhance their ability to play the games.

Bob described in great detail to Jeff a bridge-building project he did. He explained that the realism of the project gave him a clear purpose. And because he was making something that would be used, there was clear feedback provided by the environment. It was also important to him that he was building something:

> Bob: Ah, it was just fun. It felt like we were ah, taking off class time to just like, it was fun. It was like you weren't in school.
>
> Jeff: Was it because it seemed real? Because you said it a couple of times?
>
> Bob: Yeah, it was really realistic. . . . Not like school.

Aaron made a similar point. He described to Michael his disengagement with English, but then he described how he was working on a hydraulics problem that interested him, and how he sought out and read very difficult technical information to try to figure out and solve the problem:

> Michael: When you were confronted with the whole hydraulics problem, you read a text that you really didn't understand in order to try to figure it out. It's like you weren't content with not knowing it. You know what I mean? This one [assignment in English], you seem much more content [not to have figured it out or to have completed it]. And the same thing when you said, "I'm not taking the AP in English because I'm just not good at that kind of stuff." But you seemed much more content with that [not taking up the AP English challenge].
>
> Aaron: I guess it's easier for me to not know something that I don't really care to know. I'm sure it's good to know, but whether I feel at this time that it's immediately important or not makes it a lot less important to me whether or not I actually go and find out about it.

Making and designing things was a major theme that helped the boys set purposes. It made their reading, in Aaron's words, "immediately important." It also provided clear feedback. They could see what they made and whether it worked or not. It's not surprising, then, that the boys enjoyed things like making video or hypermedia documentaries (Joe, Bodey, and Ian); making bridges (all six boys in that project went on at length about it); building robots (Paul, Bodey); creating a zoo (every boy in this project talked about enjoying it); or making a formal community presentation (all six boys who were required to do this cited it as an important and engaging experience).

The Reality Principle

Figuring things out, fixing things, and making things all connected to the boys' desire for realism, a theme expressed by every one of the boys in the study. One major subtheme of realism was the importance of "getting information" about real events or situations the boys wanted to understand. Bambino, for example, insisted that he wanted to read about things that were "connected to the here and now." Pablo wanted emotional engagement when he read and maintained that "the real has more emotional punch."

Johnny was interested in the meteorology unit of his science class because it was real and immediate to him, but he was not interested in astronomy because it was distant from his immediate experience:

> I wanted to do that [meteorology] because, I mean, I want to know what the weather is like. When I look at the Weather Channel and think, do these people actually know what they are talking about? And I want to see, I can have a little bit of understanding of what they are talking about. So when I took astronomy, I knew that it was going to be boring 'cause I mean it, it's about thinking about the stars.

Johnny gave up on reading *Pale Horse* for the same reason. "I was understanding it, but like, I didn't believe it. I was just like, no, I can't read this anymore."

Maurice said he likes rap because "It's real. About reality." Marcel concurred:

> I mean, the rappers today—it is what they have experienced, it is what they have been through, you know. That is what is going on and stuff, and like, I guess that is what I like about rap mostly. It is what I see around me. It is what I have been ways around.

In contrast, Maurice refused to read more than the first two pages of de Maupassant's "The Necklace" because it wasn't about real issues; it was just dealing with these "rich people" whose concerns he did not share. For many of the boys, the sense that something is "real" requires that it relates to their lives.

Rudy reported that he liked *Into Thin Air* and *Hatchet* because they were both real, though he was fully cognizant that the first was nonfiction and the second fiction. He rejected the Harry Potter books, though, because they "couldn't happen." Several of boys rejected fantasy on these grounds.

This brings up the interesting point that the few aficionados of science fiction and fantasy books perceived "reality" in these books. Yuri vociferously maintained that the fantasy he read helped him deal with real situations, people, and emotions, and that fantasy connected to his immediate life far more than the more realistic books he had to read in school. Fantasy, he explained, gives "freedom to deal with [real] issues" in more powerful ways than could be done realistically. Fantasy, for the aficionados, connected powerfully to their real-life concerns with emotions, relationships, problem solving, and so forth. They were able to use the fantasy books as tools to think about the real world.

When boys enjoyed more canonical texts, they did so for a similar reason. Aaron enjoyed *She Stoops to Conquer* because the characters and situations struck him as real, particularly the "smart aleck guy" who reminded him of himself. When asked to write a poem from the perspective of a character from *Death of a Salesman*, Mike chose Biff. He explained the reason to Michael:

Mike: I chose him because he was like a real character. He seemed to me real.

Michael: What parts about him?

Mike: His attitudes. And the things that he did. Like he tried getting forgiveness from his mom. Like giving her flowers and stuff. And like the way that he always tried to ah, disagree, or contradict his father. He would try to persuade him, try to not do what he was told.

On the other hand, Mike rejected *The Chocolate War* as not being real, but "weird. . . . It doesn't seem real."

Liam maintained that

using something you learned is important, instead of just taking a test and learning how to use grammar or something. [In my favorite English class] we would actually go into discussions about how to apply what we learned. We would start out with discussing a book but then we would gradually slip into things that were more relevant. How to use and apply what we learned. And if you did that you would have proof that you actually learned something.

Though the boys constructed their notions of reality differently, they all privileged what they considered to be the real and discounted what was not.

Geography often played into this mix. Two students told us that reading about their own locality or a place they knew about or had personally visited made reading seem real. Nine other boys indicated that they liked to read about geographical areas they knew or that were close to home. This made it easier for them to achieve the goal of seeing a personal connection, of seeing themselves as part of the story, or of being "in the scene." By far the most popular rapper in the urban school was a rapper who grew up in that city. The local community connection helped the boys affiliate with him.

Guy said he enjoyed *The Perfect Storm* because much of the setting occurred in places he had visited, which is also why he chose it. He explained, "I picked it because some of it took place in ah, around Martha's Vineyard, Nantucket. And I have been there, so it was good." Several of the boys from Maine mentioned *Lost on a Mountain in Maine* as a favorite. And the boys from the private school enjoyed reading about places they had experienced on their class trips, such as *The Killer Angels* and its connection to a Gettysburg trip, something the school overtly planned and capitalized on.

The reality principle was also manifested in the way the boys read the newspaper. They read with the purpose of finding stories of immediate personal relevance. They tended to pay attention to the local news and local items like sports or the police report, where they would find out what was going on in their own neighborhood and might see names of people they knew. Robert made this clear to Michael:

> Michael: Do you like local stories, national stories, world stories? What kind of stories as you're going forward attract you the most?
> Robert: Local, local stories.
> Michael: Tell me why.
> Robert: Like what happened around in the area. Because I'm a hard sleeper and they be saying there be a lot of shooting going on. But, I don't be hearing that. I'll wake up, "Did you hear that shooting last night?" I'll be like, "I didn't hear nothing." I look in the paper, and it said a man got robbed. He got shot in the head in close range with a 12-gauge bullet, blew his brains out.
> Michael: And that happened close to your house?
> Robert: Yeah. And another one happened close to my house. I think he got shot in the back twice, yeah.

Keeping Track

Keeping track of things was also a major purpose for reading. Ricardo read to keep track of the upcoming movie releases and reviews. Mike and others read to keep up with the music scene. Sisqó often neglected homework reading, but he would read several sports magazines, watch news, and watch sporting events so that he could keep track. On one weekend during the NCAA tournament, he watched sixteen hours of basketball. Jeff asked him about his heavy dose of TV:

> Jeff: Now is it typical that you would watch that much sports or was it just because it was the tournament?
>
> Sisqó: Probably because it was the tournament. And it was kind of like important. I like to be informed. Like in homeroom or lunch the next day so that I can have something to talk about.

Huey, who claimed that he "hated reading" and that "reading makes me sad," nonetheless had several Internet sites that he read at least once weekly to keep up with favorite sports teams, including the Virginia Tech Hokies football team and the Baltimore Orioles. "You have to know what's going on," he explained. This keeping track connected clearly to the theme of exportability (more on that later), since keeping track allowed the boys to appear knowledgeable and to share what they knew with significant others who valued that knowledge.

Game-like Structures

As we have argued in Chapter 2, games, by their very design, provide both clear goals and immediate feedback. Game-like structures supported much of the boys' literate activity outside of school. Twenty-seven of the boys, for example, mentioned enjoying playing games on their own, particularly video games. These boys often read, especially on the Internet, to help them in their efforts. Robert talked about enjoying word puzzles that he did in the local newspaper in the mornings before he came to school. Most of the boys did some regular reading to help them pursue sporting or hobby interests.

But game-like structures helped for school learning too, though, as we note in Chapter 2, they are not sufficient in and of themselves to create flow experiences. Twenty-four of the boys talked about enjoying games that were played in class in service of learning or supporting reading. Haywood said that "Games let you act like an expert," and he enjoyed playing the role of novice expert in video games or classroom games. Bob identified Spanish as his most enjoyable class because of the games they played. He explained this to Jeff:

> Bob: Ah, like we have all these things to learn, we take notes and we study them in class and then like play *Jeopardy!* or something with them.

Jeff: So it is games that help you learn?

Bob: Yeah.

Jeff: Kind of fun structures that you do?

Bob: Yeah. That's what helps make it happen. The kids go wild. It's a lot of fun.

Helping Others/Service

Surprisingly, the boys saw a major purpose of their literate lives as putting themselves in the position of helping others. Service was an overtly cultivated idea at the private school and one of the public schools, which was part of a "Community of Caring" network. Every one of the private school students mentioned service as a purpose for learning. They talked especially about their work tutoring inner-city children. Sisqó put it this way:

> You can really help them. It feels good. Help them read and write better. Do math. They need the help and you can help them.

Sometimes, a whole school group adopted a project. The private school's football team worked on an organic farm as a project. Though most of the work was physical, some literacy was involved in promoting the farm, keeping track of produce, and so on.

Robert, who was not a student in the two service-oriented schools, also saw literacy as a way to do public service:

> I wrote a little bit about it, like I try to stop people from selling drugs or doing drugs around my neighborhood. Stuff like that.

Function as Environmental Feedback

Many of the boys actively sought out contexts in which feedback was clear and immediate. Larry, for instance, loved to write songs and perform them in chemistry class:

> I just think that it is pretty awesome that kids can create music like we do so fast. We are pretty good; chemistry is kind of boring so we kind of talk to each other a lot. We kind of have this little group going. We write songs about chemistry just for the fun of it. We call each other "Boys with Noise." Sometimes we'll do our homework in rap or something. The other kids love it.

Larry's teacher allowed the boys to do homework in rap and devised assignments that encouraged the students to create and present artifacts demonstrating their learning, such as writing newspaper articles about what happened when an element oxidized or was reduced. The boys were enthusiastic about the novelty of these assignments and the chance to perform and present what they had learned to their peers versus "just handing something in to the teacher."

Marcel was extraordinarily proud of a poem he wrote that was published in his town's newspaper. Deuce was proud of the raps he performed. Bob was proud of a country display he had made that was posted in the commons room of his school.

What This Makes Us Think About: Providing Assistance While Providing Control

The data presented in this chapter make us ask, "How can we provide the kind of assistance in becoming competent that the boys desired without taking too much control?" This is a question that is very important in literacy education, and we fear that many have answered, "You can't." At a recent conference, for example, we saw a major figure in the field argue for reading workshops in which students read texts of their own choosing without any teacher interference or assistance, precisely because she feared that any teacher intervention would lead to teacher control. In our view, many recent efforts to move away from teacher-dominated classrooms—a move we applaud—focus much more on eliciting students' responses than educating them.

But as much as the boys manifested a desire for choice and control, they also manifested a desire to be taught. And we think this teaching can take place in a way in which students feel more competent and more in control than they would if left to their own devices.

As we've stated, our belief is informed by Vygotksian notions of teaching and learning. We believe that learning only takes place when a teacher or a situation challenges what a learner already knows by addressing a misconception, building on what is known, or asking the learner to deepen or extend understanding and strategic activity in some way.

Both Vygotsky and Bakhtin (1984, 1986) highlight that learning is social and occurs in relationship. Like Vygotsky (1978), Bakhtin (1984, 1986) also argues that how we understand and act is always dependent on our past and present relationships with other people. Our consciousness is socially created. Bakhtin (1984) argues that we learn only in *dialogic* interactions through which we test and revise our perspectives as we converse with the perspectives of others: "To live means to participate in dialogue: to ask questions, to heed, to respond, to agree, and so forth" (p. 293).

Much of what occurs in school, according to our boys, works against such dialogue and fits what Bakhtin calls *monologue*. For example, textbooks and curriculum present fixed meanings. As we've seen, discussions are usually recitations with preset answers. There is no chance for what Vygotsky calls *intersubjectivity* and Bakhtin calls *interillumination*, a process through which different points of view inform and illuminate each other in a person's consciousness. (See Edmiston, 1994; Wilhelm and Edmiston, 1998.)

While teaching as the presentation of information disallows students from such dialogues and therefore from voicing their own opinions and constructing their own understandings, other models of teaching show that this need not happen. For example, Tharp and Gallimore (1988) provide a model for breaking the frame of monologic thinking that parallels the process of reading. The process starts with a learner's personal experience and understanding, which must be activated and brought to bear (hence the importance of frontloading that we explored at the end of Chapter 3). The experience is then brought into dialogue with the challenge provided by a text or situation that offers a new perspective, and it continues to dialogue and negotiate with this perspective to build a new relationship or response that reworks the frame of our understanding. It is the teacher's job not to present information but to provide challenging contexts in which students can be confronted with new and more complex perspectives. It is then their job to help students gain the strategies for "reading" or understanding those new perspectives.

Vygotsky (1978) argues that when we dialogue we connect language with thought and feeling. He identified this as happening quite often during play, which he considered to be the most natural form of learning. This play-like quality of learning, in which language, thought, and feeling are connected, can describe what the boys exhibited in their out-of-school reading but rarely inside school. Bakhtin (1984) likewise argues that we are only conscious and alive when engaged in dialogue, but again we found that dialogue was rarely invited in school, even during discussions. (See Edmiston, 1994.)

This kind of sociocultural teaching focuses on the HOW—on ways of doing things and on developing procedural knowledge—rather than on the WHAT, which is known as declarative knowledge (often presented as monologue—as unquestioned facts). Vygotskian theory therefore emphasizes activity and knowledge developed and used in activity, something that the boys in our study cried out for.

So how would this look in practice? Let's consider how this works in the case of video gaming, an activity embraced by many of the boys in our study, and the same source of inspiration that gave rise to some of the implications we discussed in Chapter 2. The boys exercised choice by selecting a game that interested them, and they set the difficulty at the appropriate level. They used what was learned at an earlier level and applied and built on this as they went to the next level. Often, friends provided assistance, helping each other to identify, understand, and use "cheat codes," which corresponded to the underlying conventions and structure of the game. This assistance occurred in the context of the game and was immediately used and applied to the task at hand. The game-like structures provided fun and a sense of clear goals and immediate feedback. As the boys improved, the challenge also increased, so the players were always operating just beyond their zone of actual development in ways that helped them improve, learn, and be able to do more.

How would a parallel to this engaging situation look in school? Since more global forms of curricular and instructional reform is the topic of our final chapter, we will address this question in more depth there. Here, we will discuss two ways that teachers might help students discover codes for reading that will help them become more competent and exert control.

Making Reading Visible

Just as friends and the Internet helped the boys see how they could more effectively play their video games, teachers can create classroom contexts that give students similar help in their reading. In a study of teacher talk during student reading, Mariage (1995) found that successful reading teachers understood their position as "a more knowledgeable other" whose role was to make their thinking and reading processes visible to students in order to support their students' efforts to comprehend and respond to text. Vygotskian instruction goes through a process of modeling (Show Me), of assistance in which expertise is gradually handed over to the student (Help Me), and then observation as the student independently uses the learned strategies in a meaningful context (Let Me).

The need to set appropriate challenges and to support the development of competence provides support for the work Jeff has done with students to make reading visible. Jeff has written extensively about using drama as one means of doing so (Wilhelm, 1997, 2001, forthcoming; Wilhelm and Edmiston, 1998), and the boys in this study spoke often of the way dramatic activities engaged them. It was perhaps the single instructional technique that was mentioned positively across the boys.

SRIs

To illustrate the importance of making reading visible, we'd like to turn instead to a technique that receives less attention: symbolic story representation. We'll use the letters SRI to label this technique as a way to differentiate it from sustained silent reading (SSR) (cf. Enciso, 1992). SRI is a technique that allows teachers to actively support particular ways of reading through the student creation and use of cutouts to dramatize not only what they are reading but how they are reading. (See Enciso, 1992; Wilhelm, 1997, 2001, forthcoming.) The cutouts (or found objects or pictures from magazines) stand for the characters, the setting, the reader, and particular moves that the reader takes to make particular kinds of meaning. Readers move the cutouts around to show where they have situated themselves, what they are doing, and how they are perceiving things at a particular point in the text.

SRIs are structured to make and highlight the student as the expert. When presenting an SRI, a student talks about his or her readerly activity, so the student is the world's only expert. The SRI requires students to explain the codes and conventions of the text. That is, in order to do an SRI, students have to understand the kind of details that are especially important in a particular kind of text, for example, the relationship between the physical setting and the emotional state of the characters in a Gothic piece or the stage directions in a play. They also have to name their skills and strategies as readers for dealing with these codes. Doing SRIs encourages students to see themselves as skilled and to understand how they are skilled, so they can transfer their strategies to new and more challenging situations.

The SRI addresses the need for competence and environmental assistance because it provides visible accomplishment, is a hands-on activity, and provides a way to talk about reading with others. It leads from reading to concrete function and performance, makes the invisible and abstract reading processes concrete, and sets new challenges by providing new strategies to try as students observe each other and borrow strategies. SRIs provide a safe forum for talk about emotions and personal response. The SRI also recognizes that students have many literacies, as it makes use of visual art, a kind of drama or puppetry, and often includes music or other arts. It brings together ways of seeing, understanding, responding, and representing that cut across various sign systems.

SRIs can also be used to teach and support the use of new reading strategies. For example, the technique can be used to model how to pay attention to key details and infer a central focus or authorial generalization. The key details and central focus can be symbolized by cutouts that are used at appropriate times in the SRI performance as the reader explains how they were noticed and interpreted. This technique can be used for any convention of reading, such as noticing and interpreting symbols, understanding irony, recognizing and evaluating the aspects of argument, and so on. For example, one low-achieving student with whom Jeff worked used the technique to show how he was noticing key details and how they contributed to the central focus or theme of the story, "A Fisherman and His Wife." For instance, the student noticed how the color of the sea changed from light blue to dark blue to black over a series of scenes to show the wife's growing greediness. The student was amazed when Jeff told him that he was demonstrating a real understanding of symbolism, a mark of an expert reader. The students' SRI then provided the basis for a whole-class discussion of symbolism and how it appeared in the reading they had been doing. (See Wilhelm, forthcoming, for full explanations.)

Using think-alouds, drama, symbolic story representation and other techniques can allow students choices into ways of studying their own reading and that of others so that procedural knowledge is shared. When students make their reading visible, they can learn from and about each other. Such activities also make reading active and foreground the fact that reading is an active and transactional meaning-making pursuit that involves them, their backgrounds, their interests, their concerns, and their opinions. All of these are needs that resounded in our data, but that were rarely fulfilled by school reading activities.

Sharing Our Secrets

In Chapter 2 we told the story of Larry, the young man who had begun to see himself as a reader because his teacher had "been kinda showing me the road and the path." In the words of Margaret Meek, Larry's transformation suggests the power of "sharing the list of secret things that all accomplished readers know, yet never talk about" (cited in Thomson, 1987, p. 109). In contrast, we saw again and again in our data, boys who were not shown the road, who consequently felt lost, especially when they encountered new text types. We do not think that reading can be reduced to algorithms, but our research here does seem to support efforts to make as clear as possible what it is that readers do.

Michael, for example, has done considerable work with developing a theoretical rationale and practical applications for assignment sequences that teach students how to read particular kinds of texts (Rabinowitz and Smith, 1998; Smith, 1989, 1991b; Smith and Hamel, 1998).

Michael's work has focused on irony and stories with unreliable narrators. However, his ideas about identifying the "secrets" experienced readers know, and sharing them with students are applicable to other kinds of texts as well.

For example, as we noted in this chapter, a number of the boys complained about the difficulty they had reading plays. As experienced readers, we realize that plays are different from other texts in a variety of ways. One of the most significant is that dialogue is presented without the commentary of a narrator. That means that readers have to provide the commentary themselves. They have to understand the subtext that gives meaning to the words spoken. One way to help students understand and take on that role might be to show excerpts from Woody Allen's movie *Annie Hall*, in which the subtext of what characters are saying appears as subtitles. Students could then write their own captions for scenes in their favorite movies and share them with the class. Having been shown the path, they could then read a play or movie script on their own with a greater likelihood of success.

Both when students create and present their SRIs, and when they are learning to apply the reading codes that particular kinds of texts require of them, they are focusing on the HOW of reading. They are learning the rules of the game, the secrets that experienced readers know. They aren't silenced by a teacher's authoritative interpretation; rather, they are invited to apply their understandings of how to read in order to develop their own interpretations.

If we, as teachers, focused more on the how of reading, our students' experiences in school would more clearly resemble their experience out of school. We would help them develop their competence, which would in turn make them better able to meet the challenge of the texts we ask them to read. By making reading visible, we demystify it, and in so doing are able to provide students with clearer and more immediate feedback. We understand the impulse that drives teachers to focus more on particular readings than on ways to read. We too have a stake in particular interpretations of favorite texts. But we think that stepping back from those interpretations, and helping students see how we came to them and how they come to their own understandings, is well worth the effort.

Meet the Crew

Bam

Wolf

Stan

Larry

Though most of the boys resisted school and school literacy in some ways, they all embraced literate activity in some form outside of school. Among the group, they did so quite differently and with different effects. Our portraits here are designed to provide some of the flavor of those differences.

Bam

Bam was an African American eleventh grader in the urban school. He was not an engaged reader, yet he had read *Of Mice and Men* over and over because his brother had given it to him. Bam had moved from Detroit to New Jersey and sometimes traveled back and forth to visit his family, who were very important to him. He was one of several students who wrote raps and poetry, but he did not write in school. He also wrote emails on an almost daily basis and felt that it was easier to express his emotions on the computer than in person. He maintained that he did "lots of writing" at home, but he said his teachers asked only for essays, which he did not consider "real writing" that dealt with real issues.

Though he loved pursuing personal research on the Internet, which he claimed he could not live without, when his English teacher tried to engage his cultural interest through a study of the Harlem Renaissance, he rejected this unit as disconnected to his life. When assigned to research the life story of Josephine Baker, he basically opted out because it did not match his preexisting interests. He wasn't a high achiever, but he kept a careful eye on his grades and planned to attend college and major in business.

We can't help but ask what would have happened if a teacher had engaged Bam's current interests with rap, his interest in humor and socializing, and his facility doing Internet searches, and had used these to develop situational interest in new topics.

Wolf

Wolf was a European American twelfth grader in the suburban school. He was in the average track, though we suspect that was more a function of his perfunctory engagement with school than with his ability. He was extremely cynical and funny about school routines, yet he was the only one of our participants who expressed a desire to be a teacher. Wolf loved history and was an avid reader of it. So was his father, and they often shared books. The passion that Wolf felt for reading only occasionally flashed in his classes. His enthusiasm for acting out *Hamlet* and for designing a coat of arms stood in stark contrast to his overt rejection of what he did on most days in most classes. Sometimes he'd sit with his head on the desk. On occasion, instead of paying attention he'd write a story to show to his girlfriend and his best friend. Literacy was crucially important to Wolf. But school literacy seldom was.

When we think about Wolf, we wonder what kind of history teacher he will be. He knows his stuff. In fact, he told us that his history teacher often deferred to him to answer questions. We wonder whether he'll tell his students all that he knows or whether he'll engage them in the kind of project-oriented work he did when he investigated the Renaissance so he could join his girlfriend as a performer at Renaissance fairs.

Stan

Stan, a European American eleventh grader, was a very engaging young man who came promptly to all the interview sessions and was totally prepared. He even came to school when he was sick on two occasions when interviews were scheduled. He seemed to take great pleasure in sharing his life and literacy experiences, and in offering opinions on a wide variety of topics. He concluded each interview by giving Jeff a vigorous handshake and saying, "Thanks, man. I enjoyed it."

His enthusiasm for this project amazed his teachers and classmates, given Stan's reputation for missing a lot of school. In fact, he had failed English the previous year due to attendance and assignment completion problems and was currently taking two English classes to catch up.

Despite Stan's failure in English and his resistance to school as "not being a very mature environment," he believed that some classes "give you free rein" and therefore worked to "free your mind." He identified art and an inquiry-based history course as classes that helped him think for himself and exercise choice.

Though he disliked and did poorly in English, he loved reading about controversial issues. He had just completed reading a biography of Marilyn Manson, explaining, "I like him 'cause he won't conform. . . . He resists expectations." He professed to enjoy "conspiracy books . . . because they catch you off guard." He also enjoyed writing song lyrics for his band. He would quote song lyrics at length and apply them to discussions of politics, gender, and ethics. He was building a website for the band, too.

Stan loved the movie *The Matrix* for "its symbolic value" and discussed its construction at length. He claimed that a life goal was "to be aware and to be mentally developed."

We can't help wondering how a different kind of English curriculum would have engaged Stan and built on his interests in ideas, in texts, and in their construction. In fact, it was hard to believe that Stan was not engaged by English until we looked at the way in which it is usually taught—as the purveyance of information about artifacts instead of as an engagement with living documents that can be used to think about relevant ideas—the kind of engagement Stan sought outside of school.

Larry

Larry, a European American eleventh grader, had suffered from a lot of in- and out-of-school trouble. He had been arrested and had been having difficulty with his parents. But he said he had seen "the error of my ways" and had done his best to make amends. He felt that he was on the straight and narrow, and he was proud of this.

Larry played basketball on the varsity team. He had one very close male friend, and he dated a variety of girls. He had only recently bought into reading and schoolwork. He particularly enjoyed creative assignments where he could exercise his creativity and perform for the class. He felt that his relationship with a couple of teachers, particularly his English teacher, had helped him. He was gratified by her personal attention and by the fact that she suggested books she thought he would like, indicating the moral and political reasons why she thought the books would appeal to him. He was eager to read these books and excitedly talked about the connections he saw between them and his own life. One day, in fact, he excitedly rushed into the library to tell Jeff, "I've just seen *Cannery Row*! Cannery Row in action, man!" It turned out that he had witnessed a strike at the local bakery and had stopped to talk to the picketers, sharing insights from Steinbeck with them.

One of the rewards of his reading was using it to pursue a relationship with his teacher. Most important, he felt that his English teacher had "showed him the way," and had explicitly taught him the strategies he needed to be successful in reading the new kinds of challenging texts that she felt he would like.

Larry offers a challenge and a possibility to teachers. He was a student who resisted school and was outside the bounds of many cultural norms, but caring teachers who knew how to assist him to competence with reading and science brought him into the fold and allowed him to embrace school and literacy enthusiastically in a way he never had before.

In short, while there was much that the boys shared, in many ways they were quite different. But when we take them as a whole, we see that all of the boys were enthusiastic about literacy in at least some regard. Some of the most vocal critics of school were also among the most passionate proponents of features of texts that schools admire. Once again, our data seem to offer a harsh critique of schooling as we know it, but also the seeds of hope.

May I Have the Envelope Please?

**THE TEXTS BOYS
ENJOY AND WHY THEY
ENJOY THEM**

5

There's a pickup truck commercial that features a heavily muscled man with what looks like a three-day growth of beard putting up fences on a ranch. As we see him working, the voiceover speaks directly to the audience, asking them whether they've seen the movie *You've Got Mail*, a movie that chronicles the developing relationship between a man and a woman who meet on the Internet. "Have you seen that one?" the voiceover asks. "Well, he hasn't."

Pickup trucks, we guess, aren't for men who liked *You've Got Mail* or other movies of the sort. But maybe they are for men who watch "Movies for Men Who Like Movies," a feature on a national cable channel. We suspect that you can guess the stars and kinds of movies featured there: Stallone and Eastwood; car chases and shoot-'em-ups.

The commercial and the movie series are clearly based on conventional understandings of the kind of texts men prefer. And we think they jibe with the understandings of educators. In classic research by Thorndike (1941), he reports that "Sex accounts for much greater differences in interests than does age or intelligence" (p. 36, cited in Monson and Sebesta, 1991, p. 666). Although in a more recent study Worthy, Moorman, and Turner (1999) argue that they found more similarities than differences between boys' and girls' reading interests, our experience with teachers and with some of the young men in our study suggests that the conventional wisdom is still intact.

In this chapter we're going to test that conventional wisdom in two ways. First, we'll return to the reading logs to identify the kinds and qualities of texts that engaged our participants, as well as to identify other influences that fostered their engagement. That is, we'll look at the reading logs to determine the various factors that promoted a focus on the immediate experience, the fourth characteristic of flow experiences that we've been addressing throughout the book. Second, we'll examine how the boys responded to four short stories that varied in terms of their emphasis on action and on the sex of their narrator.

A Focus on Immediate Experience

We have seen that the boys saw school as routine, decontextualized, and separated from real life. This kept them from enjoying and engaging with much of what they were asked to do in school. What they did enjoy about school was seeing friends and socializing. This spilled over to literate pursuits. In general, the boys rejected school literacies as being about someone else's concerns, in part because in contrast to their out-of-school activities, reading was cast as a solitary pursuit. They also often saw school literacy and the materials used to pursue it as boring, difficult, and off point. However, we have also seen that the boys would embrace literate activities, both inside and outside of school, that were fun, that possessed intrinsic and immediately functional value, and that connected to them and their lives.

Csikszentmihalyi (1990b) argues that "Reading cannot be enjoyable unless the student can imagine, at least in principle, that the symbol system is worth mastering for its own sake" (p. 133). That is, according to Csikszentmihalyi, students must have intrinsic motivation to achieve. The experience of literate activity itself must be of value to them. In this section, we will examine the features of literate experience that helped provide that intrinsic motivation to the boys in our study.

The Importance of the Social

We have seen in Chapters 2 and 3 how important the social was to these boys' lives. The social was also very important to their literacy practices. In fact, the social was the most important way to make experiences immediate and enjoyable to them. In their logs the boys talked about the social in a variety of ways: how friends and family affected literate interests; the importance of relationships with teachers; their enjoyment of working in groups; and the importance of relationships they cultivated with textual characters, authors, or directors.

In the Selection of Texts

Friendships, family, and significant others exerted a powerful influence on literate behavior. Bam's story comes immediately to mind. Bam didn't read much, at least not many books, but he did read *Of Mice and Men*, a book he had been given by his brother. He told Michael, "Oh, man. I love that book. I read that book eighth, ninth, tenth, and I have it in eleventh grade. I read it every year." Without question, Bam engaged with the characters. But also without question, the fact that his older brother gave him the book set the stage for that engagement.

Neil and Aaron told similar stories about the importance of the social dimension of their reading. Neil's friendship circle was based in part by the friends' shared reading and viewing. Aaron read *Ender's Game* and other books from series by Orson Scott Card because they had been given to him by a friend. Many of the boys said they would make a special effort to read books that were given to them by a significant other. Even highly reluctant readers like Huey said they would read books given to them or recommended by significant others so they could talk together; for Huey, friends were the most "crucial" part of his life.

Interestingly, sometimes the social connection that informed the boys' reading was a more passive one. A number of the boys discussed picking up a book they found at home that attracted their attention. In fact, doing so was a matter of convenience; the books were there when they were needed, usually when the boys had nothing else to do. But the fact that a family member had read them also seemed to matter to the boys. Making texts readily available in comfortable social situations seemed to be crucial to getting the young men in our study to read outside of class.

Unfortunately, teachers were not part of this social network for most of the boys. After Aaron described how he would read books recommended to him by friends or family, he said, "So I will read books that other people tell me I should read—except for my English teachers." This expresses the general distrust of English teachers and school reading among the boys, although as we've mentioned, there were definite exceptions in this study. The attitude could be paraphrased as follows: "English teachers generally don't understand what we really like to read, so we are unlikely to take their recommendations. But if real people we know are reading and liking the stuff, well then, maybe it is worth a try." Part of this attitude seemed to come from an impression that English teachers cared about particular kinds of texts, not about the students themselves as people or readers.

Even when the boys came to texts without the aid of a significant other, relationships were nonetheless important. But those relationships were the ones they developed with authors (or directors) and characters. Given Jeff's work in *You Gotta BE the Book* (Wilhelm, 1997), we were not surprised by the intensely social relationships the better readers took up with characters and with authors. However, our data make it clear that this tendency was also true for boys who had less success in school.

Yuri, for example, rejected most school literacy, but as he told Jeff, he became a huge fan and reader of Emily Dickinson by taking up a personal relationship with her:

Yuri: She had a, ah, kind of sadistic humorous look at the real world. The way that Mr. _____ described her also was appealing to me and told what kind of poet she was. Someone who sits at the window, and when she sees people, screams and hits the deck. It is humorous.

Jeff: She did that?

Yuri: That's what he described her as.

Jeff: I didn't know that. Ah, so his description of her personality kind of attracted you to the poems?

Yuri: Yeah. She's interesting. A real person. And some of the poems though they were four words per line just really had a lot of meaning. If you really looked at them, and that is what I like: being able to look at meanings.

Jeff: Um, um. Other things that you like about her and her poetry?

Yuri: Just that it was, the way she had of looking at the real world, it kind of looks like mine. I sit on my couch; I look at the real world every once in a while. I contemplate it, and she gave her perception to us. She shared what she thought with us. And I hear it. And I like how she thinks.

Liam talked about Alice Walker in a similar vein: "I like her. She made it [The Color Purple] relevant. I appreciate that." Ricardo closely followed the career of movie director Quentin Tarantino, knew his life story in great detail, and attempted to understand his characters and movies in terms of Tarantino's evolving life story and artistic development. He enjoyed predicting the future trajectory of Tarantino's work.

The young men also talked about relationships when they discussed the characters these authors and directors created. When Michael asked Neil his reason for reading Stephen King's The Gunslinger, for example, he replied, "Spending time with the characters. That is what it is in this book." Neil even snapped his fingers, indicating that it really clicked with him.

Neil then talked at length about how King's style allows readers to get to know the Gunslinger bit by bit, just like they would come to know a real person. Though he said he generally dislikes flashbacks, Neil appreciated how King used the technique here to unfold slowly the Gunslinger's secrets.

We saw Liam's relationship with Alice Walker above, but he also talked about the relationships he had with her characters. Not only did he sense and appreciate the intelligence behind the text, but he told us he wanted "to relate to Celie and the other characters. I want to understand and help them." He went on to say that "a good reader reads as if the characters and stories are real."

This intense relationship and care for characters was apparent even with the poorer readers, particularly in their viewing. Gohan gave a sense of the intensity of his involvement when he talked with Michael about the movie *Patch Adams*:

Gohan: If I had three thumbs, I'd give it three thumbs up.

Michael: Why did you like that?

Gohan: I loved that movie because they tried to ban Robin Williams from medicine because his medicine was laughter as he called it, and it was working sometimes. But the professionals, they weren't seeing it that way. They didn't really think that was helpful, but they started to realize that most of the patients that was being kind of stubborn were really paying attention to this guy. And, he was only a student. He was doing things that doctors for thirty years couldn't do, and he was just a student becoming a doctor. So, I really liked that. And, at the end, he became a doctor and he had a free clinic for people who didn't have the money to pay.

It was clear that taking up relationships with characters was especially important when the young men engaged in watching (or reading) a series. We found it particularly interesting that the wrestling fans recognized the wrestling shows as fictional, yet they kept track of win-loss records and cared deeply about the wrestlers as individuals. As Ricardo told Jeff, "Sure it's a soap opera. But it's a soap opera for guys. And you care about those people somehow."

Mick identified so strongly with the characters in wrestling that he would role-play as if he were one of them. In fact, he chose his pseudonym in honor of Mick Foley, the person who played some of his favorite wrestlers. This is what he had to say to Michael:

Michael: When you play wrestling, do you take on a role? Do you pretend to be one of the wrestlers?

Mick: Yeah.

Michael: Who do you pretend to be?

Mick: Captain Jack.

Michael: Oh yeah? How come?

Mick: I do the same thing he does.

Michael: Like what? What do you mean?

Mick: Jump off stuff, like tables and all that.

Michael: How many hours a week would you say you spend watching wrestling?

Mick: From nine to eleven.

Michael: Almost every day?

Mick: No, it doesn't come on every day.

Michael: So you watch it on Monday night.

Mick: Monday, Wednesday, Thursday, and Friday.

Michael: So you never miss a wrestling show?

Mick: No.

Michael: What makes you like it so much?

Mick: It's fun.

Michael: What makes it so much fun? I know, I can see your face light up when you talk about wrestling.

Mick: The people in there. They're legends. It's fun to watch. You get into it.

Twenty-six of the boys indicated that they could relate particularly strongly to villains or underdogs. Once again, this was particularly true of the wrestling aficionados. They repeatedly explained how they wanted the underdog to win; how they wanted to help the person who needed the most help; and how they admired villains because they exercised more freedom, were "edgier" (more on that later), and were more willing to stretch the boundaries of the acceptable.

Among the less engaged readers, this phenomenon of relating to characters was much more prevalent with television shows, video games, movies, and music than it was with reading. But certainly if they have the willingness and capacity to lose themselves by relating to characters on television, they should also be able to do it when they read. Though doing so in reading may be more complex, given the right kinds of assistance this achievement should be within their reach.

In Engaging in Literate Activity

The importance of social support for literacy activities went beyond selecting texts. Robert, for example, distinguished between the amount of reading and study he would do for school and the amount he would do for church, which he took very seriously. Though he did not like to share in class, he would get in front of the congregation each Sunday with ease:

> I read the Sunday school book. Read that, study the lesson. And then on Sunday, we go over the lesson and he asks us questions about it. And, we stand up in front of the church, like that.

When Michael asked Robert why he took the church reading more seriously than school reading and why he was willing to speak in front of the congregation, he replied:

> In school, it seems like when you're trying to—like, one time, we had to stand up and read something. It seemed like nobody's really paying attention. They're talking to somebody else. And in church, it seems like more people pay attention to what you're doing.

Robert's reply indicates that he was much more inclined to participate in situations where he felt valued.

On several occasions, Wolf also spoke about how his family shared their reading, particularly the powerful ideas they were reading about. He would often do his school reading so that he could discuss it with his family, though he differentiated the "contrived" nature of school activities around reading and the real, substantial work he did with his reading when discussing it with his family.

The importance of social support for literate activity extended to school itself. *In essence, when the literate activity provided the occasion for social connections, the boys had intrinsic motivation for their engagement.* This was most clearly seen in the virtually unanimous support they offered for group work. When we asked Ricardo about his favorite school memory of all time, he said:

> I think math class in seventh grade. In my old school, I think that it was that we actually learned something but also had a really good time doing it. All of my best friends were in the class and we had a good time goofing around and we also got something out of it. The teacher, she understood; she knew that she had, like, a big group of friends and it was going to be, like, a goofy experience. But I mean, she definitely, she worked with it and she got us all to, like, get good grades. We all got good grades by working pretty hard but also had a good time doing it, so. It wasn't so restrictive and it was just a good year.

Matt also insisted that getting to be active, move around, interact, and do something significant with others was what made school "fun." However, for Matt, school generally involved sitting around listening to the teacher, which completely "bored" him. When Michael asked him why he was also bored by a computer research project, he replied:

> Well it is the same thing: Somebody tells you information. Or you are doing it on your own and I think that it is the same thing. You are just sitting there looking it up for yourself.

Matt went on to equate the active with the interactive; being active requires others with whom to be active.

Similarly Robert talked with Michael about how much he preferred reading in a group:

> Robert: The plays, they be interesting because everybody in the class get a part. It would be like "Be the narrator" and it would be different people in the play. So we read, and we say the stuff that's written down in the book and we react to it.
>
> Michael: Why do you like that better than reading a story by yourself?
>
> Robert: Because it seems like everybody's participating. In it together.

When we asked what advice he'd give teachers on how to organize a class, Robert said, "Do labs. Like lab work, doing lab work. As a group, two or three people in a group, doing a project or something." He emphasized the importance not only of doing something important, but also of doing it together with other people who could provide help and with whom one could have fun.

Mike also emphasized the fun of reading together. He said he was willing to read "hard stuff" IF he was reading it and working through it with others. He complained about an assignment that "was more of this reading it by yourself. And not as fun as it should be, as it could be."

Sisqó spoke about his school's daily chapel, where students gave speeches or read essays. These in turn were discussed in homeroom. He said he would "tune out" except that he wanted to participate in the group discussion.

Ian talked about how he preferred talking to writing. In church school, he liked the study and discussion: "I like that better because it is all discussion. We don't like do any papers." He added that the discussion was always on point for life: "We apply what we are learning to our lives. It's good to learn important stuff together like that." He later described his favorite in-school reading activities as "literature circles and small-group discussions" where you "work things out and talk about important stuff" with classmates. Again, we see the importance of dealing with powerful ideas in group situations, and the privileging of talk as a way to be social.

Unfortunately, teachers often did not capitalize on this strong support for group work. The boys, particularly once they got to high school, complained about how little opportunity there was to work with others. Schoolwork was seen as an individual pursuit.

In the Use of Technology

One major tool the boys employed in their literate lives was the computer. We expected this, but we were surprised by the extent to which the fact that the computer facilitated social interaction accounted for its popularity. The majority of the high school boys, and many of the middle school boys as well, participated in instant messaging, electronic chat rooms, or regular email exchanges. We entered the study with images of boys sitting alone at the computer, playing games or surfing the Net. We found instead that they regarded it as a way to be social, to meet and communicate with others. Though a few students communicated with people they had never met face to face, most of the boys communicated with people they saw each day.

Bam talked about how the computer facilitated his social interactions. He explained that the computer gave him the power to relate to people and express himself and his feelings: "You feel you can say anything you want to. It's like I'm a shy person so I express more emotions over the computer." He also talked about the freedom to talk to people who were far away, and to explore ideas and emotions he would not explore in face-to-face conversation. He felt that he was in instant communication with the world when he was on the Internet.

The Importance of Engaging Materials

We've seen how important social relationships are in fostering boys' intrinsic motivation. But before readers can have a relationship with an author or a character, they have to read. And because the boys often rejected "school-ish" forms of literacy, they often didn't give texts, authors, and characters much of a chance to instigate those relationships. Over and over we heard that the boys expected to be engaged and absorbed by a story in the first few paragraphs. Robert explained this to Michael:

> Robert: If it's interesting, I'll read it.
> Michael: How long does it take you to decide if something's interesting? You know, you get a story and the teacher says, "Read it." How long does it take you to decide whether you're going to like it or not?
> Robert: I'll start reading. I'll start reading two or three paragraphs. That's the way I see it.

Similarly, Gohan talked about giving up on "The Necklace" during the first page because it didn't interest him:

> Gohan: There was something about the story, how the story started, that I didn't like.
> Michael: You're not very patient with stories, are you? How long will you give a story before you decide, "Forget it. I'm not reading this thing."
> Gohan: Time length, like five minutes. I get to, like, two paragraphs. If I don't like it, I'll leave the book alone.

Given that many of the boys made these kinds of quick judgments, it is important to remember the importance of frontloading to develop and build interest before students read. It's also important to note the qualities that seemed to encourage the boys to give the texts the benefit of the doubt. We turn our attention to these qualities next.

Music as Text

Popular culture texts, such as cartoons, videos, TV shows, and songs, were a favorite form of text for all of the boys. In particular, all of the boys talked about music with enthusiasm, though their tastes differed wildly, and their enjoyment of music fostered some intense literate activity. Here is Johnny discussing his favorite CD with Michael:

> Johnny: *Cuban Linx* is a rap CD by a guy called Raekwon; he's in the group Wu-Tang. It's one of the first CDs I ever got. It's got some of my favorite songs in there.
>
> Michael: What do you like about it?
>
> Johnny: I don't know, I like the music part—the songs, and whenever you have rap CDs, they use metaphors. I like when rappers use metaphors.
>
> Michael: Do you take out the lyrics and read while you listen?
>
> Johnny: No, I just try to memorize them. I memorize just about every song on that CD, and there's about sixteen or seventeen songs on it.
>
> Michael: So do you rap along with it?
>
> Johnny: Yeah, all the time.

Rudy also spent a lot of time surfing for music on the Internet, reading and memorizing lyrics, making his own CDs, and so on:

> Sometimes when I get bored doing homework, like a lot of research on the Internet, I will get an MP3 file or listen to a CD. Or I will look at the back of a CD and kind of read some of the lyrics to see if I know the song, and then I will program the songs that I want to hear.

The tremendous impact of music on the lives of the young men in our study provides testimony to scholars like Mahiri (1998) and Duncan-Andrade and Morrell (2000), who are investigating ways to use music and other popular cultural materials as a bridge to developing more canonical literacies. But that work is being done primarily with urban students. Our data suggest that such an approach would be appealing in other contexts as well.

As we explained at the end of Chapter 1, the importance of music was so great that we now see it as one important way that teachers can develop relationship with their students. Listening to one song from one kid in each class each week would not be too time-consuming. But we think the dividends it would reap would be enormous.

Texts That Are Storied

Interestingly, storied texts tended to appeal to the boys, especially in contrast to textbooks, which were almost universally condemned. Geo, who was a student in his school's lowest track, didn't want lists of facts:

> Yeah. I wouldn't really like a book, maybe I would read a person's story about slavery and how they get through. Yeah, that sounds pretty good, but I don't want to read about the whole time line of slavery or the whole time line of the Holocaust and stuff like that.

Ian, who was a very good student, concurred: "Give me the information in a story, not a textbook. I am totally against textbooks."

Jamaal enjoyed the ancillary stories and historical documents he was asked to read in history as "real stuff, by real people," but he rejected the textbook and refused to read it.

Timmy said, "There's no emotion in textbooks." He added, "There has to be emotion if I'm going to care."

We spoke earlier about how many of the boys liked wrestling. The primary reason for their enjoyment seemed to be the stories they followed. Barnabas, for example, loved the story lines, couldn't wait to see what would happen next, looked forward to Wrestlemania and Smackdown, and liked to see characters solve problems.

Action, of course, is often a primary feature of story, and the boys spoke often of enjoying action-oriented texts. Adam used a colorful metaphor to describe the action-oriented content he liked to read. He said he looked for texts "to jumpstart my head." He wanted texts that were visual, emotional, action-filled, and had a high impact. Similarly, Ricardo had trouble reading Poe because "there not enough action" and "too much description."

Fred liked the action of *Star Wars* so much that he bought the collector's edition; he loved episodic TV shows with lots of action, such as *Buffy the Vampire Slayer*. Most of all he loved suspense, a feature of stories not found in other types of texts. As Fred's selections make clear, the desire to figure things out, a desire we have already discussed, supported the boys' interest in stories.

Texts That Are Visual

For the boys in our study, the intense importance of the visual as they engaged with all forms of texts was evident, and we believe it cannot be oversold. The few engaged readers in this study all described their reading of books and stories in strikingly visual terms. The other boys described their engagement with visual or multimedia texts, such as movies and cartoons, in much the same enthusiastic way as the engaged readers described their reading. But the less engaged readers did not describe their reading in those same terms, probably, we would theorize, because they did not get the same kind of exciting visual experience from their reading as they received from media texts. All of the boys insisted that the best materials were highly visual, or stimulated visual thinking. Engaged readers like Neil said that to read well, it had to be a visual experience. It was important to "see" what he was reading.

Thirty-six of the boys ascribed their enjoyment of media texts like websites, television shows, and movies to exciting graphics and visuals. A number of the boys were devoted followers of the cartoon *Dragonball Z*, and they worked hard to describe the superiority of Japanimation to American animation. In fact, two of the boys chose their pseudonyms from that show.

There was also a substantial interest on the part of many boys in comic strips, cartoons, comic books, and graphic novels. Yuri was very taken with underground comics and with more mainstream graphic novels like *Maus*, which he liked because it told a story, it was "direct and you can see it," and the visuals symbolically helped develop meaning.

Experiencing storied texts was essentially a visual enterprise. A challenge here is for teachers to find ways to assist students who do not visualize what they read to develop ways of doing so. Otherwise they will not experience the same engagement with written texts that they do with multimedia ones. In fact, we think that the enormous popularity of drama and the powerful impact of SRIs—two instructional techniques we've already discussed—resides in large measure on their capacity to make texts and reading visible. (See Wilhelm, forthcoming.)

Texts That Are Exportable
One of the more intriguing findings of our analysis was the importance of what we call *exportability*. That is, the boys liked texts that could be easily exported into conversation. Prinz, for example, read the front page of the *Wall Street Journal* so he could talk to his father on the way to work. We mentioned in Chapter 2 that Mark checked the Internet to keep up with the scores of the local hockey team, in part because of his personal interest but more because he knew his friends would ask him about the game.

Interestingly, texts that are easily exported into conversations are those that can be easily reduced: headlines, box scores, jokes, "cool parts" of books or movies, and so on. Yet as Rabinowitz (1987) points out, complexity is one feature of texts that schools reward, as is nuanced interpretation of those complex texts. The more complex a text is, the less easily it can be reduced, and hence the less easily it can be brought into conversation. For example, both of us have been stymied trying to give a quick synopsis of a book that we were reading. These may also be features of texts and textual work that make texts less exportable and therefore contribute to boys' resistance. If we value complexity, we must ask how we can use what boys do value to help them develop toward valuing and engaging with more complex texts.

Texts That Sustain Engagement

A number of the boys talked about how they enjoyed texts that allowed them multiple opportunities for engagement. Most often this discussion came up when the boys talked about series and collections. Yuri, for example, collected underground comic books and graphic novels. Ricardo collected *Garfield*, *Calvin and Hobbes*, and *Far Side* cartoon books. Liam and Yuri collected series of fantasy books and books by particular authors whom they liked. Several of the middle school boys were reading series books such as Goosebumps, Animorphs, or sports serials.

We theorize that the boys' enjoyment of serials stemmed from the fact that the series scaffolded the boys' engagement. For readers, imagining the character, situation, and so forth in one book supports the next envisionment and, as such, provides quicker competence. The boys' enjoyment of texts that sustain engagement also seemed to relate to the importance of the social; they expressed that they wanted to "spend more time" or "get to know" a character better, or "to see what's up" with characters they had come to care about.

Repeated readings or viewing was another way the boys sustained engagement, and we think this also related to their desire for competence. Sixteen of the boys talked about their enjoyment of repeated readings of favorite texts.

Ricardo was a good reader who reported pursuing particular authors, styles, and genres as projects. He reread books and watched movies more than once "as a way to learn something new. What it means, how it was made. . . . You always see and learn something new."

Similarly, Aaron was planning to reread *Patriot Games* for the third time, and Bodey reported surfing through television channels until he recognized a movie he had already seen. He said, "Then I'll watch that. It's fun to know what will happen. And it's like seeing an old friend again if you really liked it."

Some students, like Rev, would rent a movie and, if it was good, watch it several times before returning it. Guy, who generally didn't like reading, would reread short texts that had made an impression on him.

The boy's desire to reread resonates with Carlsen's (1967) argument that first readings are for plot and pleasure, while second readings are for understanding structure and how the text works. This confirms the assertion that Clay (1991, 1993) made in her work with emergent readers. She found that initial readings focus on decoding meaning, and repeated readings help readers understand textual conventions.

When Jeff was teaching in schools overseas, he was surprised to learn that many texts were taught multiple times for multiple purposes. But the pressure for coverage makes rereading rare in American schools. At least a third of our boys would call for a reconsideration of this tendency, particularly for the texts in which students were especially engaged.

Texts That Provide Multiple Perspectives
One of the most interesting features of the texts these boys tended to like was that of multiple perspectives. Twenty-two of the boys mentioned this as a feature they enjoyed.

Jamaal said, "I like it when I hear about something from a bunch of different perspectives." He remembered a unit about the Revolutionary War in which they had read about many events from the perspectives of Tories and the Redcoats. He explained, "Whoa! Switcherooni! It made you see things in a totally new way! It was powerful."

Johnny put it this way:

> I like when it's facts, but sometimes facts get boring. I like learning the opinions of other people so I can see different perspectives, and then maybe I can think, "Well it does make a lot more sense than what I'm thinking," or then I can relate to it. Like if I can relate to something in class then I'll enjoy it more, like retain it better, than just learning facts, it'll bore me to death.

Wolf expressed a similar attitude:

> Well, I think that you can carry plays with just one person. But I think they're crap plays. You have to have lots of strong people since they all intersupport each other.

That's why he loved *Hamlet*:

> But with *Hamlet*, I kind of like that because at the same point I can see from Hamlet's point of view, from his father, from his uncle, from his mom, I can see from the different characters' points of view where they were coming from. And I like the book in that sense that I can understand where his father was coming from, being poisoned, where Hamlet was

coming from—coming back from college and all this was going on and he was like, "Hey." I can understand that. I don't know, I think that's why I liked it.

Yuri had this to say: "I want all sides looked at when I'm studying something. And I want to decide for myself what's right." Later he said, "School tries to tell you what to think, but I don't want to be proselytized. I want to see the important issues from all sides." For that reason he liked his course on comparative religions. After completing his class reading, he would go to chat rooms on religion and find people of different beliefs to share and argue with.

Texts That Are Novel
Every boy in the study looked to avoid routines they found stultifying, and this carried over to their reading and viewing habits. They desired what they described as "new," "different," or "surprising."

Rudy, a good student, railed against what he called "the routine of school. It's the same things over and over again, day after day and year after year." He enthusiastically embraced the occasional freedoms and breaks that school offered from the routine. Huey complained, "All the books and all the stories are the same. Why can't we get something different?" Yuri refused to read or finish assigned books, stating, "I know what's going to happen. All the books we read are the same. Nothing interesting or surprising ever happens, so what good is it? It's not interesting and it doesn't change the way you look at things." Mike also complained about school reading: "I like new stuff, it ought to be, I just want new stuff." In contrast, he liked reading on the Internet because it is up to date and always offers new creative possibilities.

Ricardo spoke with Jeff about why he enjoyed the "Far Side" and political cartooning:

Ricardo: Yeah, usually I just get a kick out of how they present and interpret certain situations like world events, I think it's pretty clever.
Jeff: So the cleverness is part of the fun for you?
Ricardo: I like originality a lot, so if you can present me something in a way I didn't think about it, then I'm pretty blown away by it, I'm like "Oh. . . ." I'm tired of this boring old same stuff.

The boys almost uniformly enjoyed the novelty brought by textual ruptures such as satire and irony that caused them to see in a new way. (Only one boy in the study did not like watching *The Simpsons*.) These ruptures were important for another reason. As Muecke (1969) points out, understanding irony casts the reader as a knowing insider. Given the boys' emphasis on competence, it's not surprising that they found this appealing. Neil put it this way:

> I think that there is kind of like, not a secret but just a kind of like, understood humor with *The Simpsons* and, like, kind of something that only certain people get. You know it is really funny . . . I guess that you could say it because I kind of watched it for so long I know that I actually can understand the show now, and I like things that I can understand.

Texts That Are Edgy/Subversive
Thirty-six of the boys cited "edginess" or some kind of subversive content as making reading or viewing enjoyable. They embraced material that pushed the edges of the acceptable or that presented things in a shocking way. Several boys, like Joe and Timmy, indicated that the reading assigned in English was "too tame" or "not worth arguing or caring about."

Ricardo reported loving *Hamlet* because

> it's edgy action. It's filled with surprise. You never know what is going to happen. Pirates, man. Rosencrantz and Guildenstern. Everybody is surprised. Claudius, Hamlet's mom, Rosencrantz, and Guildenstern sure were. And me! Plot twists galore. Everybody dying. Whoa. Totally shocking.

He also loved *Into the Wild*:

> I liked that he was tired of living like Gramma tells him to. He wants some freedom and variety. That's how I feel. Take the risk. And of course I like him and it blows me away to know that he dies. So I want to find out what went wrong.

The boys desired edginess along with their action as Barnabas explained in talking about wrestling:

> if there is really like no violence, like not even just a little, it would not be fun. I mean if they didn't have violence in WWF, which is, like, pretty much all the wrestling, they would just, like, have talking the whole time. And that would be just like stupid.

Neil repeatedly referred to controversy in his discussion of *Full House*, a sitcom he seemed almost embarrassed to like:

> I always liked the controversial episodes of *Full House*. You know, and like somebody gets caught with drugs or somebody, you know, has a problem with a boy. . . . The normal would be really boring. . . . I think that everybody can really say that they do like the action and the controversial parts in books instead of just talking.

Pablo repeatedly referred to "the edgy." He said he liked to read about "breaking rules, subcultures, being different, being radically different." Joe and Timmy and Bodey liked to read about "edgy stuff," "getting away with stuff," "things that are, like, totally unknown to me."

Texts That Have Powerful Ideas

Many of the boys also discussed their enjoyment of texts that expressed powerful or positive ideas. Robert said he liked rap songs and stories that expressed "positive life values." Pablo looked for "powerful ideas" in musicals, plays, movies, murals, paintings, even quilts. "That's [the powerful idea] what makes it art."

Twenty-six of the boys mentioned the importance of powerful ideas in the materials they read. The boys talked variously about the political (9), moral (13), and life-expanding appeal (16) of powerful ideas. Interestingly, though they often engaged with different kinds of texts than those assigned by schools, they often did so for the very reasons their teachers would hope—to engage in powerful ideas and expand their understanding of the world.

Texts That Are Funny

The boys desired to read humorous texts. This was especially true of their viewing choices. We were surprised that television was not more important to the boys in our study. Many had a favorite program or two they would watch, but none of the boys could be classified as a couch potato. Our findings here were in line with Csikszentmihalyi (1990b), who argues that "what people most enjoy is almost never something passive" (p. 132), such as watching TV.

But when they watched, many of the boys liked to laugh. Reruns of sitcoms were a special favorite—in part, we think, because they are often shown just before dinner. Those boys who were involved in after-school activities often watched a show or two to unwind. Laughter was an important part of their enjoyment.

But laughter was never part of their school literacy experiences. In fact, the boys struggled when asked to remember anything funny or humorous they had read in school. One of Michael's most memorable interviews involved a question that a student never answered. After Mark talked about how he enjoyed *The Simpsons* and *Seinfeld*, Michael asked him whether he ever read anything funny in school. Mark was so baffled by the question he couldn't answer. It seemed that he could not keep school and humor in his head at the same time.

We wonder why that has to be the case.

A Close Look at the Boys' Reading

One of the things that was striking about the reading logs was how seldom the boys invoked stereotypes about what men should enjoy, as in the commercial we described at the beginning of this chapter. The boys clearly expressed their preferences for reading, but for the most part, they did not seem to make selections in opposition to what they saw or expected girls' preferences to be. Mark was one of the few who did make that contrast. Here he is talking about his English class:

> We're reading *To Kill a Mockingbird* right now, and I really like that book. But there's other books like *Jane Eyre*, like all these girlie books, that I just can't relate to.

When Michael asked Mark what he meant by a "girlie book," he had a ready explanation:

> Well, *To Kill a Mockingbird*—I guess it's sort of the way they describe things. In *Jane Eyre*, they keep going over the same things over and over again, like dresses and the way something looks, is explained for pages and pages on end. But in *To Kill a Mockingbird*, they're always doing something, or the kids are going out there, messing around with Boo Radley, and things like that.

The contrast that Mark drew resonates with our discussion of how the boys liked action but disliked highly descriptive text. It also evokes Bruner's (1986) discussion of the landscapes of action and consciousness in narratives. Bruner notes that the constituents of the landscape of action "are the arguments of action: agent, intention or goal, situation, instrument," while the constituents of the landscape of consciousness are "what those involved in the action know, think, or feel, or do not know, think or feel" (p. 14). While all stories must construct both landscapes, the balance between the two vary from story to story. In Bruner's discussion of folktales, for example, he claims, citing Propp (1970), that "character is a *function* of a highly constrained plot," while character—rather than action and interaction—drives the work of Conrad.

We wanted to investigate the impact of text on the ways that the young men in our study read literature, but as we found in our discussion of the importance of school, what they said didn't always match what they did. Therefore, instead of asking them about their reading, we decided to take a more direct look at how they read by asking them to make think-aloud protocols while they read four stories.

Because conventional wisdom holds that boys prefer action-oriented stories, we selected stories that differed in their relative emphasis on the landscape of action. We also added another variable that we thought was consistent with the conventional wisdom about boys' preferences in reading: the sex of the main character. Using these two variables, then, we chose the stories presented in Figure 5.1. Apart from these two variables, we tried to match the stories as best we could. All of the stories are first-person narrations that focus on a conflict between the narrator and another person. The stories are of similar length. All have appeared in anthologies for adolescents.

Given the argument we've been making about the place of nonliterary texts in the lives of young men, it may seem strange for us to focus on literature here. We did so for two reasons. First, we value literature and have made the teaching of literature the focus of our professional lives. Second, we recognize the place that literature has in the curriculum. Succeeding in and enjoying English classes, by and large, requires successful engagements with literature.

In order to find out how the boys responded to the stories, we asked them to read them aloud and to say whatever came to mind as they read. At the beginning of the story we provided the following prompt:

> Please read this story aloud into the microphone and say aloud any response that you have while you are reading. I'm interested in anything you are noticing, asking, seeing, feeling, thinking, and doing as you read. Say anything that you are aware of thinking and doing at the point that you think or do it. And at the end of each page please stop for a minute and give an update. Thanks.

We did two kinds of analyses. First, we divided their responses into moves, segments of discourse exhibiting a single purpose. Then we categorized the moves as being one of fourteen primary processes or five ancillary processes. Michael used this coding scheme in previous research (Smith, 1991) and found that it's an effective way to describe what secondary students do when they respond to stories. Two graduate students in English did the coding and did not begin to code independently until they achieved an 80 percent rate of agreement. While they were coding, Michael read a portion of their work to make sure the level of agreement remained high. (Appendix C provides the coding scheme as well as a table that displays the nature of the moves the boys made when reading the four stories. We'll draw on that table in our subsequent discussion, but when we do, we'll highlight the findings that are most salient.)

FIGURE 5.1   The Stories

"White Chocolate"
by Robin Brancato [male narrator/character driven]

The narrator of this story is a biracial high school student. He describes his problems with his English teacher. She's pushing the narrator to work to his potential, to engage with reading in a serious way, but he won't. Things come to a head when she asks his opinion about a story that focuses on an interracial relationship. The narrator, whose parents have recently separated, goes "crazy" in class after being asked whether such a relationship could succeed, an event that leads to a conference with him and the teacher.

As the story closes, the narrator says the teacher is mistaken if she thinks she reached him: "Just let her *try* pressing me into shape, and let her see how sticky I'll be."

"The White Circle"
by John Bell Clayton [male narrator/action]

The narrator of this story is the son of a wealthy landowner. He's been given an apple tree for his birthday. He discusses the time he found the neighborhood bully, the son of an itinerant knick-knack peddler, sitting in the tree. The bully wouldn't leave and instead threw apples at the narrator. The narrator, feeling both angry and powerless, lured him into the white circle in the barn, which was drawn to warn people about the hayfork suspended above. The narrator released the fork, and the bully leaped away just in time. Stunned, he left the narrator in "the accusing emptiness of the barn."

"My Sister's Marriage"
by Cynthia Rich [female narrator/charcter]

The narrator of this story is the younger daughter of a widower who is the doctor in their small town. She and her sister take care of their father, who exerts strict control over their lives. The narrator loves her father, though she thinks her sister is his favorite. When the older daughter meets a man in whom she's interested, the father rejects him, believing he's beneath her. He forbids her to see the man. The older daughter runs away and marries. She calls the father, asking for his blessing, but he refuses. She writes the narrator regularly, asking that she intercede on her behalf, but the narrator doesn't, saying that father is not well. She does save her sister's letters though. One day her father sees her writing back and tells the narrator not to ally herself "with deception" and that now it's just the two of them. Later the narrator discovers that the father has taken the sister's letters and secreted them away in his desk. When she finds them she takes them out and burns them, thinking, "Now there is only me."

FIGURE 5.1   The Stories

"Marigolds"
by Eugenia Collier

The narrator of this story is looking back on the Depression as her African American community experienced it in rural Maryland. She tells of how she and her brother and friends enjoyed annoying an old woman, whose "crumbling decay" of a yard was marked by a dazzling array of marigolds. They would hurl pebbles at her flowers or yell and then run away. One night after hearing her father sobbing about losing his job and voicing his fears about being able to take care of his family, she wakes her brother and they run out and destroy the marigolds, a violent act that was the "last act of childhood" when she saw the "broken old woman."

The second kind of analysis we did was more holistic. Following the lead of a number of other researchers, we wanted to characterize the general approach or orientation that the young men took to each of the stories. To do so we built on the influential research of Vipond and Hunt (1984). They distinguish three basic orientations that readers take: *information-driven*, *story-driven*, and *point-driven* readings. According to Vipond and Hunt, information-driven reading "is especially appropriate in learning-from-text situations where content is relevant" (e.g., a bus schedule). As such, it resembles what Rosenblatt (1978) would call *efferent reading*. An *information-driven* reading of a story would focus on understanding the literal details of the text. It's the kind of reading that would prepare the reader to pass an objective test on the story. *Story-driven* readings are quite different in that they "tend to emphasize plot, character and event" (p. 269). *Story-driven* readings are marked by an engagement in the story world. While a reader with an *information-driven* orientation would recall plot details, a reader with a *story-driven* orientation would focus more on how events in the story affected the characters. *Point-driven* readings move beyond the details of the story to involve "the sharing and comparing of values and beliefs" (p. 263). They require generalizations that go beyond the world of the story.

In previous research Michael (Smith, 1991) identified another orientation, one that he labeled *association-driven*. This is the orientation he used to describe readers whose responses focused more on the personal associations the story evoked than on the story itself. That is, in an association-driven reading the story acts as a springboard for recalling and examining the reader's personal experience.

As we read the protocols that we collected in this study, we realized that these four orientations were not fully descriptive of the protocols, so we added two more to the list. First, some of the boys seemed to feel that it was their job simply to comment on their perception of the quality of the story as they read. We called that orientation *evaluation-driven*. Evaluation-driven reading evidenced little engagement with the characters or the ideas of a text. Rather they tended to focus on providing a thumbs-up or thumbs-down vote on its quality. Second, early in our reading we found a protocol that focused almost exclusively on what the reader was experiencing as he read. We labeled that orientation as *experience-driven*. Finally, because we wanted to recognize when the boys made took no stance and no effort to respond to the story, we added a final category, *disengaged readings*.

Figure 5.2 provides a quick definition of each of the orientations. Along with the graduate students who coded the interpretive operations, we coded the protocols for their orientation, achieving an 87 percent rate of agreement.

The students' orientations are important to us as teachers. We want students to do more than simply remember details so they can pass a test. We share Booth's (1988) belief that stories are important because they are usually centered on characters' efforts to face moral choices. He explains, "In tracing those efforts, we readers stretch our own capacities for thinking about how life should be lived" (p. 187). Consequently, we value story-driven readings. And we value point-driven readings even more than story-driven readings if they are built on a genuine engagement with the story world. (Some point-driven readings seem instead to be attempts to reduce a story to an aphorism.) Point-driven readings, we think, have the capacity to be instructive in contexts far different from the particular context of a story. Coles (1989), for example, cites one of his students talking about how literary characters speak to him; we think they must be speaking to him about beliefs and values:

> When I have some big moral issue, some question to tackle, I think I try to remember what my folks have said, or I imagine them in my situation—or even more these days I think of [characters in books I've read]. Those folks, they're people for me . . . they really speak to me. . . . (p. 203)

In our experience, association-driven readings are of two sorts. In some cases readers seem to use stories as a way to evoke a string of what seems like unconnected reminiscences (cf. Smith, 1991b). These readings don't require the kind of stretching that Booth (1988) talks about, but they can also

FIGURE 5.2   A Summary of Orientations

Information-driven readings: A primary emphasis on learning from texts. Such readings focus on the literal level of stories.

Story-driven readings: A primary emphasis on entering the story world. Such readings focus on engaging with the characters.

Point-driven readings: A primary emphasis on identifying the major morals and values that ground a story. Such readings focus on the ideas that a story evokes.

Association-driven readings: A primary emphasis on the personal associations the story evokes. Such readings focus more on the reader's prior experience than on the story itself.

Evaluation-driven readings: A primary emphasis on determining the quality of a story. Such readings focus on passing judgment rather than on entering the story world.

Experience-driven readings: A primary emphasis on the emotions the reader experiences during the course of the reading. Such readings focus on the immediate emotional experience of the reader.

Disengaged readings: Primary emphasis on simply completing the task.

involve a more thorough self-examination. While we worry that substituting their own experience for the experience of literary characters minimizes what readers can learn from authors and characters (see Rabinowitz and Smith, 1998; Smith and Strickland, 2001), as long as that examination involves an interplay between the reader and the text, it's a kind of reading we would be glad our students did. On the other hand, evaluation-driven, experience-driven, and disengaged readings don't provide what Santayana calls "imaginative rehearsals for living" (cited in Booth, 1983, p. 212), which we want for our students.

Except for three boys who received permission to do the protocols during class time, we asked the boys to do the protocols on their own time, supplying them with tapes and recording equipment if need be. We have all four protocols from eighteen boys; three protocols from eight; two protocols from eleven; and one protocol from two. We also have one protocol that was unidentified.

This is a very large data set, but it's worth noting at the outset that it's less complete than our other data sets from this study. Some of this is due to technical problems, for example, a few boys recorded over protocols they had already completed, and we lost a few tapes as we sent them to transcribers. Once we realized that Mick couldn't read the stories, we told him that he didn't have to do them. Nine of the boys simply decided not to do the protocols. We think this is further evidence of a major point we made in Chapter 4: many of the boys made a link between reading literature and school, and they were reluctant to do schoolwork when they didn't have to. Although we don't have a complete data set, the data we do have are interesting and surprising.

What We Found: An Overview

Table 5.1 indicates the distribution of orientations for each of the stories. Please keep in mind that a different number of boys responded to each of the stories: thirty-three responded to "The White Circle," twenty-nine responded to "White Chocolate," twenty-seven responded to "Marigolds," and thirty-two responded to "My Sister's Marriage."

Our analysis of moves indicates the dominance of story-driven readings. The two interpretive operations that most clearly reflect story-driven readings, Making Local Inferences and Putting Things Together (Appendix C), comprise 44 percent of the total moves the students made. The boys focused on the characters' motives and worked to understand them as human beings. In essence, they focused on playing what Rabinowitz calls the narrative

TABLE 6.1   Orientations by Story

	WHITE CIRCLE	WHITE CHOCOLATE	MARIGOLDS	MY SISTER'S MARRIAGE	TOTAL
Story	20	14	12	19	65
Evaluation	6	6	7	6	25
Information	3	3	3	4	13
Association	2	6	3	0	11
Point	0	0	2	1	3
Experience	1	0	0	0	1
Disengaged	1	0	0	2	3
Total	33	29	27	32	121

audience (1987; Rabinowitz and Smith, 1998). They treated the characters as people worthy of their attention and concern.

Our holistic evaluation jibes with our microanalysis, for as Table 5.1 reveals, there were more than two and a half times more story-driven readings than any other orientation. To give a sense of the involvement the boys had with the characters, we'll share some final remarks boys made, one about each story.

Here's Zach on "The White Circle":

Wow! I don't know. I don't know which of the two characters I like better. Anvil. Yes, he was wrong in being a bully, but that might not have been his fault. And from what I think, I think it was kind of a product of the environment that he lived in and response to having such a crazy dad. He had to be a tough kid, and he didn't really have much. So it's bad, but I don't think it's that bad. And, I think he comes out the better man in the end because he gives back the apples and he makes his point clear. He's like, "You know, Tucker, you're greedy and it was a scary greedy and I'm leaving." And he didn't respond and didn't turn back because he was too proud to accept second-thought charity. So, I think Anvil ended proudly.

Now, Tucker. Tucker in the first part, you actually kind of, or at least, I felt sorry for him because he was getting beat up by this big bully. The whole drawing out of the barn scene kind of reminded me of "The Cask of Amontillado" by Poe where you take him along a path toward death and suddenly it all clicks in the guy's mind, the victim's mind, although this time he didn't kill him. It's just you feel sorry for Tucker, but then all of a sudden you get a real quick—or I got a real quick feeling for him and I pitied Anvil more and I didn't like Tucker. You know, that was almost like crazy. I mean, he had such an attachment to that tree and those apples that stood so much for him that it was like it was *too* much, too much of a good thing. He was obsessed, and being obsessed about anything isn't healthy, and it drove him although the story didn't necessarily say that. But he had some weird psyche going on there. I don't know. I thought it was a really good story, and it had a twist in the end, which was good. I thought it was well-written and fun to read, if you can believe it.

And Geo on "White Chocolate":

So like, she had a talk to him, but he's really hard to get to. He had a strong mental mind. I think his dad is probably Black and his mom is White, the way things is, know what I mean? The way the mom was acting it sounds like she could be White. The kids in there, they sound mad funny. I think the kid act more Black than he do White. That's the way it went down. I think this story's good, I mean, I think the boy had a little bit of a problem, but that's about it. I mean, nothing that you can't fix, but it's kind of funny if you think about it. It's a good story.

And Gohan on "Marigolds":

I don't see why she had to destroy the marigolds. I did really understand because she was going through all this pressure she ain't never go through before. She ain't never seen her dad cry. She thought he was the man of the house—a rock, like she said. And, I guess that was the only thing. Since the town she lived in was ugly, that was the only pretty things to destroy. I guess that's how she was feeling so she just broke it. She started stomping on them and pulling them out. I guess she was feeling like a marigold until she pulled it out, she thought. I don't know. About her brother, her brother, after what he seen, he's gonna understand things that's going on because it's like she said; it's from childhood to womanhood was her last act. It makes sense. Ignorance, it was. But what I don't understand was Miss Lottie didn't say anything. It didn't have her remarks on there when she seen the destroyed garden, and they should have had something there. I don't know. The lady passed away as they said, and her being so nice, she planted some more marigolds at the end of the story. I like that. That's really nice. That's it, I guess.

And Buda on "My Sister's Marriage":

I don't think she meant it to be. Maybe she meant to be a little selfish, but I think she did it for her father. He wants to forget her because she betrayed him—he thinks, anyway. But she really didn't. She did what's best for her. And I like this story. It's odd in a way, but he either needs to get on or forgive her in a way that he can and start trying to get her back in his life or he'll never be completely happy. I mean now he just thinks that she's the bad daughter and Sarah Ann is the good one and thinks that she's going to stay with him forever. And as soon as she wants to marry, he's going to be all alone, and he just realized that. He needs to realize that even though they're going to be married, they'll still be in his life. He needs to figure that out.

In these responses, the boys evidenced that they were treating the characters as more than artistic creations about whom they needn't care. Rather, they demonstrate the kind of concern they would have for another human being. It's this concern that is the hallmark of story-driven readings as we have defined them. Not all of the boys who evidenced a story-driven orientation spoke at such length or with such intensity, but more than 70 percent of them manifested a similar concern for the characters in at least one of the stories.

Two of the boys (a total of three protocols) built on their engagement with the characters to develop a point-driven reading, looking for abstract principles that seemed to inform the characters' behaviors. But as was true in Vipond and Hunt's work, such readings were very rare.

We've spoken throughout the book of the emphasis the boys put on relationships, especially their relationships with friends, family, and teachers. The protocols support the claim we made early in this chapter that this emphasis on relationships extends to developing relationships with literary characters, at least for most of the readers.

Moreover, point-driven readings, a kind of reading very much valued in school, can be built on story-driven readings, and thus may be in the boys' zones of proximal development. In other words, they are likely to be within the boys' reach if students are given appropriate instruction.

Another manifestation of the boys' emphasis on relationships was the prevalence of *relating*, the second most common move that they made. It comprised 18 percent of their total moves, a substantially higher proportion than what typifies classroom discussions of literature (Marshall, Smagorinsky, and Smith, 1995). For the most part, the boys regularly used their life experience as a way to understand the characters.

For example, when Stan read that Anvil threw an apple at the narrator of "The White Circle," he commented, "Wow, I would totally give him the knuckles after that."

After reading the complaints from the narrator of "White Chocolate" about "useless" classes, Jamaal noted, "I feel like that sometimes."

When Clint read the beginning description of the setting in "Marigolds," he commented, "I can relate to that because I grew up in Ohio, where there is a lot of dirt, and ran around in bare feet all summer, no cares in the world."

Similarly, when Brandon learned that the father in "My Sister's Wedding" didn't encourage his daughters to read, he noted, "Yeah, neither do I. I can relate to that." But he also used his life experience to question the narrator's judgment. When she explained that they didn't need to read because their father had read everything and because talking to him was better than reading, Brandon said, "That's maybe not the truth. But maybe I read a newspaper or watch TV to get my information."

On occasion, the boys' thinking about their life experience seemed to supplant their engagement with the characters. On those occasions, we coded their protocols as association-driven. Here, for example, are Pablo's final comments on "White Chocolate":

> Wow, it's almost sad because I've been told that I have a way with words too and sometimes I get out of control, and I have before. I had two classes with Ms. _____ this year and one time I got out of control. Not like that. Not like I was going to punch her. But she just said, "It's a real waste." And it is. It's a real waste to have such a talent and to not use it.

And Robert's final comments on "Marigolds":

> This part, all the lady did—that's all they talked about she did was planted different kind of flowers and stuff like that. It seems like to me she wasn't bothering nobody by doing that, but the children still tried to destroy her garden and try to get on her nerves. I guess that's what they was doing. Some lady that live across the street from me. She always in her garden planting flowers and different kinds of plants, and people be walking by. They walking by eating a snack or something. They be walking by and throw the wrapper down in her yard or stuff like that, and she got to be the one to get out there and pick it up. So one day I asked her did she need help because anybody just walk by. She wasn't that old, but she looked helpless sometimes because they walking by and she planting her garden. It's looking pretty. She wetting it, and they're throwing bottles and stuff in there and different kind of potato chip bags and stuff like that. I used to always help her out. Then, her sons started coming around, helping her.

Using a story to challenge one's behavior, as Pablo did, or to support it, as did Robert, requires a real engagement with the literature. For the most part, the association-driven readings all evidenced the kind of engagement we want our students to have. In the unidentified protocol, however, the reader's use of personal experience, in this case previous literary experience, seemed to interfere with that kind of engagement. Throughout his reading of "The White Circle," the reader made references to texts he had read in school, especially *To Kill a Mockingbird* and *Richard III*. More than any other boy, he seemed to construct the protocols as a schoolish performance. He explained that this interfered with his ability to enter the story world:

> Right now, I'm imagining what they're doing. My mind's kind of flowing with the story. All of my spare thoughts are kind of readying what I'm about to say. But I can clearly say if I wasn't going to have to dictate into the microphone I would just kind of allow my mind to fixate me into the story, probably as a bystander or a tree or something. Something relaxing, just not having to think about anything else, or symbolic terms or anything, but just to see what action is going on.

Smagorinsky's (1998) argument about the implied audience of protocols is useful in understanding this protocol. Smagorinsky argues that protocols do not provide a clear window into the mind of the reader. Doing a protocol, he argues, like all human activity, is affected by the sociocultural context in which it takes place. One aspect of that context, according to Smagorinsky, is that protocols are addressed to someone, even though that person is not present. In this case, though we explicitly told the boys that we wanted them to share whatever came to their minds, what they chose to share was undoubtedly affected at least to some extent by the fact that we're university professors, that we were interviewing them about reading, and so on.

Smagorinsky also points out that the context of the protocol may have an influence. Although the boys did the protocols at home, we gave them the stories and trained them at school. Both of these factors could have affected the way that all of the boys construed and hence engaged in the task. Our guess is that they especially affected this unidentified reader. He seems to feel a tension between what he would like to do and what he feels he's being asked to do. For this young man, schoolish reading is at odds with the story-driven readings he seems to want to do. He seems to think that we expect him to keep his distance rather than to enter the story world.

Thus far, we have focused on the majority of boys who either willingly engaged with the stories or seemed to want to. But some of the boys did not evidence that engagement. This was most obviously seen in the few protocols we coded as disengaged reading and in the one protocol we coded as experience-driven, a protocol that focused almost entirely on how confused the reader felt. But it also characterized the majority of protocols we characterized as evaluation-driven.

Here's how Barnabas responded after reading the first page of "The White Circle":

> That's a pretty good story so far. It sounds pretty interesting. It's better than "White Chocolate" because "White Chocolate" was just kind of boring because it was trying to be interesting but it wasn't. This one seems interesting because it sounds like *Happy Gilmore*. All right. I'm going on.

We're not sure what in the story evoked the Adam Sandler movie, nor can we be sure that Barnabas' response didn't go deeper than what he chose to share. But we are sure that his construction of the task as reviewing the story (thumbs up or thumbs down) kept him from manifesting engagement with the characters the way other readers did.

For other students, their dislike of the story seemed to motivate their evaluation. This was evidenced in Neil's final remarks on "White Chocolate":

> Well, this story didn't have an ending, which I do and don't like. Well, it had an ending but not an exact ending like where he goes back to class. It wasn't a happy ending either way. This is very good as a novel because if you did want to open it up, you could easily do that. I'm saying like a ratio, like if you took this story and made it into a novel about something different, you could probably get a good sequel out of it—the way it's set up structure-wise. The style of writing with the children does kind of annoy me, but I'm getting used to it after reading a lot of short stories in English. Again, I prefer books with a lot more subtle action and getting more in-depth about a particular character. That's about it.

Interestingly, Neil seemed to reject what he saw as the author's attempt to be relevant to young people, the kind of effort he saw in stories he read in his English class. As he took pains to make clear throughout the interviews, he was more interested in texts, both print and nonprint, that he considered to be more adult.

More typically, the boys were more dismissive when they offered an evaluation, as was the case in Rudy's final comments on "Marigolds":

> Well, this probably hasn't been the best story I ever read because it's just a bunch of imagery and description and I don't really like reading about that much of that kind of thing. I like reading about imagery and descriptions of actual things that happened, but not about like a setting or anything else because it just makes me feel weird. And it's just hard to actually picture all that stuff because I have so much more than a lot of things than they talk about. I don't really think that there was a big connection that was made, like I expected there to be, because all they really say is, "I too have planted marigolds," but I think this story kind of

leaves the imagery and connection open to you to, like, think of it how you want. But I still don't really think this story is something I'd really like to read that's in a book that would take me a lot longer to read.

Bambino was more succinct in his comments as he read "My Sister's Marriage":

Right now, I'm feeling very ticked off because this story is long and real boring and had better get better. OK, I changed location because I was getting bored laying down. I'm downstairs now. TV's on again, like I said, and here goes.

These last two comments resonate with the expectations with which we began this study. Although we selected "Marigolds" because of the action at the climax of the story, it was more descriptive than any of the other stories. And as we pointed out earlier, many of the boys expressed impatience with too much description. When we selected "My Sister's Wedding," we fully expected many of the boys to reject it as Bambino did. But as we'll explain in the next section of this chapter, we were surprised by how few did.

When the boys seemed to construct their task as summarizing the story, what we called an information-oriented reading, they also evidenced less engagement with the characters. Such was the case in Ian's response to "Marigolds." Throughout the story he worked to provide a synopsis of what happened, as the following portion of his final remarks reveal:

'Cause it was kind of like the whole story of like ah, a girl who ah, was really childish. I mean she, like, began almost like deep thinking and she matured and then she ah, describes the whole of her adult mind and ah, realized that, and it was like she was, it was ah, and it was like she just, she just, kind of she realized that, that it was almost like ah, just kind of like the childhood in her just kind of forcing the last bit. Kind of like the last hurrah.

In contrast with the story-driven readings we presented earlier, Ian seemed less engaged. Once again, we want to stress that we are not arguing that Ian was unengaged. Rather, following Smagorinsky (1998), we are arguing that his protocol reflects a different conception of what the task was.

The influence of the way the boys constructed the task, on the way they responded, seems to us to have important implications. If we condition their task construction with tests that focus on the literal level of stories, or with the identification of literary devices, or with writing that only requires them to repeat what has been said in class discussions, then we can't expect them to evidence the kind of engagement in a story world that makes reading so compelling to so many of us. We can't expect them to use stories to think about their own lives or to transact with them in any of the other creative ways that highly engaged readers do.

The good news is that fewer students than we expected seemed to manifest the kind of conditioning that does not support an engaged response.

Instead, our analysis thus far is consistent with much of what we have argued in our previous chapters, primarily in the emphasis that the majority of the boys seemed to place on relationships. As we read the protocols, we saw other points of connection with what we saw in our interview data. Fred, for example, spoke about the importance of action. He enjoyed reading "The White Circle," expressing amazement that he was asked to read a story with so much fighting and such a "sick and twisted ending." This enjoyment is consistent with our discussion of the appeal of novel and edgy texts earlier in this chapter. On the other hand, he dismissed "My Sister's Marriage" because "the only thing interesting that has happened is the girl threw a brush at her father."

Bambino expressed surprise that he was asked to read a story ("White Chocolate") that was "actually funny." Again, this comment resonates with those we cited in our last chapter when we talked about the importance of humor.

The protocols' consistency with the interview data was manifested across stories. Although the boys sometimes made distinctions among the stories, ranking them on the basis of a variety of criteria, the differences among the stories did not result in substantial differences in the way that they read them. Instead, the boys tended to adopt a characteristic style of response. In fact, of the eighteen boys from whom we have protocols of all four stories, nine had the same orientation for all of them and four had the same orientation for three of them. Of the eight boys from whom we have protocols for three stories, four had the same orientation for all of them and three had the same orientation for two of them.

Indeed, the most striking finding of this data set is not the differences we did see, but rather that we didn't see more differences, especially in the boys' reading of "My Sister's Marriage," to which we now turn.

A Look at "My Sister's Marriage"

As we noted, we selected the stories with an eye toward what we see as conventional beliefs about boys' reading preferences. When we began our study, we shared those beliefs. We expected that the boys would be attracted to the action and the violence in "The White Circle." We thought that they would be engaged with the conflict the narrator of "White Chocolate" has with his teacher. Though we looked hard to find a more action-oriented story than "Marigolds," we thought that the narrator's destruction of the flowers was the kind of dramatic event that might appeal to at least some of our readers. But we thought that "My Sister's Marriage," focusing as it does predominantly on the emotions of two young women, would be a story that most of the boys would reject. In fact, much as was the case with the impulse behind our writing the profile of *Andre* in Chapter 3, we selected the story *in order* to allow the boys to reject it.

While some of the boys did reject it, many more did not. Overall, the boys talked more about "My Sister's Marriage" than they did about any of the other stories, making an average of 12 percent more moves than they did in response to "White Chocolate," 26 percent more than they did in response to "Marigolds," and 29 percent more than they did in response to "The White Circle."

For some of the boys, most notably Johnny and Robert, the story was appealing because they saw it as more wholesome than the others. Both of these young men dismissed the narrator of "White Chocolate" for disrespecting his teacher and praised the girls in "My Sister's Marriage" for taking care of their father. Either they did not pick up on the psychosexual implications of the girls' competition for their father's affection, or they ignored it. Geo enjoyed the story because the father was "mad phat" because of how smoothly accomplished he was. Other responses were less idiosyncratic.

Some of the boys seemed to enjoy the complexity of the story, the psychological puzzle it presented. Mark, whose comment about "girlie books" we cited earlier, began his protocol dismissively:

> I don't know what this girl is talking about. She's talking about her sister and all kinds of other weird stuff. I don't like this. Hopefully she gets into the story eventually.

But by the end of the story he was clearly engaged, though he admits being so only begrudgingly:

> This girl's got a lot of sadness. Her father never paid attention to her. And then the way her father told her not to hide anything—now he's hiding things. I think the whole family is just really crazy. After the mother died, he's like using his daughters as his wife and stuff. Then the one girl runs away and he doesn't even want to meet the husband, and there's all kinds of deception and plot twists. I guess the story was OK; I didn't like it particularly, but I guess it was all right. It was kind of weird; I guess I like that part of it. It's sort of like a mystery I guess. Sarah Ann—

she's kind of weird. I guess I like this story for the most part. It's kind of neat the way everything twisted around. That's about it.

The boys' interest in the psychology of the characters was much more common. Joe pronounced near the beginning of the protocol that the story was "lame" and that "I am not used to reading stories about girls either." Throughout his protocol, he counted the number of pages he had left. But by the end of the story, almost despite himself, he evidenced a kind of engagement:

> OK, this story is just getting weirder and weirder. Personally I shouldn't say that, but I don't know, she was just getting married. I don't—her father seemed like the type of guy that would understand, and I don't know why she had to keep it a secret. So the father is mean.

The boys' anger with the father's attempts to control his daughters marked their readings. At one point in the story, after the narrator's sister had called to tell her father of her marriage, he turned to the narrator and said, "Would you have done this to me, Sarah Ann? Would you have done it?" Upon reading that section, Wolf could hardly contain himself:

> Oh, that is crap. "Would you have done this to me?" Do you know how much crap that is? He's putting Sarah Ann through a lot of shit doing that. It's a psychological ploy right there.

Chris took on an information-driven orientation for three of his protocols, but not for his response to "My Sister's Marriage." Here are his final remarks:

> That was deep. I think that he was wrong to just take them and claim that he was going to burn them and he didn't. And I think it was wrong of her to burn them because that was like burning all the essence that he actually didn't have a daughter left. And I don't know, I think that he was too dependent on Sarah Ann, and I think she was too dependent on what he thought about her. When he was to die, she would be lonely and she's saying that she didn't necessarily hate Olive but she was still jealous, I think, that [Olive] found a love for someone or another to have last with her forever and that she had just got her father. It's sort of like leftovers, but I don't know, I think it was wrong for both of them. And I think that her father should understand that sometimes you do fall in love at first sight. But I guess he was too set in his ways and so was Olive and so was Sarah Ann, because Sarah Ann didn't want Olive to have her father have more love for Olive than to her and she always wanted that. And I think that Olive was always looking for a reason to get away from her father's love. And I think that her father was looking for a reason to keep Olive as his favorite daughter, and I think that Sarah Ann was jealous of it. I think that, really, they need to get together and talk because it just wasn't

right what happened to them. And one way or another, either Sarah Ann or her father will eventually lose one another, and then who will they have? That's what I think about that story.

Chris seemed to us to go far beyond summary here. And he did so despite the fact that his personal circumstances could hardly have been more different than those of the characters in the story. In fact, while most of the boys tended not to relate the story to their lives (the proportion of relate moves in "My Sister's Marriage" was one third less than for any other story), their lack of relating did not seem to interfere with their desire to respond.

We are not saying that personal relevance isn't important. We discussed the importance of linking boys' reading to their interests in our analysis of the reading logs. Moreover, in this data set we saw a number of boys talk about the importance of relevance to their understanding. But we are saying once again that the picture our data paint is a complex one. Generalizing is once again complicated by the different and surprising responses we received.

Although the picture is complex, it may be hopeful as well. If so many boys could get involved in "My Sister's Marriage" when they read it on their own, we think that even more could be engaged with appropriate instruction—instruction that attends to the conditions of flow experience and that provides assistance in ways of reading that Vygotskian educators would endorse.

What This Make Us Think About: Cultivating Concern for Characters

This chapter makes us ask, *How can we help readers develop relationships with characters?* The importance of relationships was a major theme in both the reading logs and in the protocol study. Our data suggest that when the boys developed relationships with characters, they were far more apt to have positive reading experiences than when they did not.

This isn't a radical idea. We think that many teachers address it through their selection of texts. That is, they seem to feel that if they select texts of high interest, then the relationships will inevitably follow. We don't want to minimize the importance of this effort. As we noted in the first half of this chapter, many of the boys had reading preferences that were seldom met by school. However, some of their preferences were quite surprising. Bam, for example, loved *Of Mice and Men*, but he didn't enjoy texts that his teacher selected even though the teacher believed they would be culturally relevant to him. Moreover, if boys have a characteristic orientation to reading, then changing the materials alone won't be enough to help those boys who tend to do information- and evaluation-driven readings experience the unique and powerful kind of knowing literature provides. Instead we'll have to create contexts that help them enter story worlds and think about the meaning of those story worlds.

When we asked this question, we thought immediately of a presentation we saw at last year's NCTE conference. Betsy Verwys, Jennifer Haberling, and Brian White (2000) shared their ideas on how to help cultivate concern for literary characters. Their work was built on the notion that if students regard literary characters as completely different from them, then it is far easier for these students to dismiss the characters as simply ink on paper rather than as people worthy of their attention and concern. They shared a number of activities they had used to overcome that barrier.

One approach they took was to simulate the conflict that a character faced before students began to read. For example, as a frontloading activity before assigning students to read "The Devil and Tom Walker," they handed students cards that had different priorities written on them: new car, friends, intelligence, and so on. Students first ranked their priorities. Then they had to try to accumulate as many of their top priorities as they could, either by finding classmates with different priorities or by persuading classmates to rethink their priorities. They then wrote about one trade they made that they would never make in real life and one trade they would absolutely make in real life.

Before they devised the activity, when their classes read the story many students responded, "This is stupid. Who makes these kinds of trades?" However, after the frontloading activity was used, students realized that they made trades and that they did so every day. Consequently, rather than dismissing Tom Walker, they regarded him as a fellow human being who faced some of the same issues they faced.

The presenters also developed a series of scenes that raised the same issues as a story (cf. Smagorinsky, McCann, and Kern, 1987). For example, when they assigned a series of texts about discrimination, they developed scenes that detailed different kinds of discrimination and asked students to consider how the character who faced discrimination felt and how that character should respond to the discrimination. Once again seeking to have students make personal connections, they began with scenes that they thought would be immediately relevant: two teenagers followed by a security guard in a mall; a Christian teen who was denied a job because he couldn't work on Sundays (their community is made up overwhelmingly of practicing Christians). But then they moved farther afield: a woman denied a promotion because of her gender; a young man who couldn't try out for a school activity because of his race; and so on. Their scenes, then, were devised to help students provisionally adopt the perspective of the characters, a kind of perspective taking that they encouraged throughout the unit. The students were able to draw on their personal experience, and the sequence assisted them to move from experiences that were closer to their personal experience to those that were further away from it. However, the scenes would not allow them simply to substitute their own personal experience for that of the character.

As part of their work on discrimination, they also addressed the issue of identity. They wanted students to think about three questions: How do we define ourselves? How do others define us? How do we define others who are different from us? They began their work by having students develop a four-panel coat of arms as a visual representation of their identity. Then they talked about what kind of coat of arms the characters they read about would devise for themselves.

The possible permutations of these activities are endless. If, as we would argue, it is also important to cultivate relationships and conversations with authors (a feature of point-driven readings) as well as with characters, students could trade value cards as though they were an author. In determining what trades to make, students would have to think hard about what values authors believed were most important. They could adopt the persona of an author when they responded to a scene: How would Martin Luther King suggest responding to one of the discrimination scenes? Malcolm X? Authors like Mildred Taylor or Walter Dean Myers? What kind of coat of arms would an author choose for a character? And on and on.

As we've noted throughout this book, the young men with whom we worked sought relationships. But, unfortunately, some of them never found relationships through reading, and few of them engaged in relationships with authors, the intelligences that create and communicate through text. We think that with the right instruction they could be helped in doing so.

We'll now turn to the more global implications of our study. But before we do, we'd like to share portraits of four more of our respondents.

Meet the Crew

Barnabas

Aaron

Mike

Marcel

Barnabas

Barnabas, an eleventh grader at the urban school, was one of the very few European Americans there. He had chosen to attend his school's learning community that featured the most traditional academic curriculum because he couldn't bear the thought of having to attend a class for eighty-four minutes, as he would have had to in the other communities, all of which were block-scheduled. He didn't read much for school, but he wondered why all of the reading he did about video and computer games didn't count more. He claimed it was all the reading he could fit into his schedule, which included much socializing and many hours working at a fast-food restaurant.

Collecting data from Barnabas was a chore. He regularly broke appointments and had to be dissuaded from cutting classes to schedule make-ups. And when he did come, he always brought friends along who waited, not so patiently, for him to finish his interviews. He did finally complete all four protocols, though he seemed to race through them and focused primarily on passing judgments on them. But he seemed also to surprise himself by enjoying them, at least a little, especially "White Chocolate," which surprised him because it left the conflict unresolved. In that case, he rushed because he wanted to finish and get on to the next story, but also because he wanted to find out what happens next.

Aaron

Aaron, a twelfth-grade European American, was one of the very best students in our study in terms of high school achievement. He had just applied to MIT and was anxiously waiting to hear whether he had been admitted. He was in AP English. He was one of the seven boys who named himself as a reader in the activity interviews. We expected to see highly elaborated protocols, but we didn't. Aaron seemed to like the stories, but, as he noted in response to "Marigolds," "if it is nice, why mess with it" by talking about it? Aaron seemed to construe making the protocol as schoolish work that would interfere with his enjoyment. Despite his great success in school, schoolish reading was something he did not embrace.

Mike

Mike, a ninth-grade Asian American in the honors track at his suburban high school, wasn't much of a reader outside of school. But he was a serious student who worked hard to get his assignments done. Whatever time that left him, he devoted to his friends and to his trombone and bass guitar. But he did like stories, at least the ones that "hooked" him, as two of the stories did in the study. He said he loved "White Chocolate" because it was "cool" and unlike anything he had read before. He seemed especially interested in the conflict between the narrator and the teacher and extended the story in his mind to create something of a happy ending. "Marigolds" hooked him as well. As he explained in his final remarks, "The descriptions were what got me hooked. The connections between all these things: the time, the characters, events. I loved it. It was pretty cool." Reading can be cool for Mike, it seems, but not cool enough to be something he does outside of school.

Marcel

Marcel was a Puerto Rican eleventh grader in the lower track of the suburban school. One of the most outspoken believers in the importance of school in theory, he was also one of the most resistant to school in practice. At the time of the study he was well on his way to failing English yet again. His protocols gave some insight into why. He rejected "The White Circle" as uninteresting, complaining throughout of his inability to understand it. But he felt much more positively about "White Chocolate." He said he understood it better, perhaps "because it kind of relates to me a little bit," especially in the way the narrator rejects school. Upon reading about that rejection, he commented,

> Like I said, I relate to this somewhat. Not like from this school, but from my previous school, especially, and elementary, like in my eighth grade, seventh year, back there, that's how the teachers were, and that's how I had to act sometimes, because I mean, if we were just learning useless stuff, and if it was so important, how come I don't know it now? Because I mean, the only things I remember are the fun things, and that's what I remember.

His English teacher made every attempt to choose relevant texts and to teach them with engaging activities, but for Marcel, the line between school and reading on the one hand, and his enjoyment in life on the other, was a hard one. He had drawn that line years before, and he wasn't willing to cross it now.

We've talked throughout the book about how our data give us some reason to be hopeful. But as we see in these four portraits, they also present a real challenge. In our final chapter, therefore, we won't be offering easy answers. Instead, we will try to share the directions in which the study's complex findings point us as teachers and teacher educators.

A Profound Challenge

IMPLICATIONS FOR CLASSROOM PRACTICE

Oh, the mornings that we have spent an extra five minutes in the shower, breathing in the steam and worrying about the day ahead. Or stayed awake late into the night considering how to deal with the escalating recalcitrance of a student not unlike Rev or Marcel. The problems that kept us awake usually involved particular kids, often boys, who were overtly resistant to our classes. So we lingered in the shower or stayed awake, considering how to invite these students into the classroom community and engage them in some of the work we thought was so important—and they obviously did not.

The findings from our study would have helped us in those earlier efforts. Even more important, we believe that our findings offer a profound challenge to the most prevalent forms of teaching and of organizing curricula. We say profound because our data indicate that the young men in our study would benefit if teaching in American schools were changed in fundamental ways.

As well, our data challenge or complicate commonsense understandings of boys and their literacy. Yet the difficulty of enacting the kind of changes we feel our data cry out for has been documented (e.g., Zeichner and Tabachnick, 1981).

We began our study wondering whether the category of "boys" is useful to think with. After all of our research, we can offer only an equivocal answer: yes and no. As we noted throughout, the theory of flow experiences helped us understand all of our data, but if Csikszentmihalyi (1990a, 1990b) is right, it would be equally explanatory for girls. As well, while the boys in our study consistently spoke of the importance of competence and control, the need for an appropriate level of challenge, the desire for clear and immediate feedback, the enjoyment of losing themselves in the immediate experience, and the importance of the social, at the same time, the boys were very different. They had different values, interests, and goals. Consequently we're wary of lumping them together in a category called "boys," and we're suspicious of research that homogenizes them.

But as we said at the outset of our book, we did this research with a teacher's eye. We asked ourselves whether our findings would give us something to go on in planning curricula and instruction. And we think they do. We think we can proceed believing in the absolute centrality of social relations

in the lives of our male students. We think we can proceed with the understanding that most boys recognize the importance of school and of literacy,
at least in theory. We think we can proceed with the understanding that they
have had meaningful transactions with a wide variety of texts, though it's unlikely that those texts are the kinds of short stories and novels traditionally
taught in school. We think we can proceed on the belief that many of them
draw a hard line between school and home and that their school lives have
featured more procedural than substantive engagement (Nystrand, 1997),
meaning that they usually just go through the motions to get the work done
with minimal effort rather than engaging deeply with ideas and ways of doing
things.

Recognizing these starting points doesn't relieve us of the obligation to
fulfill our end of the social contract our students expect from us (see Chapter 4). We still have to get to know them as individuals. But it does give us a
place to start in thinking about how to do a better job of teaching boys (and
maybe girls as well). Instead of identifying their achievements and needs
through statistical averages in which their differences are lost, we need to
recognize and work with individual difference, variety, and plurality and make
that diversity a strength of our classroom.

Implications for Teaching

Throughout the book, we've discussed a number of instructional implications
that were suggested to us.

To begin, we want to look at the more global instructional implications
of our work. We do so cautiously, mindful of an argument made by Purves in
a symposium on the usefulness of literacy research (Saks, 1995). In that symposium, Purves questioned the value of much literacy education research. He
argued that too often research is undertaken simply to advance a professional
agenda rather than to make a difference in teaching and learning. He also
claimed that as a consequence, researchers make overblown claims, minimize
and misrepresent the work of other researchers, develop general instructional
prescriptions that are insensitive to the nuances of human behavior, and
oversimplify the messiness and complexity of teaching and learning.

We want the research we have undertaken on boys and literacy to matter. It has already affected our thinking and teaching deeply, and we hope
that through us it has affected the thinking of the teachers and prospective
teachers with whom we work. In this chapter we will explore some of the key
implications of our research, taking care to avoid the oversimplifying of which

Purves speaks. Some of the implications drawn from the data are comforting to us as teachers, as they support work we've done in the past. But some are discomfitting, as they challenge us to move in new directions. The data, in fact, challenge us to rethink our answers to the most fundamental questions we ask as teachers: Why do we teach? What do we teach? How do we teach?

Why Do We Teach?

Rethinking Our Goals

We always ask preservice teachers to try to clarify their goals for teaching, often by posing "Would you rather?" questions. Here are a few we have used:

- Would you rather your students read the newspaper every day OR a novel once a month?
- Would you rather your students read lots of a series like Animorphs OR a very occasional Newbery winner?
- Would you rather your students always did their homework but rarely read for enjoyment OR that they often read for enjoyment but often did not do their homework?

Of course, none of the questions have to be either/or propositions, but we craft them in this way to provoke our students' thinking. The questions always spark a lively discussion, which we do our best to stay out of.

But if we face the questions and others like them honestly, we realize that both of us tend to come down on the side of schoolish answers. We've devoted much of our professional lives to thinking and writing about ways to make academic literacies more accessible to more kids. We have tended not to question the primacy of literature in English/Language Arts curricula. *However, the research we have reported here is pushing us to do just that.*

Although our data provide testimony to the power of canonical literature to provoke an in-depth exploration of important moral issues for some students, our data also provide evidence of the value of being willing and able to read an instruction manual, of being able to ascertain what's worth reading by thumbing through the pictures in a magazine, of being able to figure out a whodunit when watching a suspense movie. The list could go on. Our study has made our schoolish answers to the "Would you rather" questions problematic for us. The stories we've told here of boys who saw school literacy narrowly, who were seen by teachers as nonreaders, and who sometimes even defined themselves as nonreaders (although they pursued literacy with popular cultural texts in very constructive and engaged ways) call into question the very definition we have given to literacy.

It seems to us that we need to redefine literacy in semiotic terms. Semiotics is the study of all meaning-making signs. Such a redefinition would include the ability to communicate and make meaning with various sign systems, such as music, video, visual arts, and electronic technologies, and would build on the interconnections among various forms of literacy. Redefining literacy in semiotic terms will help us offer more choices and explore the meanings of different kinds of texts with particular powers to engage and express. It will also recognize and celebrate both who the boys are and the literacies they currently practice, which will allow them to see themselves and what they see as important in the classroom. At the same time, it may offer opportunities to build on boys' strengths and interests in popular culture and media literacies as a way to develop more traditional forms of literacy. Finally, conceiving of literacy more widely will help us prepare students for a modern world that uses a profusion of multimedia signs. As the classics scholar Jay David Bolter (1991) asserts, those who do not read and compose hypermedia are already illiterate by the historical standards of literacy. Our work has caused us to wonder how we, both personally and as a profession, have taken school definitions of what counts as literacy so much for granted when this definition excludes so much of what passes for literate activity in the world.

The Question of Caring

Our data have also pointed out a profound difficulty we face as teacher educators. George Hillocks (1995), a man who has had a powerful influence on both of us, points out that teaching is a transitive verb. Specifying a different direct object changes the nature of the activity considerably. In our work with preservice teachers, we've found that they tend to construct their role as teachers in one of two ways:

> I teach English (or literature or reading).
> I teach kids.

Similarly, during a recent conversation with colleagues, we found that some teachers took the position implied by making the English (or the equivalent) the direct object. "My job is to teach my subject. To give kids the information they need," one of the teachers in the group intoned. Another teacher argued, "I'm not the school counselor and I'm not trained as a counselor. I love English and I teach English. I didn't sign up for any more than that." But others took the opposite position, arguing that you can't teach a subject until you have reached your kids, that caring and connecting are necessary prerequisites for any meaningful instruction.

Our data have helped us understand that neither formulation would be enough for our participants. To be sure, they wanted teachers to recognize them as individuals and to be concerned for them, the kind of orientation suggested by the statement "I teach kids." But at the same time, they wanted to be taught something. They valued literacy and wanted to become more competent in it. They have helped us see that the best way we can care for them is to use what we learn about them to help them develop the attitudes and abilities that will both prepare them for success in the future and provide pleasure in the present. We've come to see that our goal ought to be to teach English to kids or to teach kids English.

These goals may have slightly different emphases, but *both* recognize that we have to know both our students and our subject. And as our work in this project has taught us, in seeking to know our students, we become students ourselves. Our boys taught us about themselves. They taught us much about what it means to be literate in different contexts. They taught us what it is like to be adolescents at this moment in time, something we can only learn about from them. They taught us what it is about activities that make them worth doing. They taught us about teaching and learning. They taught us about the importance of developing relationships. And they taught us that we must be alert to their evolving views, attitudes, and perspectives.

Like a basketball player who must adjust to the changing dynamics of a game or a traveler abroad who must not only phrase her questions in a foreign language but understand and respond to the answer, our boys taught us that we can teach best by teaching responsively. They taught us that we need to attend to our students and how they are learning. We must make adjustments and change our strategy as needed. We must teach as if we are surfing on the crest of the future's breaking wave.

What the boys taught us is troubling for us as teacher educators. We can teach our students how to make lessons and units and how to implement the plans they develop. We can encourage them to respond to evolving needs and changing situations. But we can't teach them how to "noodle" (Lopate, 1975, cited in Gere et al., 1992) around with kids during the passing periods or notice and remember the musical artists adorning their T-shirts. We can't teach them to care, even though doing so seems to be a prerequisite for fulfilling the social contract the boys described.

What Do We Teach?

Our study has raised questions for us about *what* we should teach. But it has also given strong support for a position we have both long taken: we need to engage students in thinking through ideas that matter to them—as Robert liked to say—in the "here and now."

We saw the motivating power of purpose and interest for boys in their out-of-school literacy. Wolf pursued his interest in psychology as he grappled with the question of what makes people evil. Mick struggled to read magazines so he could make a car go faster. Drake read and consulted widely in his quest to refurbish a vintage motorcycle. Buster inquired into the strength of materials and various design features to choose the best mountain bike and to think about designing his own. Rev read widely, rented videos, and watched the History and Discovery channels to pursue inquiry into interests he had in archaeology and philosophy that had no connection to school. Ricardo scoured the Internet and trade magazines to find out about future movie releases and to keep track of his favorite directors.

On the surface, these might seem to be radically different pursuits, but we don't think they are, for in all of these cases, the boys were motivated to learn because they wanted to solve a real problem. Perhaps the single most significant implication our work raised for us is the importance of creating contexts that encourage problem solving. Because we think problem solving is crucially important, we want to spend some time talking about how it might be done.

The Power of Inquiry

One way to encourage the kind of problem solving the boys found so motivating is to structure units around critical questions so that students' reading and writing can be in service of genuine inquiry. That's what motivated most of the boys' literate activity outside school, whether they were reading newspapers or magazines or electronic texts. (It's also what motivates our own reading and work, including all that we did to pursue this study.)

One reason reading literature is so compelling, both to us and to the committed readers in our study, is that we use it as a form of inquiry. Through literature, we think about issues that matter to us while we are engaged with characters whom we come to know and care about.

By expanding the kinds of texts that students read and by placing the study of literature in an inquiry framework, we can address the complaint expressed so eloquently by Rev that "English is about nothing." Through inquiry—the process of gathering and developing information, analyzing it, and organizing it in an effort to "figure out" or deepen understanding about a contested issue—reading can become the means through which students converse with authors about the vital human concerns we all (adolescent boys included) share.

A inquiry frame also provides a meaningful and immediate context in which to teach strategies, concepts, and textual knowledge that we have privileged as a profession. In an inquiry context, this knowledge is immediately situated and applicable. And our data compel us to believe that inquiry will be embraced and used by the students in ways they do not typically embrace and use school literacy.

In every case where true inquiry environments were introduced in school in place of asking students to report on what the teacher already knew, they were embraced. Huey and Guy, two of the more disengaged students, spoke at great length about their interest in and enjoyment of their bridge-building project, in which they experimented with and tested different bridge designs. The inquiry-oriented history class at one of the high schools was identified as their most engaging class by the students who had taken it. These students passionately described projects such as investigating and dramatizing Supreme Court cases in the roles of justices, and participating in "What If?" scenarios to explore what the present might have been like if those decisions had been different.

Organizing literacy curricula around inquiry has received much recent interest. Hillocks (1999) makes the case that reading and writing are forms of inquiry and are best taught in contexts of inquiry. Beach and Myers (2001) argue that students engage more deeply with literacy when they use it to inquire into issues connected to their own lives. Smagorinsky (2002) bases his work on developing instruction in large measure on the belief that *"people learn by making, and reflecting on, things they find useful and important"* (p. vi, emphasis in the original). These researchers critique traditional forms of literacy instruction as being disconnected from students' immediate interests and the demands of their lives. They offer inquiry (though they may name it differently) as an alternative that helps students see that various social worlds and the concepts within these worlds are socially constructed through multiple literacies, languages, and texts. These concepts and ways of doing things are therefore open to examination, critique, and transformation.

Designing Inquiry Units
All inquiry begins with a problem and a question. The nature of the question (or questions) can vary widely. When Jeff and his team-teaching partner

Paul Friedemann pursued inquiry with seventh-grade students, many of whom were labeled as at-risk, they organized the curricula around *contact zones*. According to Pratt (1991, see also Bizzell, 1984) contact zones are geographical spaces where different perspectives come into conflict and are competing for supremacy. For example, colonial America was a space where the views and interests of Native Americans, the British, the French, and various groups of colonists competed for supremacy.

We think her idea can be extended to intellectual spaces as well. The central questions asked in such units include the following: What voices were most clearly heard and why? What voices were silenced and why? What voices ought to have been heard and why?

A wide range of readings helped students consider these questions. An environmental saga like *Cod: A Biography of the Fish That Changed the World* could be coupled with folktales and fiction about Maine coastal life as well as with a whole range of informational texts. The boys' arguments for the importance of including multiple perspectives and their resistance at being told what to think suggests why such a contact zone inquiry is engaging.

As Fecho (2001) points out, teaching such a unit brings with it some risks, because questions that matter are deeply felt. But we believe with him that the risks are well worth taking, particularly when we compare the risk of emotional engagement to the risks of the complete disengagement that we repeatedly witnessed during our study.

Many very different questions could work as well. What does it mean to be mature? What counts as success? What makes a good parent? How, if at all, have the roles of women changed in popular culture? When is disobeying a law justified? What causes readers to respond to stories in different ways? And on and on and on.

Once the teacher, class, or small group of students selects a question, the inquiry begins. The next step is to read widely. (See our description in Chapter 3 of the unit Jeff built around the question *What are the costs and benefits of the American emphasis on sports?*) Most important questions have been addressed by a variety of writers, so students can access the Internet; check out magazines, newspapers, television shows, and so on; and read relevant literature. With each new reading comes a new perspective that students have to contend with.

In fact, inquiry units force students to cope with conflicts within and between the various social worlds they inhabit. For example, Flower, Long, and Higgins (2000) discuss pursuing "intercultural inquiry" as a way of developing literacy strategies in a context that is immediately meaningful. In intercultural inquiry, students explore differences between each other's cultural beliefs and expectations regarding gender, class, race, and other issues. Their research indicates that when students inquire into "rival hypotheses" or competing claims about the world and how it should work, they were highly engaged and learned to recognize, interrogate, and more deeply understand various perceptions and constructions of the world, including their own. Wells' (1999) very similar work with *dialogic inquiry* reached the same conclusions.

The culminating event of inquiry units is for students to display their position by creating some kind of artifact. Research in educational psychology (cf. Lehrer, 1993) has established that learning is not internalized or owned by students until it is reorganized, transformed, and represented in a new set of signs that is the students' own. They will not achieve deep understanding until this kind of "transformation" or "transmediation" has occurred. The knowledge artifact could be a piece of writing, a hypermedia stack, a poster, a video, a musical composition—anything that clearly communicates their position on the question. Inquiry units, then, encourage students to become both critical consumers of a wide variety of texts and informed producers of them for the purpose of staking out a position in a meaningful conversation.

Inquiry and Flow

Although we have advocated units of this sort throughout our careers, our work on this project has helped us better account for their power, for inquiry units work to create the conditions of flow experience that the boys found so compelling. First, inquiry necessitates *a sense of competence and control.* In inquiry units, teachers can help students develop competence because students will have extended experiences pursuing the issue in question. That means what students learn as they read one text can be applied when they read the next. Moreover, when students have a stake in using texts to grapple with a question that matters, they'll be very motivated to learn the reading strategies, search techniques, or data collection tools they need.

The topic of inquiry can be negotiated with students. But even if the teacher or curriculum determines the topic of inquiry, students will still be able to make choices about how to approach their inquiry, what to make of what has been learned, what position to take on the issue (since issues always have multiple perspectives), how to present findings to others, and what kind of social action should be taken as a result of a position.

Inquiry also provides *a challenge that requires an appropriate level of skill,* because any rich topic about a contested issue can provide many possible questions and many levels of research. Students can choose a subtopic that interests them and pursue it by reading whatever texts are available that are appropriately challenging. In this way, everyone in a class can be working at an appropriate level of skill and still be involved in the democratic classroom project of exploring and teaching each other about their various findings around the common issue. (See Wilhelm and Friedemann, 1998; Wilhelm, Baker, Dube, 2001.)

Students are motivated to learn because the learning is contextualized in a situation that provides *clear goals and feedback*. The students in an inquiry classroom need to know certain things to pursue and conclude their inquiries, so they can represent and share what they have learned. Feedback is provided continuously as they see to what degree they have understood the multiple perspectives around the issue and to what degree they are ready to stake their own position.

This kind of sharing ties into the theme of *the importance of the social*. Inquiry is best conducted in groups for the purposes of informing and convincing others. In inquiry situations, students learn literacy strategies and practices with a variety of different texts through active participation in what Tharp and Gallimore (1988) call "joint productive activities." In these activities, a community works together in complementary ways to reach a common goal, instead of working individually and in isolation from real-world concerns. Moreover, because inquiry results in taking a public stance and creating an artifact to represent that stance, it makes students' learning visible and accountable to the classroom community in ways traditional instruction does not.

All of these factors together suggest that in inquiry units students will *focus on the immediate experience*. To be sure, they'll be gaining skills, strategies, and knowledge they can apply in the future. But they'll be gaining them in the healthy work of the present.

How Inquiry Challenges the Traditional
Conducting inquiries of the sort we have described here takes time. Although this works for the boys' desire for competence, sustained engagement, and in-depth explorations of ideas, it also works against much current curricula and the current reform and testing movements with their push for the coverage of information. The conditions of flow require that we reconceive how time is used and spent in schools.

Inquiry also shifts literacy curricula from the traditional "teacher/information-centered" model, the aim of which is to transmit information, and it goes well beyond a "student-centered model" of natural discovery. Instead, it provides "learning-centered model," which aims to capitalize on the expertise that students bring with them to class, and to teach them what we know as more experienced readers and writers so they can become more expert in ways of reading, writing, and thinking that are valued in the classroom and the workplace. (See Wilhelm, Baker, and Dube, 2001, for a full discussion of these competing models of teaching and learning.)

Inquiry-based instruction also challenges the prevalence of the "literalist" model of instruction (Seitz, 1999, cited in Beach and Myers, 2001), which focuses on "conveying literal information or stated positions." Instead, inquiry-based instruction encourages adopting a "metaphoric" model that "emphasizes the uses and practices of language in constructing meaning" (p. 7). The learning-centered or metaphoric approach helps students learn about the power that texts have and work that texts can do. This approach emphasizes learning ways to negotiate and invent meanings around crucial issues and leads to using language to take action around these issues. In these cases, language is part of meaningful and transformative project as we saw in our discussion in Chapter 2 of Jeff's unit on the impact of sports.

How These Findings Challenge Us

Our research has not only supported our advocacy of inquiry-based instruction, but it has also challenged the way we have enacted it in the past. The boys' emphasis on the importance of choice has helped us understand that we could have done more to negotiate inquiry topics with our students rather than choose them ourselves, as was our tendency. We argued in Chapter 4 that because the boys saw reading and writing as schoolish activities, they seemed not to have their own critical standards for judging their work. Rather, they waited to see their grade before they were willing to say how they did. We think now that we should have done more to develop grading criteria with students, particularly with regard to the culminating activities of the units. This seems especially important because we have learned just how much more than us many of the boys know about alternative ways of representing their ideas (e.g., through music or computers).

We realize that we have given just a brief description of what we see as an important implication, but we hope that we've been sufficiently persuasive about the power of inquiry that readers will seek out other sources that more fully describe how teachers can create inquiry-based classrooms. One place to start would be *Strategic Reading: Guiding Students to Lifelong Literacy* in which Jeff and his colleagues Tanya Baker and Julie Dube discuss inquiry units drawing on research that Michael and others have done. In making this recommendation we are aware that we run the risk of opening ourselves to

Purves's critique that educational research is done simply to advance a professional agenda. We hope, though, that readers can see how our data have led us to make this recommendation.

The Selection of Texts

Whether text selection occurs within an inquiry unit or a more traditional classroom, the question of who gets to choose what kind of texts has a profound impact on the resulting instruction. Our data have opened our eyes to new ways of thinking about selecting texts.

Why Literature?

Although our longstanding belief in the importance of inquiry-based units was supported (though the way we have enacted that belief must now be critiqued and revised), almost all of our thinking about the selection of texts has been challenged. We've already discussed how our data have caused us to question whether preparing students to read literature ought to be our primary goal. That questioning has brought with it questions about the primacy of what are traditionally considered to be "literary" texts, or at least questions about the definition of what constitutes the "literary."

For example, the question of what counts as success in our culture, an important question to the boys in our study, is a major theme in canonical literature. Michael developed a unit on that question that included such texts as *The Autobiography of Benjamin Franklin* and *The Great Gatsby*. Our work with the boys has caused us to reflect that this theme is also clearly at play in newspaper accounts of dot.com entrepreneurs, in rappers' dueling over their preeminence, and in movies such as *American Beauty*. Michael has advocated using nonliterary texts as a bridge to reading literature, but he has not advocated giving nonliterary texts the same status in the classroom. While our discussion about the importance of story and many of the boys' surprising engagement in the protocols suggest that literature could be appealing to the young men in our study, we also saw that their reading was dominated by more information-oriented texts, such as newspapers and magazines. Given the boys' repeated statements about the importance of feeling competent, perhaps these more familiar text types should play a more important role.

How Hard Is Too Hard?

Another challenge our data raised for us is how to balance the importance of competence with the importance of an appropriate level of challenge. Maybe some texts are just too hard for too many boys for them to be worth teaching.

Our daughters' elementary school teachers have taught them the "five-finger" rule. When they pick up a new book, they open to a page at random and begin reading. When they encounter a word they don't know, they raise a finger. If five fingers are up before they finish the page, they seek out another book. In this way, they can bypass texts that will frustrate them. Some of our seventh graders still used that tool.

Oh, but how things change in senior high, when difficult texts are the curricular norm. The difficulties the boys faced included much more than vocabulary. As Rabinowitz (1987) points out, schools canonize texts that allow readers to provide nuanced interpretations. Schools value identifying motifs much more than they value solving mysteries. Texts that are densely detailed and subtle are more prestigious than those whose joy or anger are more overt.

We have worked to devise ways to teach the texts that are privileged in school more effectively. Our data are causing us to wonder whether we should spend more time thinking about whether they should be taught. We see from our data that if boys are not first engaged emotionally with texts—if they do not care about the characters and issues presented—then they will never proceed to more nuanced readings. In the past, we chose texts that were more complex and that required nuanced readings at the expense of addressing students' immediate needs and possibilities for emotional engagement.

For example, our research leads us to ask why it is important to read *The House on Mango Street*, a book that left a number of our boys in the dark. We wonder how our selection of texts could better capitalize on the boys' desire for competence and their desire to figure things out and apply what they have learned. We wonder how we can build on boys' current interests to help them outgrow their current selves.

The inquiry environments we already discussed may begin to provide an answer. *The House on Mango Street* may be important to read when pursuing certain kinds of inquiry into cultural experiences or into the influence of our past experience and social worlds on our current understandings. If we are to ask our students to read difficult and highly nuanced texts, we should take care to do so in contexts that help provide both understanding and enjoyment. After all, a number of the boys told us they were willing to read and learn from texts that were quite challenging IF they were interested in the topic or had a functional reason to use what they were learning. The kind of interest and purpose that can be cultivated through inquiry-based units will encourage students to tackle difficult texts that they might otherwise reject.

How Long Is Too Long?

In our experience, many curricula are built around particular texts, and these texts are almost always novels or long plays. One of our key findings is that ALL of the young men with whom we worked were readers even though only seven named themselves as readers in a conventional sense, the kind of reader who regularly sought out books to read for enjoyment. The other readers gravitated to shorter texts, especially those in magazines. We've already talked about expanding the range of texts appropriate for study, but the boys' interest in shorter texts has caused us to question the dominance of novels in literature curricula. Shorter texts allow more perspectives to be brought into class, something the boys valued. A number of the boys told us they experienced short pieces as less daunting and more enjoyable. We're not saying that novels and long plays should not be taught, but our data have helped us realize that we have not always been aware of the potential costs of teaching them.

Where's the Laughter?

When we asked students if they had ever read anything funny in school, we received a resounding no for an answer. That's too bad, for as many of our boys' reading and viewing habits made clear, humor helps people lose themselves in the enjoyment of the immediate experience. Many times during the study we asked ourselves, *Why didn't we assign anything funny? Why didn't we engage in more activities to promote humor?* The possibilities for using cartoons to teach text structure or conventions such as irony, for using *Seinfeld* episodes to explore various critical lenses to understand social issues, for providing students the opportunity to talk back and make fun of authors and texts through comedy routines, for simply using humor to engage them with ideas seems full of promise. And this offers a strong challenge to the seriousness of our previous teaching and the seriousness of the texts we typically assigned.

There is also the documented importance of fun to consider. Bloom's (1985) studies of how talent is developed indicate that having fun in the introductory phases of learning an activity is of paramount importance to sustained interest, engagement, and the eventual development of expertise. As Hillocks (1995) puts it, "Perhaps the most important principle in designing and sequencing [instruction] is to ensure that the students enjoy doing the work" (p. 180).

Csikszentmihalyi, Rathunde, and Whalen (1993) studied examples of students who were engaged in various activities such as academics, athletics, and the arts. The top reasons they gave for their engagement were: (1) "I enjoy it"; (2) "I get satisfaction from getting better or from learning"; and (3) "It is interesting to me" (p. 138).

Our informants loved sustained projects that were significant and that engaged them over time, and virtually all of them professed to enjoy activities that involved game-like structures, such as debates and dramas, which were also social, active, engaging, and fun. Our data encourage us to have more fun with our students and to read more material that is humorous.

Whose Choice Is It?

The centrality of choice also challenges our past practices. Our data have convinced us that we provided too few ways for our students to make choices. By far the most prevalent piece of advice our boys offered to teachers was to give students choices.

We believe that we need to work harder to provide options and choices regarding curricular content and the way that content is pursued in class. We need to work harder to help students see what their options are so they can make meaningful choices. To do so, we need to know more about young adult literature and popular culture texts, something that we can learn through relationships with our students.

Other ways to incorporate choice are to provide free time to read in the classroom or to incorporate literature circles and book clubs in which students choose books that will help them pursue inquiry questions of interest or follow authors or ideas they have come to know about. Even when the boys had only a limited choice, such as the chance to select a book from among several suggested by a teacher or to select one of several topics upon which to write, they embraced the opportunity to exercise some freedom, explore possibility, pursue interests, and assert their own identity.

Seeing that the invitation the boys received to pursue home literacy was so appealing and broad (particularly when compared to the weak invitation offered by school forms of literacy) made us ask how can we use this to our advantage. The data have helped us understand that one of the features of this invitation was the role of choice, so that boys could pursue preexisting or developing interests in ways that made sense to them.

Our data suggest that summer reading programs that offer limited lists of texts and require factually oriented reading tests work against the purposes of control and choice and may very well undermine their purpose of encouraging lifelong reading. We wonder how much more positively a summer reading program would be received if students could read widely in an area of interest (perhaps with some guidelines on the number and kind of texts that students should read) and then document the reading they did in whatever way they chose.

How Do We Teach?

Once again, when we think about this question, our data both support practices we've already advocated and push us in new directions.

The Importance of Frontloading

The boys' insistence on the importance of being competent and on being faced with an appropriate challenge bring home the need to do much of our teaching BEFORE we ask students to read texts. Because particular kinds of texts present a variety of challenges to readers, we must activate our students' background knowledge and help them build procedural knowledge of how to recognize and meet the expectations the particular text type requires. As we noted in Chapter 4, many of the boys had difficulties when they encountered new text types. For example, the most consistent difficulty the boys had in responding to the four protocol stories was their failure to see the symbolic significance of the marigolds in "Marigolds." Prereading activities in which students first work with common symbols and then move to familiar texts—both written (e.g., fables) and visual (e.g., horror movies)—would heighten their attention to how symbolism works and how they can recognize and interpret symbolism. Helping them apply this interpretive knowledge in their reading would give them a chance for a more complete, competent, and satisfying reading.

As another example, a novel told through letters or diaries requires readers to write what Eco (1979) calls *ghost chapters*, in which they work to fill in the events that occurred between the dates of the letters or diary entries. Helping students understand that this kind of filling in the blanks is part of the reader's role and providing practice in doing so would make such texts more immediately accessible. For example, students could fill in the "gutters" or spaces between cartoon panels where time has obviously passed.

This kind of frontloading helps students recognize their existing competence and become more competent. It helps them feel up to the challenge that more complex texts provide.

Making Reading Social

As we have noted, one of the most salient themes in our study was the importance of the social. Again and again the boys stressed how working with others provided intrinsic motivation. Their emphasis on the social suggests the importance of pursuing and presenting inquiry projects so that the ideas presented can be taught to each other, shared, argued over, and critiqued. It shows how group structures such as literary letter exchanges, book clubs, literature circles, cooperative learning groups, reading buddies, reciprocal reading groups, and others can provide motivation and assistance to students.

The importance of the social is something we will always keep in mind during our future planning and teaching. The boys' home literacy, which was so eagerly embraced, was always social, contextualized, and enmeshed deeply with significant relationships. We need to use group structures and projects and to emphasize sharing and group problem solving throughout our teaching.

Literacies grow out of relationships—whether these are teacher to student, student to student, parent to child, or mentor to mentee. While researching the lives of highly creative individuals, John-Steiner (1985) found that at young ages they had been introduced to particular activities, texts, and ways of doing things through relationship with significant others that profoundly influenced their future lives and work:

> [I]n all fields, the personal interest of a caring and knowledgeable adult is critical, just as it is in encouraging youngsters to reach their potential. (p. 37)

John-Steiner posits that the relational activities these people engaged in

> depict for us the ways in which they were filling up, in their youth, some invisible notebooks in their minds. . . . The shape of their more conscious efforts cannot be determined at such an early stage, but in their youth they collect some of the raw material they will draw on later. (p. 42)

Thus far in our discussion of how we teach we've shared ways that our data support work we've previously done. And we'll confess that we felt pretty good about that support. But the clear value that the boys placed on home connections—and the extent to which connections with parents inform the activities they most enjoy—challenge us to do more to develop the home-school connection.

Our data push us to think about ways to tap the *funds of knowledge* (Moll, 1992) that exist in students' homes. In a recent classroom observation, Michael saw Jennifer Saniscalchi work with her eleventh-grade students on reading *Pygmalian.* Her classroom was very diverse both culturally and economically. Students were reporting on interviews they had done with significant others, usually parents but occasionally siblings. Some students interviewed their parents on the way language is used to stratify society. Immigrant parents shared stories with the children about their experiences with discrimination because of the way they used language. Other students interviewed their parents about the extent to which they had had to conform to conventional expectations to succeed in the business world.

In this class, home became a valuable resource for students' developing insights into the characters in the play and the politics of the play. Students were highly motivated. They saw why the reading they were doing mattered. Such teaching breaks down the clear divide that so many of our boys saw between home and school. Our research has drawn our attention much more forcefully to the importance of tapping the funds of knowledge that students have at home, an instructional strategy that both of us have neglected.

Through the two years it took us to complete this study, we have come to feel quite passionate about the impact the implications of our findings could have for the boys we studied and other boys like them. In our final sections, we want to consider the impact making changes to our teaching could have on boys who are suffering to various degrees from the way school typically works, and to recognize the challenge that making such changes will exact from us.

Meet the Crew and Just Imagine

We believe that many of our boys could benefit from the recommendations for transformed practice provided in this chapter.

Joe

Joe was a European American seventh grader from the rural school who loved computers but hated the computer projects in school. He perceived these projects as "busywork" because the topics were assigned and the design of the final products was predetermined. He also rejected these projects because they were "so basic," not challenging him by making use of or extending his already considerable computer skills. He noted, "It would be fun to make something cool or do something of your own, but it is uncool to just fill in the blanks and do what the teacher tells you, which I already knew already."

Joe read on the Internet and returned to his favorite sites, like Stickmen, that use emergent systems programming. Yet he rejected schoolwork and school reading. Joe was clearly bright and had the highest standardized test scores in his school in math, but he hated reading. He refused to participate in classes or discuss issues in school. His handwritten reading journal in his English class was illegible and incoherent, yet he refused to do the journal on the computer. He also refused to keep the journal for this study on his computer, indicating that he only liked to use the computer for challenging things, which he necessarily had to pursue on his own. He perceived school as being "fake." He presented a totally passive but noncompliant, exhausted, and bored demeanor to his teacher and classmates.

Let's just imagine, what would happen if Joe were allowed the choice to negotiate an inquiry topic about an issue he was interested in, one that helped him communicate and stake out his identity in ways not typically allowed in school. What if he were helped to create his own emergent systems program with a program like StarLogo (something his teacher was capable of teaching him) to test out hypotheses about future outcomes of issues surrounding the environment or overpopulation—issues that would marry his interests and his math and computer skills to literacy? And if he were in a class with a less computer-literate teacher what would happen if he were allowed to develop and showcase his computer skills, teaching his teacher and his classmates in the process, instead of "wasting time" doing perfunctory assignments that he already knew how to do? We suspect that Joe's negative attitude toward school and his passive resistance could be transformed.

Rev

Then there was Rev, a European American eleventh grader from the rural school, who hated school so much he maintained that it depressed him to attend. He went to great pains to leave school early, taking a job in a university cafeteria and taking university classes part-time to fulfill his graduation requirements. He dismissed school, and English in particular, as being about "nothing." Yet he loved history, read widely in archaeology, watched the Discovery and History channels on television, wrote and discussed philosophy, and wrote music in a different style for each of the three different bands of which he was a member. He had very high critical standards for the scoring and the performance of these pieces, often spending extended time revising his compositions and rehearsing. He also sometimes critiqued his band members' lack of commitment to quality performances. He maintained that his songs were "always political" and were written to "express my philosophies" and "to wake people up." He argued that his peer group, and their popular culture (including their music), were "vapid" and "asleep."

Here was a young man who was smart, who loved ideas, and who used various sign systems such as words and music to create meaning and make political commentaries. He was passionate about real-world issues such as the environment and politics, but school was so "dead" that he saw no way to engage with it meaningfully. What would happen if we helped him inquire more deeply into issues that already concerned him? What if he were confronted with opposing points of view, encouraged to wrestle with rival hypotheses, and allowed to compose songs or video documentaries with original music to represent his findings?

Brandon

Brandon was a European American eleventh grader from the private school. He did not understand why school worked the way it did, particularly why he had to do the assignments or readings (e.g., Shakespeare plays) that were required, but he bought in to the nature of school and refused to question or resist it. He said, "I'm not going to sit here with a grudge and not do it!"

Brandon was scrupulous about doing his homework and was dedicated to success at school. And indeed his grades were good and his teachers were happy with his work. But his orientation was to the future, and he saw his current schoolwork as a way to get to college so he could get a job and hence gain the ability to support a family and live the life he wanted. He in no way saw school as having immediate or intrinsic importance.

And though he worked hard, he did not display any of the passion for school that he displayed for the community service project that he had planned, or for baseball, his favorite sport, which he pursued through the school team and throughout two summer leagues. Brandon also resisted required courses in the arts because he didn't see how they would help him achieve his goals of getting into a good college or getting a good job. He was bitter about the time these courses took away from his "real schoolwork."

What would happen if Brandon were allowed to engage in more projects like the one he was doing for community service? What if Brandon saw an intrinsic value to school? Although no teacher would identify Brandon as having a problem, it's also clear that he experienced little enjoyment in what he did. We wonder how much further beyond his current understandings a real substantive engagement could take him.

Robert

Finally, there was Robert, an African American tenth grader who was attending his urban school's alternative learning community. Though he professed not to like reading in English and not to be able to remember even what he had just read, he did assert that he enjoyed reading when people participated together to create drama or discuss important ideas. He critiqued reading in English as being too superficial, as jumping from topic to topic, as being about texts instead of ideas, and as not being useful.

He contrasted English with reading in health class, which he found useful and connected to his real life. He maintained that reading in health was about powerful ideas and that "everybody has something to say," demonstrating the importance of engaging ideas and the opportunity to express opinions and negotiate them. He also cited his health teacher as someone whose commitment he appreciated because that teacher made sure that he understood.

Robert also enjoyed watching television shows that explored "social issues," and he engaged in reading, study, and oral presentations in church. He read the newspaper to keep up on local events, and critiqued the lyrics of rap songs. While he gave stories assigned in school only a few paragraphs to grab his interest, he was constantly on the lookout for new magazines to subscribe to, which he found he could do for free by filling out cards offering trial subscriptions.

Robert also rejected much school writing, which he saw as being about correctness, but embraced writing that came from a personal lived connection and that allowed him to explore himself and his ideas. Robert repeatedly mentioned the importance of function and service; he clearly wanted to help others and to improve himself and the world through his work.

What would happen if Robert's schoolwork was centered on group projects, labs, and activities, a kind of teaching for which Robert was an articulate spokesperson? What if he could read action stories about young people engaged in realistic issues of interest to him? What if he chose work that gave him a sense of pride and ownership?

Robert's portrait is a perfect coda to this book. He could have written the implications himself.

Overcoming Habitus

In our first chapter we talked about the impact of habitus, the entrenched and unexamined commonsense way of doing things that is accepted as natural and that constrains both thought and action. We found that when the boys talked about school, their comments illustrated the power of habitus. For example, on those occasions when the boys described a project or a class that engaged them, we asked them why all of school could not be more like this. Buster, who enthused about his inquiry projects in history, offered a typical response to why school could not incorporate more inquiry: "It just can't." When we pressed him to explain why not, he responded, "Because school isn't like that. Look," he explained, "I lucked out on this one. You can't expect to luck out all the time." In other words, the boys saw school as reified and not susceptible to change. Any time an assignment or class substantively engaged them, they believed it was a lucky exception to the rules that govern school.

The power of habitus was evident in the boys' attitudes toward teachers, school, and school reading, as the following quick catalog of their comments suggests:

Rev: I kind of see school as a necessary evil.

Scotty: You know, you can't change a teacher.

Buster: Reading boring stuff is just something we have to put up with.

Stan: I think a lot of schools, they are just stuck on not wanting to change. Because whenever something changes it is stressful for at least one person, plus you know there is bound to be some phone calls and conflicts of interests and things like that from the parents.

Bob: The teachers are still, yeah I think the teachers are still old-fashioned a little, but I don't really mind it. I mean, it's just the way they are.

Marcel: I'm not goin' to be lookin' for no adjectives, conjunctions, pronouns, and all that, you know what I mean? I mean, I understand they have to teach it because that's the material you have to teach and all that, but it's just that, like, why, what for, that's a waste of brain space to me.

Zach: I mean, like, I think school is, I don't know, kinda old-fashioned, but I think that's the way it has to be.

Barnabas: I've been going to school for a while, and it's like I got used to it. Schools ain't going to change for . . . nothing. Maybe, like a hundred to a thousand years, it might change when everything gets faster.

Again and again the boys suggested to us that school had to be the way it was. It might be a bitter pill, but it was one they would have to swallow.

We hope that the boys are selling us short. But if we're going to overcome their habitus, we first will have to overcome ours. If we don't, our data suggest, we may continue to disenfranchise boys—and many girls, we would venture to say—at a huge cost to the students themselves, to us as their teachers, and to society at large.

APPENDIX A
MAJOR CODING CATEGORIES

Reading
    Positive features
    Negative features
    Links to other media
School
    Positive
    Negative
Gender Comments
Importance of Competence
Importance of Challenge/Competition
Importance of the Social
    Being yourself
    Spontaneity
    Family connection
    In other activities
    Shared interests
    As means of improvement
    Trust
    Shared values
    Variety
Importance of Identity
    Differentiating self from others
    Assertion of major marker
    Group identity
Importance of Unexpected/Variety
Importance of Activity
Importance of Getting Away
Importance of Visual

APPENDIX B
READING LOG DIRECTIONS

Your Reading Log

Perhaps the most important part of the information you are going to help us gather during this project will be from your reading log. It is very important to us that you record any time you "write" or "read" any kind of "text" that is longer than a STOP sign!

By "writing" we mean that you compose something meaningful; by "reading" we mean that you try to make meaning out of a "text." And by "text" we mean anything that you make meaning with that requires your involvement, including things like videos, websites, books, magazine articles, video games, drawings, photographs, pictures, etc.

This log should be kept for the whole day, both in and out of school, from the time you wake up until the time you go to bed. You should record what you read every hour on the hour, or—while in school—every period. On weekends we'd like you to record your reading each hour.

We'd like to know what you read and write and for how long. We'd also like you to make some brief comments about why you were reading, and what you thought about it.

Remember, it's important to record ANY reading and writing you do, no matter how unimportant you think it is, or how short a time you spend on it.

Each month we will talk with you about your reading. We'll pay special attention to themes and contrasts and ask about them. For example, we might ask something like, "We notice that you start each day by reading the sports section. Why do you do that?" We would also ask, "Can you tell me how your reading of a website is and isn't like your reading of the newspaper?"

Here are a couple of models:

NICK

ELEVENTH GRADE

THURSDAY

6:30 A.M.:   Woke up. Read *Spawn*, a comic book I really like, while waking up. 10 minutes.

7 A.M.:   Read the back of the Honey-Nut Cheerios box. About Olympic athletes and good nutrition. Because it was there. Maybe 5 minutes.

7:30 A.M.:   Read a couple of comics while waiting for the bus. Garfield and Foxtrot. I like these because they're funny. (I NEVER read Cathy.) Maybe 2 minutes while waiting for the bus. I read Foxtrot aloud to my sister. Thought she'd think it was funny.

first period: math—no reading

second period: science—no reading

third period—study hall: read science textbook to do outline of a section for homework. 10 minutes. Because I had to. Read *North American Fisherman* magazine. 25 minutes. Because I like to fish. And I want to try this new virtual bass fishing game I read about.

fourth period—English: no reading. We're discussing *A Tale of Two Cities* but I'm not reading it. I watched the video last weekend, though.

fifth period—Psychology: watched film about people meeting on the Internet. Cool. 30 minutes. You'd call this "reading" because you had to figure out a lot of stuff, like who was going to meet who.

sixth period—lunch

seventh period—American history: no reading, but writing assignment - biography of Davy Crockett. Yikes!

3 P.M.:   lifted weights, talked about *Tale of Two Cities* test with Joe. He hasn't read the book either.

4 P.M.:   Played Legend of Zelda video game. 50 minutes. Had to look up "dispel" in the dictionary. I guess that's reading. It's a cool game.

5 P.M.

6 P.M.

7 P.M.:   On Internet, found info on Davy Crockett. Skimmed through it and printed it out for history assignment. 20 minutes. Have to get info for my writing assignment.

8 P.M.:   Watched Seinfeld on TV. 30 minutes. I like the humor.

9 P.M.:   Worked on Davy Crockett essay for 20 minutes. Because I had to.

PETE

NINTH GRADE

SATURDAY

8:30 A.M.: Get up. Read box scores for Baltimore Orioles baseball game in the *Baltimore Sun* newspaper. 2 minutes. I'm a fan of the Orioles. Skimmed a little bit of the story about the game to see how Cal Ripken did. Another 5 minutes.

9 A.M.

10 A.M.

11 A.M.: Read a recipe for lentil soup to my mom while she made the soup. 5 minutes. Because she asked me to.

noon

1 P.M.

2 P.M.: Watched Orioles game on TV—2 hours. I wanted to see how they did and was just vegging out.

3 P.M.

4 P.M.

5 P.M.

6 P.M.: Surf the Internet. Visited some skateboarding sites. 20 minutes. I'm looking for a new board.

7 P.M.: Read an article in *Thrasher* magazine. 15 minutes. About new boards for doing tricks.

8 P.M.: Listened to album of *Godspell* two times. We're doing the musical at school and I'm in the play. We're all going to be like skater punks. About an hour. I guess this is reading because I really listened to the lyrics and tried to figure out what they meant and how I should act during the song and all that.

9 P.M.

10 P.M.

Appendix C
Category System for the Protocol Analysis and Distribution of Moves by Story

PRIMARY PROCESSES

Getting the Literal Level (GLL)—defining a word, paraphrasing a statement, figuring out syntax, or understanding the plot.

Making Local Inferences (MLI)—making inferences based on details from limited portions of the text. These inferences may be about the plot, characters, genre, setting, or structure of a story.

Putting Things Together (PTT)—making inferences requiring a number of pieces of information from different portions of the text. These inferences may be about the same aspects of the story as are local inferences or they may be about the point of the story.

Making Sense of the Whole (MSW)—attempting to understand the entire story. Retelling, summarizing, or explaining the point and the ways readers might make sense of the whole.

Relating (REL)—citing a correspondence between the story and the life, knowledge of the world, or literary experience of the reader.

Reacting (REACT)—giving an emotional response to the details of the story.

Expanding (EXPAND)—using the text as a springboard for the reader's own beliefs.

Evaluating (EVAL)—commenting on the quality of the story or of some portion of the story.

Monitoring (MON)—evaluating one's understanding or reading performance.

Narrating (NAR)—explaining what one does or usually does.

Noting Text Features (NTF)—noting the existence of some feature of the text without using the existence of that feature to make some further point.

Rereading (REREAD)—rereading a portion of the text without using the textual information to make some further point.

Imaging (IMAGE)—creating a concrete image of the story.

Making Peripheral Remarks (MPR)—saying something unrelated to the story.

ANCILLARY PROCESSES

Affirming—asserting approval of some process.
Qualifying—moderating some process.
Specifying—clarifying some process.
Supporting—substantiating some process with reference to the text, knowledge of the world, personal experience, or literary experience. Unlike relating, supporting uses information in service of some other process.
Testing—assessing the accuracy of some process.

TABLE 1   Interpretive Orientations by Story

	WHITE CIRCLE	WHITE CHOCOLATE	MARIGOLDS	MY SISTER'S MARRIAGE	TOTAL
GLL	28	21	15	19	83
MLI	537	530	418	798	2283
PTT	145	175	153	344	817
MSW	44	31	31	60	166
REL	299	405	291	264	1259
REACT	102	95	73	70	340
EXPAND	15	37	17	15	84
EVAL	154	150	137	179	620
MON	151	94	106	100	451
NAR	162	131	106	180	579
NTF	13	16	35	23	87
REREAD	11	4	3	11	29
IMAGE	4	2	4	0	10
MPR	35	51	34	78	198
Total	**1700**	**1742**	**1423**	**2141**	**7006**

Note: Ancillary processes were added to the total of the primary processes to which they were in service. Thirty-three students responded to "The White Circle," twenty-nine responded to "White Chocolate," twenty-seven responded to "Marigolds," and thirty-two responded to "My Sister's Marriage."

BIBLIOGRAPHY

Abrahamson, S., and Carter, B. (1984). *From Delight to Wisdom: Nonfiction for Young Adults.* Westport, CT: Oryx Press.

Alloway, N., and Gilbert, P. (1997). Boys and Literacy: Lessons from Australia. *Gender and Education* 9(1): 49–58.

Alpert, N. (1991). Students' Resistance in the Classroom. *Anthropology & Education Quarterly* 22: 350–366.

Applebee, A. N., Burroughs, R., and Stevens, A. S. (2000). Shaping Conversations: A Study of Continuity and Coherence in High School Literature Curricula. *Research in the Teaching of English* 34: 396–429.

Bakhtin, M. M. (1986). *Speech Genres and Other Late Essays.* (Trans. Vern McGee.) Austin: University of Texas Press.

———. (1984). *Problems of Dostoevsky's Poetics.* (Trans. Caryl Emerson.) Minneapolis: University of Minnesota Press.

Bandura. A. (1993). Perceived Self-Efficacy in Cognitive Development and Functioning. *Educational Psychologist* 28: 117–148.

Barrs, M. (1993). Introduction: Reading the Difference. In M. Barrs and S. Pidgeon (Eds.) *Reading the Difference*, pp. i–xx. London: Centre for Language in Primary Education.

Beach, R., and Myers, J. (2001). *Inquiry-Based English Instruction: Engaging Students in Life and Literature.* New York: Teachers College Press.

Bettelheim, B. (1976). *The Uses of Enchantment: The Meaning and Importance of Fairy Tales.* New York: Knopf.

Biddulph, S. (1997). *Raising Boys: Why Boys Are Different—And How to Help Them Become Happy and Well-Balanced Men.* Sydney: Finch Publishing.

———. (1994). *Manhood: A Book About Setting Men Free.* Sydney: Finch Publishing.

Bissex, G. (1980). *GYNS at WRK: A Child Learns to Write and Read.* Cambridge, MA: Harvard University Press.

Bizzell, P. (1984). Contact Zones and English Studies. *College English* 56(2): 162–169.

Bleach, K. Ed. (1998). *Raising Boys' Achievement in School.* Stoke on Trent, UK: Trentham Books.

Bloom, B. (1976). *Human Characteristics and School Learning.* New York: McGraw-Hill.

Bloom, B. Ed. (1985). *Developing Talent in Young People.* New York: Ballantine.

Bolter, J. D. (1991). *Writing Space: The Computer, Hypertext and the History of Writing.* Hillsdale, NJ: Lawrence Erlbaum.

Booth, W. (1988). *The Company We Keep.* Berkeley: University of California Press.

———. (1983). A New Strategy for Establishing a Truly Democratic Criticism. *Daedalus* 112: 193–214.

Bourdieu, P. (1990). *The Logic of Practice* (Trans. R. Nice.) Cambridge: Polity Press.

Brown, J., Collins, A., and DuGuid, P. (1989). Situated Cognition and the Culture of Learning. *Educational Researcher* 18: 32–42.

Bruner. J. (1986). *Actual Minds, Possible Worlds.* Cambridge, MA: Harvard University Press.

Bryant, A. (1993). Hostile Hallways: The AAUW Survey on Sexual Harassment in America's Schools. *Journal of School Health* 63(8): 355–357.

Bushweller, K. (1994). Turning Our Back on Boys. *The American School Board Journal* 181: 20–25.

Campbell, J., Voelkl, K., and Donohue, P. (1998). *NAEP Trends in Academic Progress. Achievement of U.S. Students in Science 1969–1996, Mathematics 1973–1996, Reading, 1971–1996, Writing, 1984–1996.* Washington, DC: ED Publications.

Canada, G. (1999). *Reaching up for Manhood: Transforming the Lives of Boys in America.* Boston: Beacon Press.

Carlsen, R. (1967). *Books and the Teenage Reader: A Guide for Teachers, Librarians, and Parents.* New York: Harper and Row.

Cherland, M. (1994). *Private Practice: Girls Reading Fiction and Constructing Identity.* Bristol, PA: Taylor & Francis.

Children's Literature Research Centre. (1996). *Young People's Reading at the End of the Century.* Roehampton Institute: Children's Literature Research Centre.

Chodorow, N. (1978). *The Reproduction of Mothering: Psychoanalysis and the Sociology of Gender.* Berkeley: University of California Press.

Clark, M. (1976). *Young Fluent Readers.* London: Heinemann Educational.

Clay, M. (1993). *Reading Recovery: A Guidebook for Teachers in Training.* Portsmouth, NH: Heinemann.

———. (1991). *Becoming Literate: The Construction of Inner Control.* Portsmouth, NH: Heinemann.

Cohen, M. (1998). "A Habit of Healthy Idleness": Boys' Underachievement in Historical Perspective. In D. Epstein, et al. (Eds.). *Failing Boys?*, pp. 19–34. Buckingham, UK: Open University Press.

Cole, N. (1997). *The ETS Gender Study: How Females and Males Perform in Educational Settings.* Princeton, NJ: Educational Testing Service.

Coles, G. (1998). *Reading Lessons: The Debate About Literacy.* New York: Wang and Hill.

Coles, R. (1989). *The Call of Stories: Teaching and the Moral Imagination.* Boston: Houghton Mifflin.

Connelly, F., and Clandinin, D. (1990). Stories of Experience and Narrative Inquiry. *Educational Researcher* 19(5): 2–14.

Csikszentmihalyi, M. (1990a). *Flow: The Psychology of Optimal Experience.* New York: Harper and Row.

———. (1990b). Literacy and Intrinsic Motivation. *Daedalus* 119: 115–140.

Csikszentmihalyi, M., Rathunde, K., and Whalen, S. (1993). *Talented Teenagers: The Roots of Success and Failure.* Cambridge: Cambridge University Press.

Curtis, M. (1990). The Performance of Girls and Boys in Subject English. *The Teaching of English* 57: 3–20.

deBeer, E. (2001). *Beyond the Label: A Narrative Analysis of College Students with Learning Disabilities.* Unpublished doctoral dissertation, Rutgers University.

Dewey, J. (1916). *Democracy and Education.* New York: The Free Press.

Donalson, Margaret. (1978). *Children's Minds.* London: Fontana.

Duncan-Andrade, J., and Morrell, E. (2000). *Using Hip-Hop Culture as a Bridge to Canonical Poetry Texts in an Urban Secondary English Class.* (ERIC Document Reproduction Service No. ED442893.)

Dunne, J., and Khan, A. (1998). The Crisis in Boys' Reading. *The Library Association Record* 100(8): 408–410.

Edmiston, B. (1994). More Than Talk: A Bakhtinian Perspective on Drama in Education and Change in Understanding. In *National Association for Drama in Education Journal*, 18: 25–36.

Elley, W. B. (1992). *How in the World Do Students Read?* The Hague, Netherlands: International Association for the Evaluation of Educational Achievement.

Enciso, P. (1992). Creating the Story World. In J. Many and C. Cox (Eds.). *Reader Stance and Literary Understanding: Exploring the Theories, Research and Practice*, pp. 75–102. Norwood, NJ: Ablex.

Epstien, D., Elwood, J., Hey, V., and Maw, J. (1998). *Failing Boys? Issues in Gender and Achievement.* Buckingham, UK: Open University Press.

Equal Opportunities Commission and OFSTED (1996). *The Gender Divide: Performance Differences Between Boys and Girls at School.* London: Office for Standards in Education.

Esslin, M. (1987). *The Field of Drama: How the Signs of Drama Create Meaning on Stage and Screen.* London: Methuen.

Faludi, S. (1999). *Stiffed: The Betrayal of the American Man.* New York: William Morrow.

Fecho, B. (2000). Critical Inquiries into Language in an Urban Classroom. *Research in the Teaching of English* 34: 368–395.

———. (2001). "Why Are You Doing This?": Acknowledging and Transcending Threat in a Critical Inquiry Classroom. *Research in the Teaching of English* 36: 9–37.

Finders, M. (1997). *Just Girls.* New York: Teachers College Press.

Flower, L., Long, E., and Higgins, L. (2000). *Learning to Rival: A Literate Practice for Intercultural Inquiry.* Mahwah, NJ: Lawrence Erlbaum.

Fordham, S., and Ogbu, J. (1986). Black Students' School Success: Coping with the Burden of "Acting White." *The Urban Review* 18: 176–206.

Fueyo, J. A. (1990). *Playful Literacy: First Graders as Meaning Makers in the Literacies of Play, the Creative Arts, and the Language Arts.* Doctoral dissertation, University of New Hampshire.

Gambell, T., and Hunter, D. (1999). Rethinking Gender Differences in Literacy. *Canadian Journal of Education* 24(1): 1–16.

Garbarino, J. (2000). *Lost Boys: Why Our Sons Turn Violent and How We Can Save Them.* New York: Anchor.

Gee, J. (1989). What Is Literacy? *Journal of Education* 171(1): 18–25.

Gere, A., Fairbanks, C., Howes, A., Roop, L., and Schaafsma, D. (1992). *Language and Reflection: An Integrated Approach to Teaching English.* New York: Macmillan.

Gilbert, R., and Gilbert, P. (1998). *Masculinity Goes to School.* Melbourne: Routledge/Kegan Paul.

Gilligan, C. (1982). *In a Different Voice.* Cambridge, MA: Harvard University Press.

Gilligan, J. (1997). *Violence: Reflections on a National Epidemic.* New York: Vintage.

Greene, M. (1988). *The Dialectic of Freedom.* New York: Teachers College Press.

Gurian, M. (2001). *How Boys and Girls Learn Differently!: A Guide for Parents and Teachers.* San Francisco: Jossey-Bass.

———. (1999). *A Fine Young Man: What Parents, Mentors and Educators Can Do to Shape Adolescent Boys into Exceptional Men.* New York: J. P. Tarcher.

———. (1997). *The Wonder of Boys: What Parents, Mentors and Educators Can Do to Shape Boys into Exceptional Men.* New York: J. P. Tarcher.

Hall, C., and Coles, M. (1997). Gendered Readings: Helping Boys Develop as Critical Readers. *Gender and Education* 9(1): 61–68.

Hampton, S. (1994). Teacher Change: Overthrowing the Myth of One Teacher, One Classroom. In T. Shanahan (Ed.). *Teachers Thinking; Teachers Knowing*, pp. 122–140. Urbana, IL: NCTE.

Hamel, F., and Smith, M. (1997). "You Can't Play the Game If You Don't Know the Rules": Interpretative Conventions and the Teaching of Literature to Lower Track Students. *Reading and Writing Quarterly* 14: 355–378.

Harris, S., Nixon, J., and Rudduck, J. (1993). Schoolwork, Homework and Gender. *Gender and Education* 5(1): 3–15.

Heath, S., and McLaughlin, B. (1993). *Identity and Inner City Youth: Beyond Ethnicity and Gender*. New York: Teachers College Press.

Hidi, S. (1990). Interest and Its Contribution as a Mental Resource for Learning. *Review of Educational Research* 60: 549–571.

Hillocks, G. (1999). *Ways of Thinking/Ways of Teaching*. New York: Teachers College Press.

———. (1995). *Teaching Writing as Reflective Practice*. New York: Teachers College Press.

Hillocks, G., and Smith, M. (1988). Sensible Sequencing: Developing Knowledge About Literature Text by Text. *English Journal* 77(6): 44–49.

Huff-Sommers, C. (2000). *The War Against Boys: How Misguided Feminism Is Harming Our Young Men*. New York: Simon & Schuster.

Hunter, I. (1988). *Culture and Government: The Emergence of Literary Education*. Basingstoke, UK: Macmillan Press.

John-Steiner, V. (1985). *Notebooks of the Mind: Explorations of Thinking*. New York: Harper and Row.

Inglis, F. (1981). *The Promise of Happiness: Value and Meaning in Children's Fiction*. New York: Cambridge University Press.

Kelly, P. (1986). The Influence of Reading Content on Students' Perceptions of the Masculinity or Femininity of Reading. *The Journal of Reading Behavior* 18(3): 243–256.

Kessler, S., Ashedon, D., Connell, R., and Dowsett, G. (1985). Gender Relations in Secondary Schooling. *Sociology of Education* 58: 34–48.

Kimmel, M. (2000). "What About the Boys?" *Women's Educational Equity Act Resource Center Digest* (November). Newton, MA: Education Development Center, Inc.

———. (1999). "What Are Little Boys Made Of?" *Ms*. (October/November): 88–91.

———. (1996). *Manhood in America: A Cultural History*. New York: Free Press.

Kindlon, D., and Thompson, M. (1999). *Raising Cain: Protecting the Emotional Life of Boys*. New York: Ballantine Books.

Kivel, P. (1999). *Boys Will Be Men: Raising Our Sons for Courage, Caring, and Community*. New York: New Society.

Klein, H. (1977). Cross-Cultural Studies: What Do They Tell About Sex Differences in Reading? *The Reading Teacher* 30: 880–885.

Language of Life. (1995). Public Broadcasting System.

Latshaw, J. (1985). *An In-Depth Examination of Four Preadolescents' Responses to Fantasy Literature*. Unpublished doctoral dissertation, University of Saskatchawan, Saskatoon.

Lave, J., and Wenger, E. (1991). *Situated Learning: Legitimate Peripheral Participation*. New York: Cambridge University Press.

Lehrer, R. (1993). Authors of Knowledge: Patterns of Hypermedia Design. In S. Lajoie and S. Derry (Eds.). *Computers as Cognitive Tools*, pp. 197–227. Hillsdale, NJ: Lawrence Erlbaum.

Lopate, P. (1975). *Being with Children*. New York: Simon & Schuster.

Mac An Ghaill, M. (1994). *The Making of Men: Masculinities, Sexualities and Schooling*. Buckingham, UK: Open University Press.

Mahiri, J. (1998). *Shooting for Excellence. African American Youth and Culture in New Century Schools*. Urbana, IL and New York: National Council of Teachers of English and Teachers College Press.

Mariage, T. (1995). Why Students Learn: The Nature of Teacher Talk During Reading. *Learning Disabilities Quarterly* 18: 214–234.

Marshall, J. D., Smagorinsky, P., and Smith, M. W. (1995). *The Language of Interpretation: Patterns of Discourse in Discussions of Literature*. Urbana, IL: NCTE.

Martino, W. (1998). "Dickheads," "Poofs," "Try Hards," and "Losers": Critical Literacy for Boys in the English Classroom. *English in Aotearoa (New Zealand Association for the Teaching of English)* 25: 31–57.

———. (1995a). Boys and Literacy: Exploring the Construction of Hegemonic Masculinities and the Formation of Literate Capacities for Boys in the English Classroom. *English in Australia* 112: 11–24.

———. (1995b). Gendered Learning Practices: Exploring the Costs of Hegemonic Masculinity for Girls and Boys in School. Proceedings of the *Promoting Gender Equity Conference*, February 22–24. Canberra: ACT Department of Education.

———. (1995c). Deconstructing Masculinity in the English Classroom: A Site for Reconstituting Gendered Subjectivity. *Gender and Education* 7(2): 205–220.

———. (1994a). The Gender Bind and Subject English: Exploring Questions of Masculinity in Developing Interventionist Strategies in the English Classroom. *English in Australia* 107: 29–44.

———. (1994b). Masculinity and Learning: Exploring Boys' Underachievement and Under-Representation in Subject English. *Interpretations* 27(2): 22–57.

Maybe, D. (1997). Boys Read Less Than Girls: True or False? *Books for Keeps* (September).

McCarthey, S. J. (1998). Constructing Multiple Subjectivities in Classroom Literacy Contexts. *Research in the Teaching of English* 32(2): 126–159.

McCormick, K. (1999). *Reading Our Histories, Understanding Our Cultures: A Sequenced Approach to Thinking, Reading, and Writing.* Boston: Allyn and Bacon.

Michaels, S. (1981). Sharing Time: Children's Narrative Styles and Differential Access to Literacy. *Language in Society* 10: 423–442.

Miedzien, M. (1991). *Boys Will Be Boys: Breaking the Link Between Masculinity and Violence.* New York: Doubleday.

Millard, E. (1997). *Differently Literate.* London: Falmer Press.

———. (1994). *Developing Readers in the Middle Years.* Buckingham, UK: Open University Press.

Minns, E. (1993). Three Ten Year Old Boys and Their Reading. In M. Barrs and S. Pidgeon (Eds.). *Reading the Difference: Gender and Reading in the Primary School.* London: CLPE.

Moje, E. (2000). "To Be Part of the Story": The Literacy Practices of Gangsta Adolescents. *Teachers College Record* 102: 651–690.

Moll, L. (1992). Literacy Research in Communities and Classrooms: A Sociocultural Approach. In R. Beach, J. Green, M. Kamil, and T. Shanahan (Eds.). *Multidisciplinary Perspectives on Literacy Research.* Urbana, IL: National Conference on Research in English/National Council of Teachers of English.

Monson, D., and Sebesta, S. (1991). Reading Preferences. In J. Flood, J. Jensen, D. Lapp, and J. Squire (Eds.). *Handbook of Research on Teaching the English Language Arts*, pp. 664–673. New York: Macmillan.

Morimoto, K., Gregory, J., and Butler, P. (1973). Notes on the Context for Learning. *Harvard Educational Review* 43: 245–257.

Muecke, D. C. (1969). *The Compass of Irony.* London: Methuen.

Mullis, I., Dossey, J., Foertsch, M., Jones, L., and Gentille, C. (1991). *Trends in Academic Progress, 1971–1990: National Assessment of Educational Progress.* Princeton, NJ: Educational Testing Service.

Newkirk, T. (2001). The Revolt Against Realism: The Attraction of Fiction for Young Writers. *Elementary School Journal* 101(4): 467–477.

———. (2000). Misreading Masculinity: Speculations on the Great Gender Gap in Writing. *Language Arts* 77(8): 294–300.

Nystrand, M., with A. Gamoran, R. Kachur, and C. Predergast. (1997). *Opening Dialogue: Understanding the Dynamics of Language and Learning in the English Classroom*, New York: Teachers College Press.

OFSTED (1993). *Boys and English*. London: HMSO. (Ref: 2/93/NS).

Osmont, P. (1987). Teaching Inquiry in the Classroom, Reading and Gender Set. *Language Arts* 64(7): 758–761.

Pajares, F. (1996). Self-Efficacy Beliefs in Academic Settings. *Review of Educational Research* 66: 543–578.

Paley, V. (1984). *Boys and Girls: Superheroes in the Doll Corner*. Chicago: University of Chicago Press.

Peterson, S. (1998). Evaluation and Teachers' Perception of Gender in Sixth Grade Student Writing. *Research in the Teaching of English* 33: 181–206.

Phillips, A. (1993). *The Trouble with Boys: Parenting the Men of the Future*. London: Pandora.

Pollack, W. (1999). *"Real Boys:" Rescuing Our Sons from the Myths of Boyhood*. New York: Random House.

Pratt, M. L. (1991). Art of the Contact Zone. *Profession* 91: 33–40.

Pressley, M., Schuder, T., and Bergman, J. (1992). A Researcher-Educator Collaborative Interview Study of Transactional Comprehension Strategies Instruction. *Journal of Educational Psychology* 84: 231–246.

Propp, V. (1970). *Morphology of the Folk Tale* (Trans. L. Scott.) Austin: University of Texas Press.

Purves, A. (1992). *The IEA Study of Written Composition II: Education and Performance in Fourteen Countries*. Oxford, UK: Pergamon Press.

Rabinowitz, P. (1987). *Before Reading: Narrative Conventions and the Politics of Interpretation*. Ithaca, NY: Cornell University Press.

Rabinowitz, P., and Smith, M. W. (1998). *Authorizing Readers: Resistance and Respect in the Teaching of Literature*. New York: Teachers College Press.

Ravitch, D. (1994). "The War on Boys." *Men's Health* (October): 110.

Reynolds, K. (1990). *Girls Only? Gender and Popular Children's Fiction in Britain, 1880–1910*. Hemel Hempstead, UK: Harvester Wheatsheaf.

Rogoff, B., and Lave, J. (1984). *Everyday Cognition: Its Development in Social Context*. Cambridge, MA: Harvard University Press.

Rosenblatt, L. (1978). *The Reader, the Text, the Poem*. Carbondale: Southern Illinois University Press.

Rotundo, E. A. (1994). *American Manhood: Transformations in Masculinity from the Revolution to the Modern Era*. New York: Basic Books.

Sadker, D., and Sadker, M. (1995). *Failing at Fairness: How America's Schools Cheat Girls*. New York: Scribner.

Saks, A. L. Ed. (1995). Viewpoints: A Symposium on the Usefulness of Literacy Research. *Research in the Teaching of English* 29: 326–348.

Salisbury, J., and Jackson, D. (1996). *Challenging Macho Values: Practical Ways of Working with Adolescent Boys*. London: Routledge/Falmer Press.

Seitz, J. (1999). *Motives for Metaphors: Literacy, Curriculum Reform, and the Teaching of English*. Pittsburgh: University of Pittsburgh Press.

Shapiro, J. (1990). Sex Role Appropriateness of Reading and Reading Instruction. *Reading Psychology: An International Quarterly* 11(3): 241–269.

Silverstein, O., and Rashbaum, B. (1994). *The Courage to Raise Good Men*. New York: Penguin.

Smagorinsky, P. (2002). *Teaching English Through Principled Practice*. Upper Saddle River, NJ: Merrill/Prentice Hall.

———. (1998). Thinking and Speech and Protocol Analysis. *Mind, Culture, and Activity* 5: 157–177.

Smagorinsky, P., McCann, T., and Kern, S. (1987). *Explorations: Introductory Activities for Literature and Composition*, 7–12. Urbana, IL: ERIC.

Smith, F. (1988). *Joining the Literacy Club: Further Essays into Education*. Portsmouth, NH: Heinemann.

Smith, M. W. (1991a). Constructing Meaning from Text: An Analysis of Ninth-Grade Reader Response. *Journal of Educational Research* 84: 263–272.

Smith, M. W. (1991b). *Understanding Unreliable Narrators*. Urbana, IL: NCTE.

———. (1989). Teaching the Interpretation of Irony in Poetry. *Research in the Teaching of English* 23(3): 254–272.

Smith. M. W., and Strickland, D. (2001). Complements or Conflicts: Conceptions of Discussion and Multicultural Literature in a Teachers-as-Readers Discussion Group. *Journal of Literacy Research* 33: 137–168.

Sommers, C. H. (2000). The War Against Boys. *The Atlantic Monthly* (May): 59–74.

Squires, J. (1964). *The Responses of Adolescents While Reading Four Short Stories*. Urbana, IL: National Council of Teachers of English.

Taylor, D. (1983). *Family Literacy*. Portsmouth, NH: Heinemann.

Telford, L. (1999). A Study of Boys' Reading. *Early Childhood Development and Care* 149: 87–124.

Tharp, R., and Gallimore, R. (1988). *Rousing Minds to Life: Teaching, Learning and Schooling in Social Context*. Cambridge: Cambridge University Press.

Thomas, L. (1983). *Late Night Thoughts While Listening to Mahler's Ninth Symphony*. New York: Viking.

Thomson, J. (1987). *Understanding Teenagers' Reading: Reading Processes and the Teaching of Literature*. Melbourne: Methuen.

Thorndike, R. L. (1941). *A Comparative Study of Children's Reading Interests*. New York: Bureau of Publications, Teachers College, Columbia University.

Travers, M. (1992). Gender Differences: Adolescent Girls' and Boys' Fear of Speaking in Class—An Australian-American Comparison. *English in Australia* 102: 20–36.

Verwys, B., Haberling, J., and White, B. (2000). *Cultivating Concern for Characters*. Paper presented at the annual meeting of the National Council of Teachers of English, Milwaukee, WI.

Vipond, D., and Hunt, R. (1984). Point-Driven Understanding: Pragmatic and Cognitive Dimensions of Literary Reading. *Poetics* 13: 261–277.

Voss, M. (1996). *Hidden Literacies: Children Learning at Home and at School*. Portsmouth, NH: Heinemann.

Vygotsky, L. S. (1978). *Mind in Society*. In M. Cole, V. John-Steiner, S. Scribner, and E. Souberman (Eds.). Cambridge, MA: Harvard University Press.

Walkerdine, V. (1990). *Schoolgirl Fictions*. London: Verso.

Wells, G. (1999). *Dialogic Inquiry: Toward a Sociocultural Practice and Theory of Education*. New York: Cambridge University Press.

West, C., and Zimmerman, D. (1991). Doing Gender. In C. West and D. Zimmerman (Eds.). *The Social Construction of Gender*, pp. 13–37.

Whitehead, A. N. (1961). *The Adventure of Ideas*. Cambridge: The University Press.

Whitehead, F. (1977). *Children and Their Books: Reading Habits, 10–16*. Schools Council Basingstoke, UK: Evans/Methuen Educational.

Wilder, G., and Powell, K. (1989). Sex Differences in Test Performance: A Survey of the Literature. *College Board Report No. 89-3*. Princeton, NJ: Educational Testing Service.

Wilhelm, J. D. (forthcoming). *Reading IS Seeing: Visualization Strategies for Assisting Readers to Engage, Comprehend and Reflect*. New York: Scholastic.

———. (forthcoming). *Reading Manipulatives: Teaching Reading Processes Through Symbolic Story Representation*. New York: Scholastic.

———. (2001). *Improving Comprehension with Think Aloud Strategies: Modeling What Good Readers Do*. New York: Scholastic.

———. (1997). *You Gotta BE the Book: Teaching Engaged and Reflective Reading with Adolescents*. New York: Teachers College Press.

Wilhelm, J. D., Baker, T., and Dube, J. (2001). *Strategic Reading: Guiding Students to Lifelong Literacy*. Portsmouth, NH: Heinemann.

Wilhelm, J. D., and Edmiston, B. (1998). *Imagining to Learn: Inquiry, Ethics, and Integration Through Drama*. Portsmouth, NH: Heinemann.

Wilhelm, J. D., and Friedemann, P. (1998). *Hyperlearning: Where Projects, Inquiry, and Technology Meet*. York, ME: Stenhouse.

Willinsky, J. (1992). *The New Literacy*. London: Routledge/Kegan Paul.

———. (1990). *The Triumph of Literature; The Fate of Literacy*. New York: Teachers College Press.

Worthy, J., Moorman, M., and Turner. M. (1999). What Johnny Likes to Read Is Hard to Find in School. *Reading Research Quarterly* 34: 12–27.

Young, J. P. (2000). Boy Talk: Critical Literacy and Masculinities. *Reading Research Quarterly* 35: 312–337.

Zeichner, K., and Tabachnick, B. R. (1981). Are the Effects of University Teacher Education "Washed Out" by School Experience? *Journal of Teacher Education* 32(3): 7–11.

Index

Abrahamson, S. and Carter.
B., 11
Acceptance, 43
Accomplishment, 45
Visible signs of accomplishment, 33, 62, 118, 131
Achievement, (see Accomplishment)
Boys vs. Girls, 10
Action-orientation, 101, 147, 173, 197
Activity, 46, 130, 147, 158, 197
Activity Ranking Sheet, 29
Alloway, N., 9
Alpert, N., 80
Ambiguity, 115
Clear point, 121
Intolerance for, 121
Amistad, 56
Animorphs, 153
Applebee, A. Burroughs, R., and Stevens, A., 51
Application, (see Function)
Assistance, 128, 130, 138, 146, 187
Active learning, as assistance, 101
Environmental assistance, 131
Features of learning activities as assistance, 101
Teacher assistance, 99
Association-driven reading, 161 and *ff.*
Athletic Shorts (Crutcher), 86
Attitudes, xxii
Toward literacy, xxi
Boys vs. Girls, 10
Averages, xix

Baca, Jimmy Santiago, xv
Baker, J., 16

Bakhtin, M.M., 128–129
Interillumination, 129
Monologue/dialogue, 128–129
Balance, Importance of, 90
Barrs, M., 3, 11, 12
Beach, R. and Myers, J., 189, 193
Beloved (Alice Walker), 56
Bettelheim, B., 3
Biddulph, S., 5, 9
Biological determinism, 5 and *ff.*
Bissex, G., 12
Bizzell, P., 190
Black Like Me, 56
Bloom, B., 196
Bolter, J.D., 186
Booth, W., 162, 164
Bordieu, P., 15, 69, 203–204
Boy code, x, 6, 43
Boys Will Be Boys (Miedzien), 8
Boys Will Be Men (Kivel), 8
Bridge building project (see also Design), 122
Brown, J., Collins, A. and DuGuid, P., 84
Bruner, J., 158
Buffy the Vampire Slayer, 151
Bushweller, K., 8
Busywork, 119, 200
As disrespect, 100

Calvin and Hobbes, 153
Campbell, J., Voelkl, K. and Donahue, P., 1
Cannabis, 97
Cannery Row (John Steinbeck), 138
Caring, 186 and *ff.*
Cars, 105
Carlsen, R., 154

Catcher in the Rye (J.D. Salinger), ix
Challenge, 34, 56, 83, 103, 113 and *ff.*, 128, 131, 133, 194, 200
Appropriate level, 36, 37, 38, 51, 53, 117, 130
Importance of, 35, 48
Overmatched, 37
Challenging Macho Values (Salisbury, J. and Jackson, D.), 9
Chocolate War, The (Robert Cormier), 124
Children's literature, 14
Children's Literature Research Center, 11
Chodorow, 13
Choice, 18, 33, 34, 108, 109, 110, 121, 130, 193, 197
Boys vs. Girls, 11
Clark, 12
Class (social class), xxi, 18, 21, 78 and *ff.*, 96
Class size, 107
Clay, M., 154
Clear point, 121
Cod (Kuransky), 190
Cohen, M., 2
Coles, R., 162
Collins, A., 84
Color Purple, The (Alice Walker), 144
Community of practice, 96
Competence, 13, 30, 32, 37, 38, 40, 43, 51–53, 70, 84, 87, 96, 103, 105–107, 109, 121, 133, 153, 191, 194
Assistance to become, 96
Circumscribed area, 98
Conflict with social, 69
Cost of emphasis on, 31

Competence (*cont.*)
  Developed, 104
  Fun, 98
  Skillfulness, 97
Competition, 118
Complexity, 153, 173
Computer, 32, 43, 57, 98,
    105, 106, 109, 149
  Games, x, 179
  RPG (role playing games),
    55, 57, 110
  MUD (multi-user
    domains), 148
Conclusiveness, 120, 170
Connections, 176, 203
Consciousness, 158
Constructivism (*see* Social
    Constructivism, Vygot-
    sky), 129
Contact zones, 190
Context, 27, 84
Control, 30, 33, 37, 53, 84,
    87, 96, 106, 107, 109,
    113, 128, 191
Cooking, 30, 36, 38
Courage to Raise Good Men,
    The (Silverstein, S. and
    Rashbaum, O.), 8
Creativity, 138
Critical standards, 193,
    201
  No sense of, 118, 120
Critical theories
  Theoretical perspectives,
    13 and *ff.*, 203–204
Crutcher, C., 86
Csikzentmihalyi, M., x, 28,
    30, 33, 34, 38, 40–42,
    47, 62, 66, 67, 94, 96,
    103, 107, 118, 121, 142,
    196
Cuban Linx, 150
Cultural concerns, xxi, 18
Culture of cruelty, 6
Curricula, 192
  Negotiated, 112
  Responsive, 81
  Thematic, 112
Cyrano de Bergerac (Ros-
    trand), 116

Daily student officer, 20
Death of a Salesman (Arthur
    Miller), 85, 124
Debates, 103, 197
deBeer, E., 59
Declarative knowledge, 129
Democracy and Education
    (John Dewey), 66 and *ff.*
Depth
  Related to competence and
    control, 107
Description, 116, 158
Design projects, 103, 127, 137
  Artifacts, 191
  Bridge building, 105, 108
  Hypermedia, 105
  Video, 105
"Devil and Tom Walker,
    The", 176
Dewey, J., 66 and *ff.*
Dialogue, 128, 133
Diaries, 52
Dickinson, Emily, 52, 144
Difficulty, textual, 194–195
Disengaged reading, 162 and *ff.*
Donalson, M., 3
Dragonball Z, 152
Drama, 103, 105, 130–132,
    144–145, 148, 152, 189,
    197, 202
  Trials, 103
  Hotseating, 103
  What If Scenarios, 189
Dreams
  Practical, 68
  Fallback positions, 68
DuGuid, P., 84
Duncan-Andrade, J. and
    Morrell, E., 150
Dunne, J. and Khan, E., 11

Eco, U., 198
Edginess, 146, 156, 157, 166,
    172, 173
Education, 63 and *ff.*
  Instrumental value of,
    82–83
Efferent stance, 40
Effort, 13
Electronic technologies, 109

Elley, W. B., 2
Elwood, J., 2
Emotion/affect, 151, 190, 195
Enciso, P., 131
Ender's Game (Orson Scott
    Card), 57, 143
Engagement, 138, 149, 195
  Emotional, 123
  Procedural, 23, 184
  Substantive, 23, 184
Epstein, D., 2
Equal Opportunities Commis-
    sion /OFSTED, 11
Essentializing Students,
    18–19
Esslin, 87, 117
Ethnicity, xxi, xxi, 62, 80, 96
Evaluation-driven reading,
    162 and *ff.*
Evil, 114
Experience, xxi
Experience-driven reading,
    162 and *ff.*
Exportability, 126, 152

Failing Boys?, 2
Faludi, 9
Family, 82–83, 136, 142
Fantasy, 57, 123
Far Side, 153, 155
Fecho, B., 81
Feedback, 38, 40, 51, 53, 62,
    118, 122, 130, 133, 192
  Immediate, 38, 126
Feminism, 9, 71, 83
Fiction, 89
Figure out, 48, 120, 195
Fine Young Man, A (Gurian),
    5
Flow, x, 28, 87, 94, 103, 114,
    183, 191
Flow experiences, 38, 40, 41,
    47, 53, 62, 66, 84, 126,
    141
Flower, L., Long, E., and
    Higgins, L., 190
Fordham, S. and Ogbu, J., 78,
    80
Foucault, M., 15
Freedom, 146

Friends (*see also* Social), 42
  and *ff.*, 45, 56
Frontloading, 85 and *ff.*, 176,
  198
Full House, 156
Function / application, 104,
  107, 118, 123, 131, 148,
  180, 189, 203
  Environmental feedback,
    127
  Fixing, 121
  Immediate, 84
  Making /designing, 121
Funds of knowledge, 199
Future plans, 202
  Plans, 49
  Orientation, 80

Gallimore, R., 192
Games, 126–127
Garbarino
  Lost Boys, 8
Garfield, 153
Gee, J., 4
Gender, xvi, 2, 5, 11, 14, 18,
  50
  As superordinate category
    of identity, xvi
  History of, 16, 17
  Secure sense of, 12
Gender biased, 3
Gender regime, 14, 16
Gender roles, 7, 18
Gender wars, xvi
Geography
  Personal connection to,
    124
Getting away, 45–46, 95
Getting by, 102
Getting information, 105,
  120, 123
Getting to the point, 116
Ghost chapters, 198
Gilbert, R. and Gilbert, P., 9
Gilligan, C., 1, 9
Gilligan, J., 8
Ginsberg, A., 52
Girls, achievement, 1
Goals, 38, 53, 62, 84
  Clear, 86, 118, 126, 192

Purpose, 86
Goosebumps, 36, 153
Grades, 120
Greene, M., 108
Gregory, 107
Gunslinger, The (Stephen
  King), 144
Gurian, M., 5, 9

Haberling, J., 176
Habitus, 15–16, 18, 69,
  203–204
Hall, C. and Coles, M., 11
Hamel, F., 133
Hamlet (Shakespeare), Ix, 56,
  136, 154, 156
Happy Gilmore, 170
Harris, S., Nixon, J. and
  Rudduck, J., 14
Harlem Renaissance, 136
Harry Potter, 123
Hatchet (Gary Paulsen), 123
Heath, S. B. and McLaughlin,
  B., 19
Helping others/service, 127,
  145, 146, 203
Hey, V, 2
Hidi, S., 109
Hillocks, G., 186, 196
History, 106, 201
  Interest in, 111–112
Hoff Sommers, 9
Homework, 94, 100
  Completion, 118
Horror, 81, 198
House on Mango Street, The
  (Sandra Cisneros), 195
How Boys and Girls Learn
  Differently (Gurian), 5
Humor, 145, 157, 172, 196
Hunter, I., 17
Hyperlearning (Wilhelm and
  Friedemann), 11, 20, 185
  and *ff.*

Identity, 97, 108, 118, 177,
  197, 201
  markers, xi, 105
IEA, 2
Immediacy, 195

Immediate activity,
Immediate experience, 41, 51,
  62, 142, 192
Important ideas, 202
Individuals, xix, 100
  Getting to know them, 20
    and *ff.*
  Losing sight of, 19
Information, 89, 104, 105,
  120, 123
Information-driven reading
  etc., 161 and *ff.*
Inglis, F., 3
Inquiry, 85, 132, 136, 137,
  188 and *ff.*, 195
Instrumental value, of read-
  ing, 41, 62
Interest, 24, 31, 69, 79–81,
  85, 91, 95, 107, 108,
  112, 113, 138, 141, 175,
  201
  As resource for learning, 109
  Immediate, 94
  Situational, 111 and *ff.*,
    136
Interest inventories, 20
Internet, 43–44, 56, 98–105,
  126, 130, 136, 141, 152
Into the Wild (Jon Krakauer),
  156
Into Thin Air (Jon Krakauer),
  123
Intrinsic value, 120
Invisible Cities (Italo Calvino),
  117
Ironman (Chris Crutcher), 86
Irony, 133, 155

James Bond, 36
Jane Eyre, 158
Jeopardy!, 53, 126
Jokes, 23, 152
John-Steiner, V., 199

Keeping Track, 125, 145
Kelly, P., 11
Kern, J., 176
Kessler, S., Ashedon, A.,
  Connell, R. and
  Dowsett, G., 14

Killer Angels, The (Schaara), 111, 125

Kimmel, M., 5, 6, 17

Kindlon, D. and Thompson, M., 6, 7

King, Jr., Martin Luther., 177

Kivel, P, 8

Kliebard, H., 50

Kristeva, J., 15

Landscape of action; of consciousness, 158

Language and Life (PBS), xv–xvi

Lave, J. and Wenger, E., 97

Learn by doing, 89

Length, 115

Letter exchanges, 20

Literacy
As feminized practice, 12, 16, 71, 78
As healthy work, 84
Boy's achievement, 1
Importance of, 3, 64 and *ff.*
Redefinition of, 186
Schoolish, 96

Literature, x, 74, 185, 195

Looking for Richard, 102

Lord of the Flies (William Golding), ix

Lost Boys (Garbarino), 8

Lost on a Mountain in Maine, 125

Machine Head, 41

Magazines, xix, 93, 105, 108, 185

Mahari, 19, 24, 80, 81, 150

Malcolm in the Middle, 45

Malcolm X, 177

Manhood (Biddulph), 5

Manuals, 121, 185

Mariage, T., 130

Marilyn Manson, 137

Married with Children, 45

Martino, W., 12, 16, 59, 77

Masculinity, 6, 34, 69, 71
Changing definitions, 18
Culturally redefining, 8
Definition of, 9

Hegemonic versions of, 12

Norms, 77
Reinforcing traditional notions, 12

Masculinity Goes to School, 9

Matrix, The, 137

Maw, J, 2

Maxim, 93

Maybe, D., 11

McCann, T., 176

McCarthey, S., 18, 19

McCormick, K., 18

Meek, M., 132

Miedzien, M., 8

Millard, E., 11, 12, 14, 19

Minns, E., 12

Miss Saigon, 115

Moje, E., 19

Monologue/ dialogue (*see* Bakhtin),

Moorman, 141

Morimoto, K., Gregory, J. and Butler, P., 107

Morrell, 150

Motivation, 81, 107, 118, 188
Intrinsic, 142, 149
Lack of, 80

Movies, 23, 43, 46, 55, 56, 95, 120, 144, 153, 185, 188

Moyers, Bill, xv

Muecke, D., 155

Music (*see also* Rap), 24, 41, 43, 50, 55, 89, 90, 93, 131, 137, 146, 150, 180, 201

Mutual respect, 107

Myers, W.D., 177

Mystery, 120

National Assessment of Educational Progress (NAEP), 1

Narrative inquiry, 59

Necklace, The (de Maupassant), 149

New Boys Movement, 14 and *ff.*

Newkirk, ix–xi, 2, 34, 113

News, 39, 125, 152

Newspaper, 39, 95, 128, 152, 168

Nixon, 14

Novelty, 46, 128, 137, 155, 166, 180
Shock, 120

Nystrand, M., 23, 106, 184

Of Mice and Men (Steinbeck), 136, 142–143

OFSTED, 11

Opinions, 137, 154, 203
Voice, 106, 129

Osmont, P., 12

Pale Horse, 123

Paley, V., 13

Patch Adams, 145

Patriot Games (Clancy), 153

Peer culture, 15

Peers, 128

Perfect Storm, The (Junger), 125

Performance, 131

Personal connections, 138, 144

Personality profile, 20

Perspective
Multiple, 48, 129, 154
See from new perspective, 48

Persuasive writing, 2

Peterson, 3

Phillips, 12

Planning Instruction, 50

Plays, 52, 148

Poems/Poetry, 52, 55, 97, 128, 136, 144

Point-driven reading, 161 and ff.

Pollack, W., x, 6 and *ff.*, 43

Power of Myth (Campbell), 117

Pratt, M.L., 190

Pressley, M., 112

Pressure, 45, 49, 56, 75, 97

Problem solving, 151, 188 and *ff.*, 195, 199

Problem-centered work, 104

Procedural knowledge, 129, 133, 198

Profiles, 60–61
Projects (*see* Design),
Propp. V., 158
Protocols (*see* Think Alouds),
Psychological Health, 4 and *ff.*
Purpose, 104, 120 and *ff.*
Purves, A., 2, 184

Rabinowitz, P., 34, 133, 152, 164, 195
Race, 18, 77 and *ff.*
  Acting white, 78, 80, 81, 166
Raising Cain (Kindlon and Thompson), 6
Rap (*see also* Music), 30, 35, 63, 67, 68, 70, 97, 113, 123, 125, 127, 128, 136, 150, 194, 203
Ravitch, D., 8
Reading, 32, 72 and *ff.*
  As game like challenge, 114
  As healthy work, 83
  As schoolish, 84, 90
  Context, 112
  Definition, 48
  Enjoyment, 78
  Feminized pursuit, 12, 16, 71, 78
  Immediate interest, 39
  Immediate need, 37
  Instrumental value of, 64 and *ff.*
  Rejection of, 79
  Repeated, 153
  Short, 116
  Tension with school, 73
  Time, 116
Real Boys (Pollock), 6
Reality/Reality Principle, 123, 136, 144, 151, 170
Relationships, 44, 128, 167, 172, 187, 199
  With author, 142
  With characters, 142, 145, 146, 175
  (students) With teacher, 99 and *ff.*, 184, 187

(Teacher) With students, 21, 98, 101, 107, 138, 142, 150, 167
  With villains, 146
Relevance, 111, 120, 124, 144, 175, 190
  Immediate importance, 122
Reluctance, 97
Resistance, 24
  Situational, 80
  Linked to teacher behavior, 80
Response
  Boy vs. Girls, 11
Richard III (Shakespeare), 169
Rogoff, B. and Lave, J., 86
Romeo and Juliet (Shakespeare), 102, 121
Rosenblatt, L., 40
Rotundo, A., 17
Routine, 46, 47, 112, 136, 142, 155
Rudduck, 14

Sadker and Sadker, 2
Salisbury and Jackson, 9
Sandberg, C., 52
Satire, 155
Scarlet Letter, The (Hawthorne), x
Schema theory, 86
School
  Adversarial relationship, 100
  As prison, 110
  Change, 109
  Importance of, 63 and *ff.*, 113
School vs. home, 76 and *ff.*, 86, 93, 94, 184, 199
Schuder, 112
Sci-fi, 55
  As tool to think about real world, 123
Seinfeld, 157
Self-efficacy, 37
Self-expression, 105, 106
Semiotic terms, 186
Sense of accomplishment
  Visible, 116

Separate Peace, A (Knowles), ix
Sequencing, of activities/assignments, 51, 53, 104, 130, 133, 153, 177, 196, 198
Series books, 36, 95, 145, 151, 153
Shapiro, J., 11
Shakespeare, W., Ix, 56, 61, 80, 81, 102, 116, 119, 121, 136, 154, 156
She Stoops to Conquer (Goldsmith), 124
Silverstein, O. and Rashbaum, B., 8
Simpsons, The, 23, 45, 155, 156, 157
Situational interest, 136
Sixth Sense, 120
Skill
  Appropriate level, 34
Slam, 108
Smagorinsky, P., 169, 176
Smith, M. W., x, 4, 34, 52, 133, 162, 164
Social, x, 24, 42, 44, 50, 62, 69, 71, 74, 81, 82, 147, 148, 183, 197, 199
  importance of social, x, 70 and *ff.*, 89, 128, 142, 192
  Group work, 147, 148, 197, 199
Social action projects, 191
Social constructivism (*see also* Vygotsky), 6 and *ff.*, 16
Social contract with teachers, 99 and *ff.*, 184, 187
Sociocultural teaching, 129
Source, 105
Sports, 25, 31, 34, 35, 39, 44, 57, 67, 70, 73, 85, 86, 89, 90, 108, 114, 124, 126, 138, 190, 193
  Challenge of, 34
SRI (see Symbolic Story Representation),
Star Wars, 95, 151
Staying Fat for Sarah Byrnes (Crutcher), 86

Stereotypes, 19, 78, 79, 158
  Perpetuating them, 14
Stevens, 51
Story-driven reading, 161 and
  ff.
Strategic Reading (Wilhelm, et
  al.), 34, 38, 193
Strategy instruction, 113
Stiffed (Faludi), 9
Stress (see Pressure),
Style
  Difficulty with, 116
  Texture, 116
Substantive ideas/issues, 48,
  133, 138, 144, 147, 157,
  185, 202
Success, 194
  Ensuring it, 37
  Narrow vision of, 19
Superficial coverage, 109
Surveys, 20
Suspense, 48
Symbolic story representation
  (SRI), 104, 131–133,
  152
Symbolism, 132, 137, 198

Task construction, 171
Taylor, M., 177
Teacher
  As more knowledgeable
    other, 130
Teaching
  Responsiveness, 187
Television, 45, 48, 71, 155,
  156, 157, 168, 171, 188
Telford, L., 12, 19
Testosterone geysering, 5
Textbooks, 107, 117, 151
Texts
  Alternative, 87
  Availability, 37
  Overmatched by, 143
  Popular culture, 87
  Relating to, 87

Selection, 142 and ff., 194
  and ff.
Short, 115–116, 196
Types, 52, 133
Tharp, R., 192
Think-alouds (Protocols),
  104, 132, 159 and ff.
Thomas, L., 3
Thorndike, R., 141
Time and reading, 109, 192
To Kill A Mockingbird (Lee),
  158, 169
Tony Hawk, 27, 43
Traditional teaching
  challenge to, xii, 183 and ff.
Transformation, social, 18,
  84, 87, 189, 191
Transformative power
  Of literacy, xvi
  Social Projects, 17, 193
Triangulation, 59
Turner, 141
Twelfth Night (Shakespeare),
  116

Underachievement, 2, 4
Unfamiliarity
  Text structure, 116
Unreliable narrators, 133

Values, xii
  Positive, 157, 173
Variety, 47
Verwys, 176
Vibe, 60, 70, 108
Video games, xx, 35 and ff.,
  39, 41, 43, 51, 53, 56,
  93, 98, 105, 121, 126,
  146, 179
Violence, 7 and ff.
Violence (Gilligan, J.), 8
Visible signs of accomplish-
  ment, 33, 62
Vision of Disorder, 41
Visual art, 68, 103, 131

Visual texts
  Cartoons, comics, graphic
    novels, 152
Visualization, 48
Voss, M., 13
Vygotsky, 37, 40, 44, 103,
  128, 130, 175, 192
  Intersubjectivity, 129

Wall Street Journal, The, 152
Walkerdine, V., 12
Weightlifting, 38–39
Well-roundedness, 70
Wells, G., 191
West and Zimmerman, xvi, 6
White, B., 176
Whitehead, A.N., 11, 109
Whitman, W., 52
Whole person, 107
Wilhelm, J., Baker, T. and
  Dube, J., 34, 38, 193
Wilhelm, J. and Edmiston, B.,
  11, 103, 131
Wilhelm, J. and Friedemann,
  P., 11, 20
Wilhelm, J., x, xx, 11, 34,
  131, 143, 193
Willinsky, J., 17
Workshop design, 112, 128
Worthy, J., 141
Would You Rather?, 185
Wrestling, 23–24, 93, 98,
  145, 151, 156
Writing, 33
Wu-Tang, 150

"You Gotta BE the Book", xx,
  143
You've Got Mail, 141
Young, J., 16
Young adult literature, 14, 197

Zeichner and Tabachnick, 183
Zone of proximal develop-
  ment (ZPD), 40, 103